Shoppernomics

Mullin and Harper are very experienced Directors and have succeeded in capturing their knowledge and expertise in this fascinating book, Shoppernomics: How to Shorten and Focus the Shoppers' Routes to Purchase. *The biggest disservice that nineteenth-century economists did to mankind was to assert that consumers are rational. The fact is that they remain an enigma and any insights into their behaviour is to be welcomed. I wish I had had this book and its insights and wisdom when I was Marketing Director of a major fast-moving consumer goods company all those years ago. Well done Roddy and Colin. You have made a major contribution with this book.*

Professor Malcolm McDonald MA(Oxon) MSc PhD DLitt DSc,
Emeritus Professor,Cranfield University School of Management

Shoppernomics

How to Shorten and Focus the Shoppers' Routes to Purchase

RODDY MULLIN and COLIN HARPER

Routledge
Taylor & Francis Group
LONDON AND NEW YORK

First published in paperback 2024

First published 2014 by Gower Publishing

Published 2016 by Routledge
4 Park Square, Milton Park, Abingdon, Oxon OX14 4RN

and by Routledge
605 Third Avenue, New York, NY 10158

Routledge is an imprint of the Taylor & Francis Group, an informa business

Publisher's Note
The publisher has gone to great lengths to ensure the quality of this reprint but points out that some imperfections in the original copies may be apparent.

British Library Cataloguing in Publication Data
A catalogue record for this book is available from the British Library

Library of Congress Cataloging-in-Publication Data
Mullin, Roddy.
Shoppernomics : how to shorten and focus the routes to purchase / by Roddy Mullin and Colin Harper.
pages cm
Includes bibliographical references and index.
ISBN 978-1-4724-2485-3 (hardback) -- ISBN 978-1-4724-2486-0 (ebook) -- ISBN 978-1-4724-2487-7 (epub) 1. Communication in marketing. 2. Consumer behavior. 3. Consumers--Research. 4. Sales promotion. I. Harper, Colin, 1948- II. Title.

HF5415.123.M85 2014
658.8'342--dc23

2014005082

ISBN: 978-1-4724-2485-3 (hbk)
ISBN: 978-1-03-283746-8 (pbk)
ISBN: 978-1-315-60904-1 (ebk)

DOI: 10.4324/9781315609041

Contents

List of Figures and Tables

Figures

Tables

Preface

For the authors, a period of reflection arises while their book is being prepared for print. Fortune has smiled upon us during this agonising delay. In this rapidly moving world there is a hazard that new evidence may come to light that negates some part of the recommendations and suggested actions that those for whom this book is written; brand managers, retailers and suppliers specifically, and all those in sales and marketing generally. What we have written holds true as we hand the book over to the publisher. Indeed the Christmas 2013 retail shopping period reinforces the authors' view that it is not discounting or location that really increases sales: Fat Face did no discounting but sales went up, Asda only discounted from Boxing Day with a staggering rise in sales, other supermarkets with early discounting did not do so well, convenience stores did well. The shopper continued to ignore the dispute of whether online (now 20 per cent of sales) or bricks and mortar stores is preferred: Primark sales (no online!) rose 12.4 per cent, John Lewis and Next flourished with both, universally click and collect is proving successful. So if it is not these what is it that drives the shopper to buy? Understanding and building the engram in the shopper's subconscious seems to be the key.

As authors we still believe that there is a need for six communications with the shopper, three of which are the IPA-recognised advertising message points, to reach the shopper's tipping point – the moment when the shopper decides to buy. It is of course necessary to manage stock to avoid the 'disgusted' shopper who finds the shelf bare. Our recommendations for action are in a series of shorter chapters in Part III based on our findings in Parts I and II. We also believe that investing in your core stores and the shoppers that buy there is not only really sensible, but, in the light of information you will find in these pages, absolutely vital, not just for growth but also to avoid serious decline in loyalty. How truly loyal (and sales beneficial) is sometimes a puzzle: the surge of City workers seeking free coffee at Waitrose in Canary Wharf has caused a stir(!) but have local coffee outlets suffered? Has it helped the Waitrose engram? Unfortunately we do not have the time to address these questions within the scope of this book.

We are as ever grateful to colleagues and friends who have advised on content and to the businesses that have generously supplied case studies. Their inputs are recognised in the Appendix.

As authors we hope that more retailers, as a result of reading this book, will recognise that their epos data, properly managed, can offer a great return from coordination and collaboration down to core areas using supply chain running in harness with local brand advertising and promotions. This is a place that brands should be keen to go and retailers equally keen to encourage. The chance to increase sales *and* loyalty all round should be hard to resist.

The authors have updated and additional information relating to the book – please follow the link www.retailvitalstatistics.com to view.

Lastly, we encourage all brand owners to understand and measure the effectiveness of their messages and find out what the shopper has in their mind by developing a brand engram. If you don't know what's in *their* mind, you'll find it hard to know what appeals to them.

We commend this book to you.

Colin Harper
Roddy Mullin

Introduction

Why You Should Read This Book...

... because the tortuous route that leads to a sale starts a long time before the shopper is anywhere near making a purchase decision. It is too easy to see your product as something like a magnet drawing people in. It is a better metaphor if you see a shopper a little like a random particle with many options as to where to go and what to buy. Some of these location options may not stock the product, some may not sell it. Very few products are destinations. Often it is easier to see yourself as reducing the chances of your product *not* selling rather than actually promoting the sale. This encourages you to focus on distribution, availability and display. However, before that, you need to build the brand so people actually recognise your pack and what it is – not just let their eye skate over it to a pack, product or service they do recognise. This book explains what has to be done to secure that first recognition by the shopper (or buyer if business to business (B2B)), whatever you are selling. For business to consumer (B2C), the shopper's family and friends will need to have that same awareness and for B2B those around the buyer will also need that recognition to ensure a sale.
... because one of the huge advantages in seeing life from the point of view of the shopper is that it does point the way to where you should be focusing alongside advertising. When you advertise you pick out target markets and select the message accordingly. Shopper Marketing (which gives you Insights into the shopper both from research and in-house data) advises you to focus on where they live, what they read and how they shop, as well as what they buy. People tend to live amongst others like themselves with similar attitudes so targeting activity at them will encourage them to talk about your product, as will store staff who live in the same communities. Coca-Cola in the UK has just announced: 'Coke will garner(s) sales and volume data mapping it against external consumer, workplace, competitor and retail geo-demographics.' In effect, Coca-Cola is making each shop a major customer ... and treating them appropriately. This may sound too micro – but it's not – if you recognise that even small issues may stand in the way of a sale and that media can be targeted right down to the individual shopper.

… because for the shopper it is a complicated and fragmented journey – this book shows how retailers, suppliers and brand managers (plus those seeking a career in retail – 10 per cent of UK employees – or brand management, or those starting businesses) can influence shoppers more successfully along the shopper's path with the right message through the right channel at the right time such that the shopper will be persuaded, and then buy, a particular product or service, rather than that of a competitor. The book also describes the possible barriers to purchase that retailers introduce.

So if you are a retailer, supplier, brand manager or an entrepreneur, or are in sales or marketing, or seeking a career in retail – this book is for you.

… because new research featured here describes the part the subconscious plays in making purchase decisions for the shopper and what is required to implant an engram – the brand recogniser in the shopper's mind (described in Chapter 1) – because it is so important! As a result, alongside other researched facts, the authors believe that marketers should understand the following before deciding on the messages to send out in their marketing planning and associated budget:

- the absolute importance of the subconscious-embedded engrams;
- the need to apply Excess Share of Voice (ESOV);
- the benefits of relationship building with the shopper;
- how to assist the shopper to make comparisons and obtain product and service reviews alongside obtaining feedback and responding to concerns through social media;
- at all points on the journey, using sales promotions, signs, advertising and promotional marketing to provide interest, stimulation and fun;
- the value of creative, innovative Point of Sale (POS) material, promotion, packaging; and
- the effect of product availability and planning for it (or the dire consequence of a lack of it!).

... the authors consider that they can assist anyone selling anything to understand how the shopper buys – and then put into practice the following:

- sending the right messages (format, content, information, education about product or service, location for purchase, delivery, cost, value, social and cultural positioning, feedback from other shoppers);
- through the right media and channels;
- at the right time (there are six opportunities or points on the journey);
- including embedding subconscious brand reinforcement before the need even arises;
- while 'advising' and providing advice to the shopper along the journey to purchase;
- and at the Point of Purchase (POP) making the 'killer promotion' that secures the purchase.

This is particularly important now as the shopper has been empowered through new technologies to take control of their journey to purchase. Research shows that a shopper almost completely ignores any difference between online or offline and delivery anywhere, or collection in a bricks and mortar outlet (note that even eBay is now trying pop-up shops and is linking with Argos for its delivery outlets).

... because Tony Bryant of K3 argues that retailers have to take note of the complete journey to be truly customer centric. Jon Stanesby at Responsys reports a threefold increase in purchases when the marketing messages matched the customer-preferred communication channel.

This book looks at the whole of the Path to Purchase, the messages the shopper expects and when, and how you can deliver these messages to get the greatest impact.

The brand, supplier and retailer need to research the shopper then use the Insights and, just as importantly, discover the shopper's preferred channels – but very few do that. Measuring the effectiveness of marketing is carried out by less than 40 per cent of retailers. As for data, no retailer wants to bother with it, accepting that data can be extremely difficult both to collect and then make sense of. 44 per cent of 100 retailers questioned by *Internet Retailing* (2012) found it hard to turn the customer data they own into useful Insights and produce an output tailored to the customer. The same applies to data as to research – you just have to employ people who want to play with data or research to come up with meaningful Insights. Data can be gleaned from loyalty cards, purchase history, segmentation, customer polling, attitude and demographic research, behavioural analysis and now social networking sites. A key benefit for those retailers who analyse data is that they would find the Recency, Frequency and Monetary (RFM) value score of any shopper, which could then determine whom to target or reward As a reward for their top customers, Screwfix offer free delivery to a building site rather than the construction firm's base. There is an oft-cited statement by retailers that they are 'customer facing'. The reality is they are not. It is just a public relations (PR) statement of ambition generated by 'top-down retailer tyranny' (*Internet Retailer* said that first!) for if they just bothered with research, measuring marketing effectiveness and using their own data they would find they are far from customer facing.

... because, if you apply it correctly, loyalty can be persuasive – Australian retailer Myer, advised by Sarah Richardson of Global Loyalty Pty Ltd, who use 20 differentiators to benchmark their loyalty programme, find that, on average, members of their loyalty programme, MYER one, spend 3.8 times the value of the gift cards that they earn. (Retailers note that, for Myer, shopper data is the 'real and know' value pay off.) Myer have refined a system that allows added benefit for both staff and shoppers alike. For staff, it helps them to recognise a shopper's category; for example, a high-spending browser who showrooms a lot initially but does eventually buy. For the shopper, the MYER one programme (including the smartphone app) and the Myer Visa credit card offer a loyalty tier system which awards them a cherished status (including VIP), along with special rewards that persuade them to remain loyal. Neiman Marcus (with a clever app) reward the loyalty of those that spend more than $20,000 annually with a party. High Value, High Loyal shoppers deserve rewards. M&Co, it is reported, are on first name terms with their top 10 per cent of customers and welcome them back from holidays and remember birthdays. Space.NK.Apothecary report that 75 per cent of transactions come from their loyalty programmes. One per cent of Costa Coffee customers account for 10 per cent of the chain's overall revenue and they are rewarded with invitations to 'come and try' new products. However, analysis of European spending by *VISA* (466 million signed-up shoppers carrying out 13.2 billion transactions a year) shows that shoppers are not actually that loyal, with 69 per cent spending with competitors and 43 per cent converting their spend to a competitor from one year to the next. Other surveys confirm this and find that more than half of shoppers are no longer loyal but would be if the retailer offered them what they want; Insight provides this information. US shoppers have, on average, 22 loyalty cards; UK shoppers average 13. This book suggests what to do and where to go for help to extract the Insights – see Part III (Chapters 16 to 18).

... because promotion analysis (studying the effect of a marketing communication on the sales of a product) has been gleaned, hitherto, mainly from the perspective of the manufacturer/supplier – but now the authors of this book offer analysis from a retailer perspective, which is harder but more rewarding, for consumer and B2B businesses. For the retailer it can demonstrate the effectiveness or otherwise of promoting an existing product in a new way, which can dramatically increase sales. Typically a retailer in a chain of stores will have 150,000 Universal Product Codes (UPCs – the barcode number that identifies each product) supplied by some 1,000 manufacturers, from which 30,000 are selected to fill the shelves and, over a two-and-a-half-year period, some 20 million promotions will be offered. Managers really do need help to make effective operational decisions and that help is offered here in this book. A B2B buyer can be just as resistant to change as a consumer, but he or she can be persuaded to act as they consider placing an order by appropriate messages delivered from a reputable, trusted source. This book also describes how to avoid 'failures to deliver to the shopper' which, from research given in this book, is anathema to some shoppers who will not buy from that supplier again. We describe how to overcome shopper dismay – such as the 2013 Easter egg shortage which could so easily have been avoided by the five major retail chains – more anon!

... because it has always been the case that the shopper or buyer took advice before they tried and bought for the first time but now they are getting the advice from elsewhere and this book shows how to be part of that advice chain. Fifty years ago, the advice might have come from advertising copy or a shopkeeper suggesting and recommending, or a salesman calling at the factory door. Latterly, it might come from many more variations of advertising, friends real or virtual (social media!), celebrities, from POS, or from the product itself via the packaging and, of course, there are many forms of experiential marketing, putting product in the hands of more or less receptive shoppers or buyers.

... because today the advent of social media means the shopper or buyer can be in touch with almost anyone, almost anywhere, at any time, to ask for advice and, as we write, this is moving away from Facebook to Pinterest and

Instagram, along with a growing preference for access through mobile. This wealth of communication potential can help the supplier and retailer: it is now possible, for example, to analyse social media and adjust the offer and the message. But how does the supplier or retailer cope with the fear of taking the wrong decisions on communication with the shopper or buyer, which channels or media to employ and what message to put across and when, to the seemingly ever-demanding, ever more knowledgeable customer? Knowledge dispels fear. This book has the knowledge retailers and suppliers need to overcome the seeming enormity of the problem they now face – communicating with the customer in a ROI rewarding way (except for B2B where an alternative – described in this book – is required).

... because retail in the UK employs 10 per cent of the workforce (12 per cent of the UK spend on training) and if you are a bright young person and intend to make a career in something – try retailing rather than remain unemployed and if you do select retail then you need to understand the customer and how to reach them. This book provides what you need to know.

... because some are saying this book (they have heard about our writing) is the logical sequel to *Why We Buy – The Science of Shopping* by Paco Underhill, still an essential book to own though published in 2000. This book also encompasses the reports over the intervening years produced by Deloitte, the Institute of Practioners in Advertising (IPA) and others such as Booz and Company. This book not only includes the latest research findings at the time of going to print, such as the Mobile Outlook 2013, but goes further in that the authors have provided for you, in the text of the book itself and in Appendix, the websites from which you can access up-to-date information, as at the time you enter the site – today.

The *Raison d'Etre* of the Book

Big brands and their products appear everywhere. That is what being big is all about. If you want to be a big brand, by using careful messaging you can appear to be bigger than you are. A small brand can now be perceived as big as a big brand. But you need to decide that before you start – and courage is required.

This book tells you that, no matter how often you repeat a fact, it will never sink in unless you make the message appeal to the emotions and then attach this to a strong and recognisable symbol – the engram. Research by Myer finds that the shopper is driven by rational thinking only 20 per cent of the time –

the rest is emotional thinking. Once the engram is developed, any mention of the product by friends, family or the web helps to cement this engram in place more firmly. Every product, POP, advert, article or discussion reinforces and locks this engram in place.

Much work has been done over the years on Share of Voice as a key predictor of advertising success. This book shows that ESOV is what you need on the Path to Purchase if you want to build a brand and sell at the same time. We show you why this is important, how you get it, where you put it and how you can measure it.

The approach this book recommends is designed to work for any brand anywhere, although many illustrations are drawn from fast-moving consumer goods (fmcg), since data is more readily available in this market.

Companies that want to move forward need to see their sales and marketing budget as one resource, building both short-term sales and long-term marketing. Most companies still have a vast divide between these budgets. The authors pose this question to you – 'Do you Dare to be Different?' Go for both short and long term at once. Hardly anyone is – they have separate budgets. Dare to be Different. Short-term discounting affects long-term sales which affects the brand.

The process of getting as many people in touch with, and then regularly buying, your products in bricks and mortar outlets, or indeed online, is as much about removing barriers as it is about building bridges. Retailers and suppliers need to keep both existing shoppers and business buyers and attract new ones. Getting the balance right is important or both will be lost.

The customer has also shifted their buying habits and is doing so even more in the recession, moving from a habitual shopping routine to much more savvy purchasing, causing an overreaction by retailers (for example by WalMart and Tesco) which has cost them sales. Tesco in the UK also suffered from the horse meat in beef products exposure. In June 2013 reports indicated a 4.2 per cent footfall drop for Tesco. One way to increase purchases may be daypart merchandising (see Chapter 5). The Japanese introduced daypart merchandising some years ago. This most sensible way to cross-sell, increasing per visit purchase, has yet to be widely adopted in the West but, when it is – even in such diverse outlets as hotels – customer loyalty and buying increases.

Barriers such as price can be removed with special offers – the International Grocery Distribution (IGD) say that 60 per cent of all products are tried at offer price. Poorly trained staff or too highly trained staff, prone sometimes to 'showrooming', can also affect closing the sale. On a tube journey approaching Sloane Square, three young men were describing how they were going to look at very large television screens in Peter Jones, using the expertise of the sales staff to describe the benefits and features, which they then planned to go online to buy. For a time another retailer used advertisements to say: 'visit John Lewis then buy more cheaply from us'. Now retailers offer in-store screens to make comparison easier for shoppers. The price is now similar in-store and online in any case. Sainsbury are campaigning for a tax on online sales to level the playing field and balance the cost of business rates paid on bricks and mortar outlets – such a tax is difficult to achieve in a global marketplace so it may be wishful thinking. Other barriers, such as actual or functional non-availability of product (for example, Waitrose do not stock all the products on their promotional labels – more anon) can be addressed by work with the supply chain, the pack design or category/product signage and the employment of Field Marketing Companies (see *The Handbook of Field Marketing* by Alison Williams and Roddy Mullin).

Customers look for a store to be in stock on promoted items – otherwise a percentage (20 per cent – see Chapter 6 for the sources quoted here) will leave without purchase. Failure to fill shelves due to Out of Stock conditions will lose retailers an estimated 15 per cent in sales. Insufficient stock is reportedly due to ordering 'what we did last time' rather than looking at last time sales or any other parameter such as the effect of price on sales. It is a system that does not learn. Chain-wide ordering also leads to over or under-ordering for each store as does ordering quantities relative to the store size or equal quantities to each store. Category size allocation by store does not necessarily relate to sales either. The industry system of measuring 'lift' over baseline is flawed. Ordering by case (12 units per case) can grossly overweight errors for slow-moving items (this means too much sits on shelves – but the supplier in error believes the demand to be there). Part III of this book suggests a better way to assess what quantity to order. The argument for the need to measure marketing effectiveness of promotions is a no brainer! Yet *The Grocer* reports 61 per cent of retailers have never measured any marketing effectiveness.

Brand manufacturers and their agencies need to realise that you cannot just address one issue without looking at the rest to balance their offer to the shopper – the Customer Value Proposition (CVP). Overcoming the silo mentality and operation through creating a single customer focus is now being shown by research to be a key organisation structural necessity.

Research findings by IBM are demonstrating that removing silos dramatically changes the shopper view of product and services. For example, Willie Walsh of British Airways has removed all the customer-facing silos, placing the people within them under a single boss, and is now discovering dramatic improvement in customer bonding. The business executive is recognised as the same person when booking economy class with the family as they are when paying top rate – and the treatment is consistent. The 'shopper' loves being treated in the same way where status is recognised – no surprise there then.

The approach that maximises the value of investment behind brand growth, bringing all of the above factors into focus, is called Shopper Marketing. It brings into sharp clarity the real importance that contacting the shopper or the B2B purchaser – the gatekeeper to the family budget or the business budget – is at a stroke nowadays both easier and much more difficult. Easier in the sense that if you know who they are it can cost you almost nothing to talk to them. Harder because if you do not know who they are, getting value for money from media becomes ever harder as the media proliferates. In this book we seek to extend the Shopper Marketing concept from the moment a shopper or B2B buyer starts the journey to purchase and extend it into ownership, after the money exchange has been made.

The value of maintaining any single link in the chain rises as you unbalance your spending in any one area. An exact simile would be car maintenance. Replace the engine with one twice the size and you will rapidly appreciate the need for a brake and suspension upgrade. To say nothing of retraining the driver!

Every retail outlet appeals to shoppers from a defined area. You can spend a fortune on a national advertising campaign and get only a modest increase in sales in any single store. However, spend very much less in that one store and you can double the sales. The impact of doubling sales in a few stores for one retailer would be an increase in distribution as your products can be seen to be improving their share of store and category sales. The retailer/manufacturer Zara is opening five new stores a week (as at January 2013) – simply advertising each outlet opening. They keep up with this growth rate because they keep in close contact with the customer to ensure that products manufactured are near exactly what the customer needs, little stock is available for more than a few weeks and they price wisely. For B2B the same rewards of more product sales overall is achieved through concentration on just a few customers each time. The similarity between B2C and B2B applies to a larger extent than realised.

Investment behind shopper sales needs to be balanced between those which will impact on store by store sales and those that build a brand nationally (making it easier to gain national distribution in other stores). Meanwhile, access at store level is guarded by retail chains that are increasingly (as this book is written) concerned with extracting the maximum value from a brand to retain customer loyalty and company growth. Does this really work? The answer is no. The customer actually should determine the ideal brand parameters, not some agency trying to be clever. This is how Zara works – Zara's sales staff listens and observes and reports back to Zara's manufacturing. In this way the customer dictates what they are happy to buy. A win–win cycle.

Overall, there is the need to understand the comparative impact of investment behind the myriad opportunities that present themselves. Approaches to build immediate revenue or long-term loyalty might be objectives. Customer satisfaction is also a parameter faithfully reported on by the UK Customer Satisfaction Index (UKCSI) who every six months survey 26,000 consumers in 13 business sectors. Increasing customer satisfaction above the market share means more sales; 9 per cent sales growth has been reported. Or, if awareness is the aim as opposed to impact, produce a presentation on the category versus what is top of mind in the home or office. Throughout the book the generic term 'shopper' is used – assume it to include the B2B buyer unless especially specified.

How Have We Written This Book and Why is it Special?

This book takes you through the steps in the chain from that desire stimulus in the shopper to the product in use at home or in business and gives you a vision of how you can approach each step of the shopper journey with appropriate messages. The customer is generally acknowledged to follow four stages on the route to purchase which varies by category and can also be changed by the trigger that starts the process. The authors think there are six message points on that journey.

The Importance of the Customer

Long gone are the days when the customer was told what was available (Ford Model T and it is black!) and that was all that was offered. The customer today may well arrive at a shop with a very clear idea, and with the most detailed specification, about the product they wish to buy (ask any car salesman), but the concept has spread to all categories. The customer expects a high standard of sales service, relationship building and communication. A whole chapter is devoted to the modern customer. Unsurprisingly! It is of course the customer who pays the money and provides the profit. The largest part of this book describes how the customer shops and gives the research findings to enable the targeting of messages through the appropriate media at the appropriate stage of the customer's route to purchase.

Has the recession hammered retail? Yes, if the supplier and retailer have not understood the customer. No, if they have understood – look at Zara (up to March 2013 – where Zara's owners are reporting a 22 per cent increase in profits). In a recession the prevalence of customers is to become deal seekers (not loyal to brand), who switch to buy whatever is on deal this week particularly in these categories: food, drink, household.

Not everyone subscribes to the importance of the shopper and *The Hub* magazine (March 2013) reports a growing split into those who believe the shopper is king (who think strategically, and plan and collaborate between retailer and supplier) and those who support the category (who measure nothing, operate opportunistically and in an ad hoc way).The facts as far as can be ascertained (the opportunists tend to be part of the 42 per cent who do not measure anything) show that the strategy planner collaborators – shopper marketers – either for themselves or their clients do achieve better sales and a higher Return on Investment (ROI). Shopper Marketing has two key benefits – first is 'a better understanding of how target customers behave as shoppers resulting in more relevant and effective programming' and second is 'improved collaboration, now much more strategic than in the past'.

The Changing Face of Shopping, Work and Living

It is not the purpose of this book to describe the environment in which people live and work now and in the future. This is well researched by such authors as Cor Molenaar in his book *Shopping 3.0*, and the authors, in general, support its conclusions. *Shopping 3.0* sees buyers using all channels for information and shopping (on the internet first, then checking in-store), before making the buy decision. Molenaar, writing in 2010, perhaps makes too little of the influence of social media and the weight placed by customers on advice taking from others, preferring to task the retailer with first ensuring the product data is consistent across all channels and then that the internet or in-store experience is fast, efficient, customer-focused, pleasurable and that the system delivers.

This book does not seek to redress the old habits of transaction driven service: fixed price, fixed opening hours, fixed layout. What this book does is seek to open the eyes of retailers and suppliers to the points at which customers need messages on their journey to purchase, rather than the old habit of reliance on newspaper and leaflet advertising.

High Tech Communication and Data Processing

This features in great part in this book. The customer has access to so much more in improved communication and the ability to question and seek advice along the way. But the retailer and supplier can also follow the way the shopper shops and adjust their operation accordingly. Carphone Warehouse is developing a seamless connection experience through their 'roller apps' for shoppers connected, if they wish, with a single sales colleague. It will also allow any shopper within three kilometres to be 'on the radar' and offered promotions and rewards.

Why Alternatives to Discounting Are So Important

There are people who will buy on price. Then again there are people who will buy for the unique values of your brand. If you feel that competing on price is what you want to do, then this book is not for you. You need to invest, instead, into a continuous process of cost saving. Your strategy always runs the risk of being nullified by brands that appeal for other reasons, such as coming down to your price point and being much more competitive. If, however, building a launch pad for growth is your objective then read on. Infinitely better are the four alternative sales promotion tools offered to replace price discounting (see *Sales Promotion* – fifth edition by Roddy Mullin).

What Is Not Covered in This Book

How business operates and how marketing fits into a business and the tools available to the marketer are not within the scope of this book. A short resume is given in Roddy Mullin's other books (see *Sales Promotion* or *The Handbook of Field Marketing*).

An Overview of the Book

The book is in three Parts. Part I describes the players and drivers. Part II examines the components of the route to purchase for message opportunities and dares you to be different with marketing and sales messages that are for both the short and long term – taking up the six message points but also ensuring the supply matches the take-up. Part III examines how each component can be successfully improved with timely messages to optimise the return, looking also briefly at strategy, organisation and the future.

How to Use This Book

For background reading, to discover the authors' context, you should at minimum skim the first two parts and read Chapter 13. The third part describes what you can do to enhance your sales.

PART I
The Shopper Analysed

Chapter 1
Inside the Mind of the Shopper

Over the last few years there have been four major changes:

- the rise of the internet as both a means of communication (advertising, direct mail) and also interaction (social media);

- the increase in ownership of mobile phones;

- the increase in the ability for businesses to target people in many more places than ever before with a more personalised message;

- the increasing ability to measure campaigns and gain feedback from and Insight into the minds and actions of consumers – the targets for a product or service. It is research and the resulting Insight that has led to the discovery of the importance of the engram.

The pace and scale of change mean that as a business you need to continually re-evaluate the way that marketers select and achieve the best strategy to reach their target market – the shopper. (More on strategy in Part III and also developing the organisation to take it on.) To gain a benefit from all of the new opportunities requires a sea change in the way that a marketing plan is put together. Using these four significant market changes (the bullets above) to frame these opportunities requires a basic and simple understanding of how they can be integrated together. This understanding is developed below.

The immediate need is to consider how exactly the advertising and promotion communication budget work together. The following are questions with which you may well be familiar.

- What will build and nurture product sales best?

- Why should I spend in one area rather than another?

- When should I be investing (in communicating with the shopper)?
- How should I spread the budget?
- Where should my message appear?
- Who should I be reaching?

You will develop and mature your own theories about this, the most taxing element of the marketing spend. Why is this taxing? Put simply – because few communication strategies actually deliver in a direct and measurable way in the short term. It is possible to find short-term measures but these come from oblique understandings of why people buy. This was covered as long ago as 2000 by Roddy Mullin in his *Value for Money Marketing*. In the long term – at minimum a two-year period for most B2B businesses – ROI measures can be seen to operate. Charities may use direct marketing, for donations, where results can be easily understood, but they still invest in advertising to pass across their core message. In part, of course, it is because many of the charities have a campaigning element to their *raison d'etre*. But another key reason is that consumers need to recognise them to even open the envelope in the first place. The fast.MAP Marketing Gap survey (fast.MAP is a company!) which has run consistently across four years to 2011 shows every year that the main reason people open up a direct mail piece is that it is from a 'brand or company I know', with 55 per cent of people agreeing.

The survey goes on to identify other reasons why customers open a mailshot. These are, in order:

- personally addressed to me (46 per cent);
- interested in the product or service (46 per cent);
- may contain a voucher or coupon (38 per cent);
- see it contains a free sample/voucher (36 per cent);
- local service or event (21 per cent);
- because it is a competition (18 per cent);
- interesting package (15 per cent);

- looks fun/humorous/attractive envelope/design colour (less than 10 per cent).

In essence, what this says is that familiarity or some internal trigger (the engram) matters even before a shopper actually sees any advertising messages at all. As you read on through the various chapters you will see this reflected in many other places than direct mail.

What is now coming to the fore is the realisation that the shopper's subconscious plays a key part in buying. Something inside the shopper's head which they do not articulate when questioned is prompting their behaviour. This may be subconscious but it can be encouraged. To understand what's going on let us share a small amount of history to explain the part played by the engram.

At the beginning of the last century most basic advertising models described the customer journey as being a gradual route to a purchase. There were several of these models, but the best known was probably AIDA.

Awareness
Interest
Desire
Action

This was a formula invented by St Elmo Lewis, a salesman for the National Cash Register Company, over 100 years ago. It was expressly designed as a basis for face-to-face selling.

Other models then added detail or context to this original idea. Perhaps the most cogent expression of this is in the Unique Selling Promise (USP), invented by Rosser Reeves, Chairman of Ted Bates ad agency, and described as the 'one thing that would make people buy your product'.

There is a logic underlying all this. The unvoiced assumption was that a purchase decision of any kind was a rational, conscious decision. Responding to this USP model, Gordon Brown of Millward Brown developed an ad tracking system based on recall, and the details they could recall.

The reasoning is that if your advertising or sales models were correct, you should be able to draw some kind of direct line between measured awareness and sales success. Millward Brown asked two simple questions: 'Which of these advertisements do you recall (from a selection)?' and 'the details they could recall about the ad'. The basic theme is that advertising is there to deliver conscious information, and deliver attitude and behaviour change. This you can measure and also, to an extent, predict.

However, Andrew Ehrenberg had another take. When he was appointed as the Professor of Marketing and Communication at the London Business School he had, by his own admission, read nothing about either of the subjects in his title. With a background in statistics, and quite unburdened with prejudices or preconceptions, he pointed out:

1. there was a lack of empirical evidence showing sales increases resulting from advertising;

2. small and medium brands persist despite the massive advertising of the majors;

3. brands usually survive even when ad spend is cut;

4. new products have a catastrophic failure rate.

Using consumer panel data Ehrenberg showed that few products had 100 per cent loyal users. He also found that often attitude change was behaviour led – people tried the product first (more in Chapter 3).

He asserted that 'advertising's main role is to reinforce feelings of satisfaction with brands already being used' (Ehrenburg 1974: 33). This model is called Awareness–Trial–Reinforcement (ATR).

In order for advertising to persuade, the message needs to be understood. However, most advertising is not consciously read, it is just there. Andy Tarshis (AC Nielsen Co. quoted in Mayer 1991: 179–80) said: 'We find advertising works the way that grass grows. You can never see it, but every week you have to mow the lawn.'

It seems that advertising can actually work better in some cases where it creeps under the radar; where it may even be designed simply to convey a feeling from elements that 'qualify' a message rather than communicate a specific message, it gets under the skin of the shopper and then gets into their mind. Take, for example, the O2 campaign in the UK. This telecoms provider competes in a very competitive area. In 2001 they started a TV campaign involving a bubble, doves taking off with some lilting music in the background. This was up against Orange network's 'The future's bright, the future's Orange' and One-2-One's slogan 'Who would you like a one-to-one with?'. By 2005 O2 had become the market leader, with an advertisement that communicated a range of good feelings, without any specific message. In many cases, if you awake a conscious process, you invite counter arguments. On the other hand, if you share an emotional message without awakening this conscious process and the potential censoring this might involve, then the message can get through more easily.

This process of communicating through elements that are not recognisably communicative is called 'metacommunication'.

In fact a great deal of research shows that we notice things without knowing that we notice them; that we can actually learn without knowing that we are learning. This is something called Implicit Learning. People pick up cues from their environment all the time when making decisions about what to buy. Think, for examples, of the cues you pick up when you meet someone in the street even before you start talking. Do they look tired, are they walking slowly or with a spring in their step? Similar cues are carried in the bubbles and the music of the O2 advertising, rather than any words.

Work carried out outside of a supermarket in 2007 by Jonah Berger and Grainne Fitzsimons (2008) at and following Halloween showed that shoppers mentioned orange-coloured chocolate bars and soft drinks 50 per cent more often before Halloween when orange pumpkins were on display, than after, when they were not. In a second experiment they asked people to fill in a questionnaire with an orange or a green pen. Afterwards they asked them to choose from ranges of orange, green (and some other coloured) items (drinks, detergents, food). As before, those using the orange pen selected more orange products, and those with the green pen, more green ones.

What seems to be clear from this is that a preference at a point of decision is rarely a conscious process for many decisions, and as a result could hardly be a rational one. The weighing up of the options and choosing the one with the greatest utility (or bang per buck) is random. Recency of influence looks as if it might have an undue influence on a decision, particularly if it does not involve an item or service that is a *critical* purchase.

This discovery may appear intuitive. Few buying decisions are life threatening, and if we spent all of our time pondering the merits of one lunch ingredient over the next we would not actually have time to eat the lunch. All of which might be very disappointing for a marketing director about to spend a fortune on a new product or service launch.

If we accept that the subconscious is an important part of shopping, how is it affected by a brand? The mechanics of communication are dealt with in the next chapter. But let's look at recent research on the subconscious mind as it reacts to a brand.

Placing a Brand into the Subconscious Mind: Building a Long-Term *and* a Short-Term Property – Brand Engrams

Everything that a brand *does* or a shopper experiences about a brand has an impact on the image that a shopper has of the brand at any place along the journey to purchase.

The construct in the brain that holds this unique vision is called the engram. The process of building a recognisable engram is called encoding. It is not only the pack design that has a real part to play in maintaining and building this engram but it may be this that triggers an action.

An engram is defined by Schacter (1996) as 'the brain stores (memory networks) by increasing the strength of connections between different neurones that participate in encoding an experience'.

The engram is built from experience of episodes such as advertising, personal recommendation and product experience and is framed around by other, similar products or experiences so it has a context. Elliott defines this as the 'adaptive subconscious'. Research shows the shopper takes 70 per cent of purchase decisions at the POP and that decision is highly influenced by brand engrams.

An organism (animal or shopper) focuses on selected features of their environment. Because of the exposure to messages (some 600 to 625 ads per day) consumers adopt low attention strategies – subconsciously storing information. It is possible for any brand manager however to have their creative people draw up engram-friendly designs that reinforce and build the component parts of a brand in the mind.

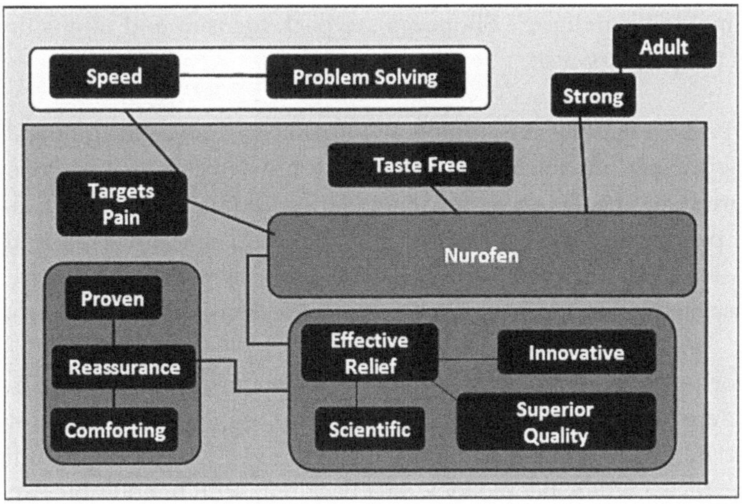

Figure 1.1 A mental engram built around the idea of a Nurofen pack

The packaging itself needs to trigger the engram in a very brief glance. The elements on the pack that trigger this are the visual mnemonics of the pack. Shoppers look for *unique* visual clues in prioritising shape and colour over any words.

When developing a pack, it needs to have the kind of standout that reinforces the engram. Meaning it must be distinctive and unique. This involves learning and using Visual Language: imagery or symbols, in preference to words, to illustrate the 'story' which describes in highly encapsulated form your product or service. Here, as an example, is a mental engram built around the idea of a Nurofen pack (Figure 1.1). The pack itself was designed expressly to reinforce the engram.

The standout 'target' for pain in the modern-style pack is linked to 'urgent' red features that make it hard to pass by if you are wanting to cure a headache! Pick one up yourself and see.

The shopper absorbs marketing communications and advertising messages into the adaptive subconscious before entering the store. The shopper may be consciously smart, sophisticated, cynical of marketing and advertising, time scarce and highly selective. The in-store environment is immensely complex. With often some 25,000 products on display and several thousand promotions, other shoppers and staff, how does the shopper set about the task of making purchases? Shoppers are pack-focused and interacting with packs is the primary task.

The packaging is the most important form of communication for the shopper. The shopper subconsciously pays attention only to packs that are relevant to their store visit. The shopper's attention is triggered by the unique visual clues because packaging design minimises the effort and time involved in decision making. The Core Visual Mnemonic (CVM) often has high recall. Where it does not, conscious processing is required to make the decision to select a product.

Unfortunately market researchers are often unaware that the research they undertake exposes conscious attitudes and opinions to research stimulus material but rarely identifies the subconscious. Eye-tracking studies, for example, reveal where people look on a pack but, with honourable exceptions such as iMotions studies (discussed later), do not reveal whether a dwell in one area is a result of trying to understand or high levels of interest.

Building and Maintaining an Engram

What does all this mean for a marketing communication plan?

It reinforces the significance of developing a product message that is recognisable at all points in the shopper journey. This means that you need to have some inventive, innovative, creative point of reference that the shopper can use as their engram for your product. A logo or colour or some sound (notes or a jingle) or a phrase needs to be constructed and then used in all marketing communications. Be aware that the shopper may not select your preferred engram. How to find out what the shopper has used as their engram for your product is covered in Part III.

Message consistency and frequency are important. Recognising that a message helps to build a feeling around a brand helps you to understand why a recognisable image at the exact point of decision actually becomes part of your advertising campaign. Fortunately this meets other needs that persuade the shopper to buy, described briefly towards the end of this chapter.

There are elements of your message that you cannot change with impunity. Later on in this book we instance a case study from a Tropicana campaign that had serious impact on their market share to the extent that the re-design was almost immediately withdrawn.

You cannot rely on just one channel to build your brand if you want to bring sales along with the image. The IPA report suggested that three channels are best. We suggest six are even better.

Establishing, and consistently using, an engram in shopper communication is essential to return maximum value for money from your marketing and advertising spend.

Building the Relationship between Shopper and the Brand Engram

The engram gets 'under the skin' of the shopper. To convert that subconscious implant to sales requires other marketing communications, part of the long and winding road that as a marketer you need to traverse successfully to obtain sales – these marketing communications are described briefly in the paragraphs below and at greater length in the chapters listed.

An Econsultancy/Responsys survey (2013) finds that, though 70 per cent of companies agree that building a relationship is important and that pound for pound it is of more value than going for new customers, only 30 per cent are committed to doing so. The reason given is lack of resources (22 per cent) or no clearly defined strategy (19 per cent). Sixty-four per cent acknowledge they are still committed to campaign-centric communication. Brands, suppliers and retailers that communicate with shoppers on a two-way basis benefit from the relationship they can build. See also Chapters 8 and 9.

Excess Share of Voice (ESOV)

A key determinant of success explored further by the IPA lies in achieving ESOV ('How Share of Voice Wins Market Share' – IPA Nielsen 2009). Analysis of successful IPA award-winning media campaigns show that the companies generating the best return from their advertising investment focus on getting the greatest share of media impinging on the target market. The IPA finding is supported by the earlier work of Villarejo-Ramos and Sánchez-Franco (2005) who reported '… The higher the spending on advertising for the brand, the better the quality of the product as perceived by the consumer … price deals as incentives to increase sales have been shown to have a negative effect on brand equity.' The facts and how to achieve ESOV is covered in Chapters 8 and 9 and, of course, all advertising can be used to promote engrams.

Encouraging the Shopper to Use Social Media

Shoppers may be guided to find out what others think of your product or service. Social media reaction can also be used to correct misunderstandings and rectify shortcomings; customer feedback is a part of life – benefit from it. Read more about social media in Chapter 4.

Promotions, a Marriage Made in Heaven

Research has for some time been available to show that a key persuader along the shopper journey and at the POS is a sales promotion that should be fun, benefits both seller and buyer and that also knocks out the competition. Palazon and Delgado (2005) discovered: 'non-monetary promotions are more effective than monetary promotions in affecting brand equity positively. While non-monetary promotions raise the Satisfaction and Loyalty without decreasing any other constructs; monetary promotions increase Satisfaction but lead to lower Quality, Value and Prestige.' More on promotions in Chapters 10 and 11.

Point of Sale/Purchase

In-store signing and support of the product with POP is important as this is where 70 per cent of the decisions are made. There is extensive coverage of this in Chapters 10 and 11.

Monopolising Your Shopper

Synergy works. An IPA report, following Palazon and Delgado, using some of the same source data, showed that Synergy in Approach is a key factor in winning high shopper ratings. This is totally supported by the need in The Offer to the shopper to consider the 6Cs – again described later in Chapter 3.

Investing behind Your Shopper

Many hurdles are unwittingly placed by retailers in front of the shopper, all of which have simple remedies if they are duly considered. Chapter 6 is devoted to these barriers to purchase.

Summary

Implanting and sustaining the engram is essential. There are, though, techniques that are much more adept at cutting through where the engram can be significantly more effective at reaching the adaptive subconscious. You may have the right message, but in the wrong place, and you may discount the additional value of synergy. Do so at your peril for, as the following chapters in this book show, there is more that has to be done to win in the battle for the shoppers' or buyers' purchase of your product or service. First it is helpful to understand a bit about how people communicate and learn.

Chapter 2
The Communication Canvas

Because of the rise of the mobile and the internet, brands and retailers will need to communicate directly one-to-one with the customer and expect and should, as a mutually beneficial policy, encourage feedback. A reading of the literature reveals that Communication and Learning are intertwined, so it is important for the marketer to understand the theory. This chapter is a brief guide to both subjects. The reference section includes the 234 texts on which this chapter is based.

In summary, a person (the shopper) follows a process when a 'message' is offered to them (by the marketer). The person processes, either subconsciously and/or consciously, and decides, first, whether to receive the message or not (communication), then the person tries to make sense of the message (learning), finally storing the 'processed message' into the brain – alongside or with whatever the brain has decided is an appropriate place (the engram, if it has been highlighted by the brand or retailer).

This chapter describes the concept of the communication canvases of sender (the marketer) and receiver (the shopper) and how, if they do not overlap sufficiently – that is, that there is no common realm of communication – the message is lost. The detail of the communication canvas – a device used in this book as an analogy based on the work of Chris Fill – and how a marketer can ensure 'overlap' is covered later in this chapter. The need for relevancy of the message to the shopper is also assessed here. By way of examples for relevancy, the message may be 'this is a fashion item' (important to fashionistas but irrelevant and so rejected by others); or, this is a survival message – 'the product is poisonous' (important to all); or, this is an endorsement message (only category relevant and then only if the shopper rates that category). This chapter also covers other potential sources of a failure to communicate.

The shopper, accepting the message as a communication, next processes and 'learns' from the message. There is an implied duty on the marketer in any case to match the shopper's understanding capability for any message, but the part learning plays can be used by the marketer. A marketer has the opportunity to trigger an appropriate learning technique (described later in this chapter), selected from the range of marketing disciplines available, to actually shape how the brain learns from the message. Learning from marketing messages differs by marketing discipline; to illustrate this, when the salesman in an experiential marketing situation suggests a shopper tries a new vacuum cleaner the brain has to learn the motor skills to use it – how to hold it, how to move it – that skill is then stored with the engram (logo?/noise?/shape?) – which is why experiential marketing is a powerful way to get the message across because it is per se requiring a conscious brain activity. Compare that with basic advertising, when, unless the words, sound or picture make you stop (Benetton?), absorbing the advert is just a subconscious activity of the brain. When the advertising does contradict the shopper's knowledge it makes a person stop and engage brain, which is why cognitive dissonance – a learning technique – is such a powerful creative tool in advertising, requiring the shopper to engage their conscious brain to rationalise the knowledge (more on this later in the chapter). How the message is absorbed in the brain is dependent on how the message is 'learnt'. Where it is stored in the brain comes next.

The message, in the way the shopper has processed the message, is registered and if one is given it is placed with a relevant engram. If no engram is offered, then the brain will place it dependent on how the shopper processed the message and will allot a category. Of course neither message processing nor location may be that which the marketer intended. If the message is not learnt as the marketer hoped the shopper will carry incorrect knowledge, and if the message is 'mis-tagged', that is, not with the engram, it may also be stored in the 'wrong place' in the shopper's brain.

Remember a strong marketing communication is very powerful and the shopper or buyer learns from it – it can even persuade a rational shopper to place their hand on a purse or wallet and extract hard-earned money to buy a product or service on the spot.

Communicating Theory

Communication is defined as a transactional process between two or more parties whereby meaning is exchanged, then 'learnt' and stored. Throughout, the 'receiver' must 'allow' a message to be sent to him/her. An illustration of a receiver's exclusion: research shows that regular readers of newspapers seem to be capable of ignoring all advertisements even though presented with them full face (if you read a paper this morning – can you recall any of the advertisements?). So both the conscious and subconscious can be switched off. From whom the message is sent is important, as in most communication the credibility of the 'sender' will affect how much attention is paid to the message. If credibility is high (for example, if the sender of an engram related to the message is recognised), or if the paper or writer is known, the intended receiver will give it attention and tend to believe it.

Why this 'sender acceptance' is important will be made clear in subsequent chapters. Sender message acceptability will need to conform to the shopper's communication canvas. Brands, suppliers and retailers will need to adapt their products and services' messages to the customer voice in order to be 'heard'. Some report that this will have to be as soon as by 2016 in order to compete – with format, content, information, education about product or service, location for purchase, delivery, cost, value, social and cultural positioning, feedback – with other shoppers' brands that are aligned to the shopper. In particular the package 'message', POS material and advertising should match the preferred message format and so on of the shopper. As it is recognised now that different countries may require different messages for their shoppers, in future, that may have to be extended within countries to different regions or even down to local stores to optimise communication – as Coca-Cola are now proposing to do.

So, meaningful communication is more likely when there is overlap of communication understanding between the source (that is, the sender which is you – the brand, supplier or retailer) and the receiver (the shopper). So in trying to imagine how a shopper receives messages a definition of that capability is needed:

> *The realm of perception of a person, defined and constrained by their physical and mental capabilities, the context or environment in which they receive the message and their preferred language, format, culture, social context and channels within which he or she will receive and frame any message.*

When communication between a sender and receiver occurs, how much of the message is passed depends on the overlap of their communication canvases. A simple illustration might help depict this canvas analogy (Figure 2.1). Using the communication canvas analogy to illustrate how the (shopper as) recipient prefers to take in messages, allows for a greater scope when marketers brief agencies and their creative staff as to how to optimise their advertising material to appeal to the shopper. An artist paints on a canvas using different colours,

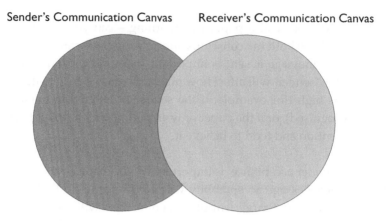

Figure 2.1 Communication – the sufficiency of the overlap

materials and shapes to portray a particular view of an image to the viewer. The recipient shopper here might be described in artistic terms – preferring one of photo-realist or impressionist or abstract communication. Colour or black and white, or reverse negative might be preferences, or the viewer might hate them. The framing of the message might be varied – simple or complex – just as the texture and the medium, say exercising a preference for 'watercolour' to 'oil'. The potential of the communication canvas is probably unbounded – but helpful in describing the target shopper in a more constructive and useful way when briefing creative staff on how to present the message.

The diagram illustrates that the communications overlap needs to be sufficient to communicate the message – and at an appropriate level. If there is no overlap between the circles this indicates that there is no realm of understanding. An extreme example would be between a wild animal and man – there is no common culture or language. However, domestic animals and man can learn to communicate. At the other extreme it is said that a couple who have been together for decades may almost fully and uniquely understand each other. A greater overlap is required for complex communication. For example, at the lower end of overlap a British scaffolder employing a number of Europeans (say Latvians and Poles) might require them to learn English, or alternatively, as their employer, to learn Polish and Latvian. Of course, the scaffolder might find it possible to communicate through demonstrating the rudiments of scaffold work using the bits of pipe and fittings. Describing the health and safety legislation that applies to scaffolding would probably require a higher level of communication overlap. In marketing communication terms there are additional local understanding and background, social and cultural meanings that require exploration. For example, describing to a shopper the technical benefits of a product may call on a higher level of education in both parties to the communication. Some salespersons may deliberately assume a higher level of the realm of understanding to bamboozle a shopper or a shopper accepts being bamboozled, not wishing to reveal a lower level of education with ignorance of the contents of the communication.

Now consider what happens each time someone sends out a message, in whatever form. How the receiver sees or hears the message depends on the *sender's communication canvas* and the *receiver's communication canvas*, illustrated by the two overlapping circles.

The amount of overlap represents the ease or difficulty of communication – the more overlap the easier it is to communicate. But the overlap depends on each person's communication canvas, and each person's communication canvas is different. For example:

- the message may be in a language or jargon that the receiver does not understand whether spoken or written;
- meanings of the same word can differ, even within a small geographic area;
- the message may require a higher education or technical level of understanding than the shopper holds;
- the message may assume a knowledge of a subject of which the shopper is unaware;
- the message may presume a social or cultural background which the shopper does not hold.

So when you are communicating messages, think about how much overlap there is between you as the sender and your communication canvas and that of the receiver – that is the individual shopper's communication canvas. Is your message within their realm of understanding?

If a spoken language is a challenge for your shopper, then use just a few key words in each person's language, or use signs or pictures. This is becoming important in a multicultural country or across border message communication. There are also a few key marketing words that trigger attention – these key words are described in Chapter 11.

If you need to put across to the shopper more complex messages, communication that is matched to the realm of understanding becomes even more important, particularly in order to be able to motivate the shopper to action.

A marketer needs to spend time finding out how the shopper communicates.

- Do they prefer the spoken word?
- Or written instructions?
- Are diagrams better?
- Or cartoons?

There is a need to research the shopper's jargon too.

Study the feedback response of people (through call centres, salespersons, social media) to increase the realm of understanding and over time set down the communication canvas of the shopper. Then, use that research to modify the messages, to match each receiver's communication canvas. And, over time, discover that this type of motivational communication is more effective and achieves better results. As a marketer this means the shopper commits to purchase. An example would be asking for comments on a new product and taking note of the words used by the shopper to describe the product or the environment or context in which the shopper describes the product, then using these words in subsequent communications.

Today, some people may prefer the web style of messages – with short bullet points, lots of headings and so on. This matches the speed with which messages have to be taken in (0.9 of a second in a supermarket), but it may equally infuriate those with a more artistic communication canvas who prefer the Waterstones' staff handwritten shelf labels relating to book content.

In summary, the marketer needs to spend time discovering how shoppers communicate: to find out their language strengths and limitations, their preferred communication channels, their preferred formats – whimsical descriptions or terse notes? Discover whether your customers prefer – speech? Writing? Diagrams? Drawings? Cartoons? What format do they like the messages in? Most people are unhappy with writing across the A4 page unless they are professionals like lawyers, preferring newspaper format with lots of short sentences and headings. Pictures alongside text may work even better.

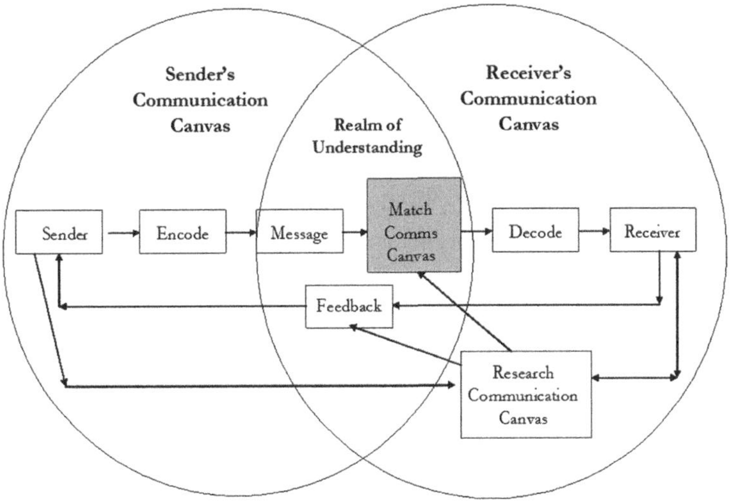

Figure 2.2 The feedback on shopper communication

Source: PhD thesis, Roddy Mullin.

When this has been done the marketer is in a position to use the research to modify the message, to match the receiver's communication canvas. The feedback on shopper communication can be illustrated diagrammatically (Figure 2.2).

Remember also that there are the basic requirements of communication:

- If it is a voice message, the sender may speak too quietly or without conviction. The receiver may be partially deaf or blind. This factor might be illustrated by varying the size of the circles on the communication canvas to indicate the extent of the communication task. If it is a written message, the font size may be too small for the eyesight of elderly shopper targets.

- If the communication is in picture format it has to be sufficiently visible and clear.

- The receiver may choose not to listen – or only to parts, or not be aware that the message is addressed to them.

- There may be too many other stimuli in the background for the receiver's brain to take in or be bothered with the message.

Communicating buy-in to change or a new product. If the marketer wishes the shopper to 'buy-in' to a change, whatever that change is, whether in the brand or the product, the message is likely to require the shopper to learn about the change and the need for change. The message has to create the vision and overcome any fears as well as motivate. Again a change message must be couched in terms that match the communication needs of the individual shopper and the way the shopper learns. Importantly the buy-in has to extend to the shopper's friends, family and social contacts. Change requires the approval of those around the shopper, described here as stakeholders, to enable the shopper to respond to questions both in their mind and asked of them such as 'Why has the brand changed?' This can be illustrated diagrammatically (Figure 2.3).

Place all the communication canvases on a circle, including the shopper and the sender (brand as well as retailer – the staff) as well as the influencers (families, colleagues and friends). Here each element of the extended circle is described as a 'stakeholder' – this is now the target of such 'change' message communications. The extent of overlap depends as before on the amount between sender and recipient. For example, if the response can be 'because it is new', then all the marketer has to put on the product or its surrounding POS is the word 'new' (more on the best choice of key words later in Chapter 11). If the product is new there may be a requirement to educate the shopper as well and provide sufficient information for the shopper to sell and explain the 'newness' to the stakeholders.

The consequence of this assessment is that there is then a need to establish the communication canvas of all the stakeholders involved with any change proposed and the provision of, and understanding the need to provide, answers for the shopper to use to explain the change. The messages on packaging and POS should be extensive, subtle and establish credibility of the change. Repetition of such messages is important as part of the reinforcement of learning (see the final part of this chapter).

Establishing that common ground overlap between sender and receiver. A common mistake with marketers is to assume that their own background, social, cultural, educational, experience and knowledge is the same as their target shopper. The fields of perception in reality are likely to be quite different. It is a human failing to make assumptions about how others think and are likely to respond to communications.

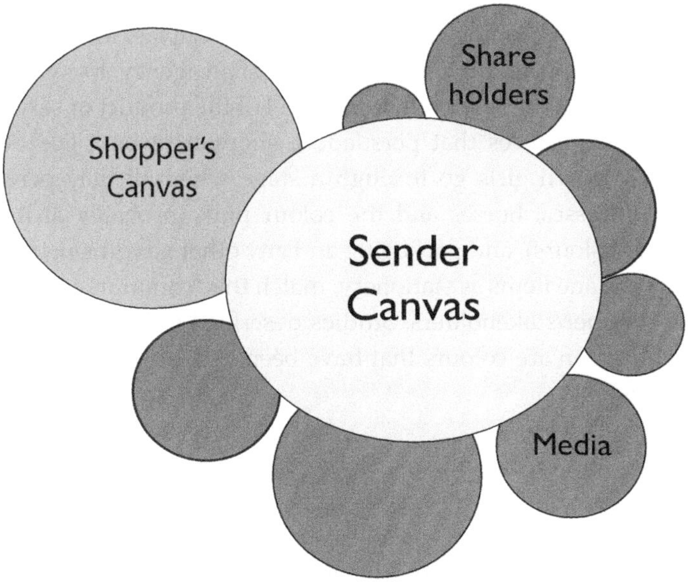

Figure 2.3 Finding the stakeholder's communication canvas

The marketer has to erase from their own mind any thinking and prejudices related to the marketer's own background. This method has been described as 'self-recognition criteria' – accepting that the way any one person – here a marketer – thinks and reacts is certainly wrong for any individual or stakeholder being analysed. A marketer has to detach themselves from all their background (and prejudices).

Finding the Communication Canvas

A business typically might research customers' needs and wants with regard to the product or service and hopefully, but with less emphasis if any in the past, seeking also the preferred communication channels, language and message formats to establish the shoppers' 'communication canvas'. Knowing which media the target shopper consumes enables the astute marketer to target accurately and avoid wasting budget on trying to communicate with people who are not paying attention or have no interest in the product. The research may be carried out through questionnaires, accessing pre-researched or global questionnaires, interviewing or by telephone and now through data accumulated through mobile and internet reactions of shoppers.

The purpose of establishing the communication canvas, for the marketer, is to use the resulting Insight (intelligence), or brief an agency, to communicate messages that are tuned to the psychological feel of the product or service with words, colours and pictures that persuade a shopper to buy. For example, the majority of Western girls go through a stage when all they perceive as wonderful is princesses, horses and the colour pink (probably at that time rejecting all other colours), and packaging and any other advertising messages, even on such mundane items as stationery, match this 'communication canvas' need of these shopper/stakeholders. Studies described in later chapters show how orange and green are colours that have been used to persuade shoppers to buy subconsciously.

Focus groups and questionnaires alone might have fulfilled the research role previously. Now the answers can be acquired from in-house data (credit card/store card data, purchasing profile and so on), asking questions of the shopper as they buy, and also now using analysis of social media. Trying to acquire all this information at once is hazardous. Research confirms that if the online shopper encounters more than three web pages at the end of a transaction (where the retailer may be trying to acquire data) the majority will abort the purchase. It is easier to build the knowledge up in small packets to create a database of information on the customer over a period of time and then convert that data to Insights.

Very often organisations only identify some of the 'louder' individual customers but fail to recognise the different needs of other quieter stakeholders. The evidence for this is difficult to qualify and quantify. However, by way of example, the media have recently made much of a UKIP MEP politically incorrectly referring to aid given by the UK to 'Bongo Bongo' land countries as wasteful. The MEP stated that such money would be better spent within the UK during hard times. The media has by its voice denigrated this view. Interviews with the 'man on the street' though have found, however, that people agree the view of the MEP and not the media, though they do infer that the MEP might have used less sensitive language.

Communication Hazards Affecting the Receiver

For completeness the marketer should also be aware of the following hazards of communication, described on the next page.

Semiotics assumes meaning will be derived socially – it is an interaction between the receiver and the message. Messages are created by re-working signs, codes and symbols within the particular social sign system in order to generate connotations and meanings. The social process involved generates pleasure as well as cognitive (or rational) activities. A receiver outside the social orbit of the sender will have difficulty understanding the true meaning of the message sent. For example many in the US and now in the UK use a 'high five' to indicate that was a 'good job' or a 'good game'. The high five is when two persons raise a flat palm and strike them together. The high five would be lost on a recipient not familiar with the symbol.

Syntactics describes the structure of communications. Symbols and signs change their meanings according to the syntax, or contexts, in which they appear. The same word can have different meanings in different sentences, or the whole message can acquire a different meaning when seen in different locations. For example, 'The chicken is ready to eat' has two alternative meanings. A recipient would not understand unless the context is clear.

Semantics is concerned with the way words (spoken or read) relate to the external reality to which they refer. It is a concept really concerned with the appropriateness of the words to the message itself. This is a barrier because, for anyone unaware of it, the phrase would be meaningless. For example, 'It is raining cats and dogs' does not mean that literally. It means a heavy rain downpour. Again a recipient would not comprehend unless they know the expression and what it signifies.

Culture. Most body language – the silent language – does not transfer well to other cultures, even when the cultures are otherwise close. The problem arises because of ethnocentrism, which is the practice of assuming that others think in the same way and believe the same things. Ethnocentrism is one of the few features of human behaviour that belongs to all cultures. For example, the two finger hand signal 'V' has widely varying meanings in different countries. The Guinness advertisement of a man carrying a girder signified strength in the UK and 'virilility' in Africa. When the advertisement first appeared, Africans thought the drink was a stimulus to procreation.

Perception is the process by which individuals select information from the surrounding environment and synthesise it into a view. Because there is so much going on around us at any one time, selection covers only that which is most immediate or interesting. Inevitably this means that there are gaps in each individual's view of their world, and these gaps are usually filled in by using previous experience or analogies drawn from elsewhere. Meanings of words can be denotative – having the same meaning for everybody – or connotative (having a meaning which is unique to the individual). Perception relates to a single matter; it might be said that a 'communication canvas' is a multitude of perceptions held by the individual.

The make-up of each individual's perception mind map – that is, their communication canvas – differs from every other individual's because it is, in part, a construct of their imagination. The process is affected by the following factors (Table 2.1):

Table 2.1 Factors influencing an individual's communication canvas

Factor	Explanation	Impact
Subjectivity	The individual's view	Whether the shopper accepts or rejects the message
Categorisation	How they store such information in their mind	If the shopper has been supplied with an engram – then that is where the message is stored. If not the message storage will be up to the individual
Selectivity	How the individual selects stored information	If the engram is triggered then that information is selected by the brain
Expectations	Their presumption towards a future message	If the engram is triggered then the expectation will be based on the information that is held
Past experience	Triggering a response – positive, neutral or negative	The shopper response will initially relate to the engram if implanted
Attitude	Is a learned tendency that responds to a thought, idea or meaning in a consistently favourable or unfavourable way. Attitudes are formed as a result of translating needs into motivation to process information and consequent exposure to stimulus	There is more in Chapter 3 on how attitude is developed

Communication Hazards That the Sender Can Cause

A sender can inject 'hazards' into the message that is sent. These are:

Cognitive dissonance (a learning process – see below) is when the brain is faced with conflicting beliefs and is uncomfortable at having to find a solution and 'striving for achievement' fits with the cognitive approach. It is a way that a person learns and useful to a marketer in that it stops a person – a shopper – for a sufficient time to take in a message. The classic example is from

Aesop's Fables where the fox failing to pick the grapes reasons they were probably sour anyway. It is perhaps most useful to indicate that a high-price item is affordable to a shopper if they rationalise the cost, say over a long period of time, or, say, for the raised status the shopper acquires (you're worth it!).

Spin is the latest hazard to communication. Skewing the information presented to meet the sender's point of view. This is dangerous for it presumes the shopper has no contrary indication and if discovery occurs later, it can damage a brand.

Measures That Improve Acceptance of Communications

For a marketer there is a lot more to think about when communicating (Table 2.2). First, the amount and quality of the information that is communicated, and, second, the overall judgement that each individual makes about the way a message is communicated.

Table 2.2 Measures that improve acceptance of communication

Measure	Reasoning	Impact
Balance	The style of a message should reflect a balance between the need for information and the need for pleasure or enjoyment in consuming the message	Too serious delivery may turn the shopper off. Too frivolous messages will have little impact and the impact may be adverse if it wastes the shopper's time
Humour and cynicism	Adds to the pleasure – accepts that many shoppers view marketing as a game and tend to disbelieve product claims that are over-exaggerated	Can put the receiver in a positive mood which means s/he is likely to process messages with little cognitive elaboration. Recognising and accepting in a humorous way that over-exaggeration has occurred is fine for some products
Conclusion or no?	An important structural feature which shapes the pattern of a message is whether the message draws a firm conclusion for the audience, or should people be allowed to draw their own conclusions from the content?	Explicit conclusions are, of course, more easily understood and stand a better chance of being effective. One researcher found this depends on the complexity of the issue, the level of education possessed by the receiver, whether immediate action is required and the level of involvement required by the receiver
Two-sided messages improve credibility	Where the good and bad points of a product or service are presented, messages are more effective	Credibility is improved with two-sided messages, which tend to produce more positive perception of the sender than one-sided messages. When the receiver's initial opinion is opposite to that presented in the message and when they are highly educated there is greater impact

Table 2.2 Continued

Measure	Reasoning	Impact
Communicating key points. Order of points made	The development of message strategy concerns the order in which important points are presented to avoid encountering objections and opposing points of view. Messages which present the strongest points at the beginning use what is referred to as the primacy effect	The decision to place the main points at the beginning depends on whether the shopper has a low or high level of involvement. A low level may require an attention-getting message component, a weak point may lead to a high level of counter-argument. A decision to place the strongest points at the end of the message assumes that the receiver agrees with the position adopted by the source or has a high positive level of involvement
Rationality and logicality	Messages should be rational and contain logically reasoned arguments and information. It is insufficient to state that a product washes whiter without saying why (because it has a new ingredient?)	Receivers must be able to complete their decision-making processes. Factual establishment of credibility is vital. Where it helps understanding, present the problem to the shopper through demonstration
Reassurance	That the product does do what it says it can	The shopper is not only happy to have found the product and any promotion but also sees on the packaging that it confirms the reason for the purchase
Appeal	Execution of the message appeal is key and must be appropriate to the receiver's perception and expectations	Without an appeal – to buy, to respond, to try – the chances of successful communication are reduced

Establishing Sender Credibility by the Receiver

Here are some of the factors that make up your credibility as a communication sender. Different factors will have significance or relevance in different contexts.

- need for recognition of sender (the engram!);
- need for conviction, authority, trust, expertise;
- need for liking of the sender – a generally favourable view of the sender (brand or commentator) – that is, the receiver believes the sender is genuinely shopper friendly, will assist;
- drip feeding of reminders – shoppers are human beings and need constant repetition (and consistency) to enhance sender credibility;
- the source – whether the brand (they would say that anyway!), or an independent commentator (belief in the media?) of a message is an important credibility factor in the communication process to the receiver;

- if a receiver perceives a source lacking conviction, authority, trust or expertise the receiver is likely to discount any message received from that source, until such time that credibility is established.

The identification of the sender is important to the effectiveness of the communication. With it, the message is more likely to be believed: without it – less belief – for example, websites that do not list an address may not be identified and hence not trusted as much. The identification process may be two-stage with endorsements from such persons as Mrs Smith of Totnes reviewing a hotel on Trip Advisor. A recent highly endorsed restaurant in Devon was found not to exist. The onus is then on the website to be diligent and honest or it loses credibility.

So the corollary for the marketer is to ensure that the appropriate messages must be included in the communication to establish the credibility of the brand, supplier or retailer as sender. This is best achieved by establishing a relationship – one of the six communication channels recommended by the authors.

As an aside, how can individual communication skills be developed by a marketer?

- Increase vocabulary – by reading widely. This particularly applies to that material read by your target shopper. Watching TV programmes will also provide the jargon used. This will increase understanding of the target shopper's communication canvas when the Insight is received.

- Take every opportunity to listen and talk – particularly to your target shoppers. It will add to the Insight obtained from data and research. This means your messages should work better in terms of matching the shortcuts and slang used. Attend lectures and talks to better understand the use of language to move an audience. Motivational phrases are valuable to acquire from accomplished speakers. There are always people who have ideas and like to talk. Join in and express a view. Sometimes by announcing a more outrageous view the discussion will be wider ranging. Talk both at work and outside work. It all helps with establishing the communication canvas concept and researching and proving that of the shopper.

- Sign up for public speaking courses. Particularly helpful if considering radio or TV and cinema advertising. The spoken word is quite different from grammatical writing. Practise talking and varying rhythm, speed, volume and pitch which will be of benefit in writing promotional scripts that are tuned to the communication canvas of the shopper through audiovisual media.

- Debating groups? Amateur dramatics? These will assist in understanding dialogue that is forceful to make a point. There are debating groups – at which the opportunity to speak should be taken. Amateur dramatic groups allow you to practise throwing the voice and applying emotion. Making a successful appeal to the shopper is key to obtaining a buy decision.

Learning

Learning, along with communication, is important for a marketer to understand. This knowledge is valuable when selecting the marketing media to apply. Marketing disciplines rely on different ways of learning.

How we learn requires a brief explanation: Marketing communication requires the receiver – the shopper – to learn from the message. So how do people learn? (See Figure 2.4.)

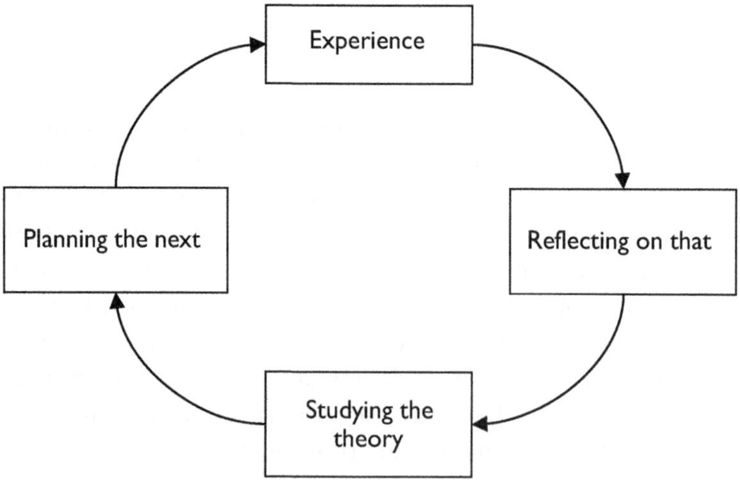

Figure 2.4 How people learn

ALL EXPERIENCE IS LEARNING

A review of the literature indicates we learn through repeating a cycle of the experience, reflecting on what happened, studying the theory and planning the next experience. There may be a need to pre-research the underpinning knowledge, acquire or hone skills such as writing, observing, listening and question preparation to enhance the learning experience. Testing assists a learner to recognise what areas require additional effort. Providing the opportunities for learning experiences is rated as important to the individual.

THE INDIVIDUAL NATURE OF LEARNING

It seems that the way in which an individual actually learns will affect the kind and extent of learning from any particular situation. There is a need to use appropriate language – if at all possible tailored to each individual – to adopt a level of language that is appropriate and ensure the complexity of argument is at the level of the learner rather than that of the subject expert preparing the course. This may seem a tall order still, but as with the accumulation of shopper data, communication data will one day follow. Some people recall that a particular teacher was brilliant – it may well be that the teacher had nearly perfectly matched the person's learning and communication needs.

In the teaching profession there is now recognition that there is a need to carry out an investigation of the learner and their communication needs in the context of their learning history, learning experience and maturity in the knowledge sense.

Different forms of media can be used to assist learning. For adults, trial and error to find the best way is one solution. Writing copious notes, 'photographing' material in the mind's eye – but see also below, which describes alternative ways that people learn.

THE NEED FOR A WILLING LEARNER

Training and learning is like hearing and listening. You can hear but not listen; you have to take an active decision to listen and that's down to the individual. A willingness to 'learn how to learn' and the ability to learn from experience are among the best ways of coping with continuous change. An adult shopper however has to commit to learning.

THE RECOGNISED ROUTES TO LEARNING – THERE ARE FIVE!

- *Learning as behaviour.* Reinforcing responses through reward is the behaviourist's way of encouraging the desired behaviours. By rewarding the desired behaviour, the behaviourist conditions the individual to perform the action again and again.

- *Learning as understanding.* Cognitive learning theories view learning as a process of understanding and internalising the principles, connections and facts about the world around us. Seen this way, the learner is like a powerful machine that processes information and internalises it as knowledge as a human being grows. This is a self-rewarding process.

- *Learning as knowledge construction.* Individuals assign meaning to knowledge that they have obtained through their own experience and only then does it become usable. The learner himself or herself is at the centre of the learning experience. Interaction and dialogue (with other learners) are used by the learner to enhance his or her own personal experiences and understanding. This is where the benefit of social media applies to the shopper.

- *Learning as social practice.* Where learning, when it arises, is applied in a social setting. Learners perform well above their age if given the chance to interact with someone older. The conclusion is that social interaction is crucial to some forms of learning.

- *Learning through understanding how the brain works.* Each human being is unique: that is their personality, life experience, knowledge, 'interest', previous social and cultural experiences influence the way an incoming sensory perception is interpreted. 'Interest' here includes attention and motivation at the time. So the learning processes in the brain mean each individual must *ipso facto* have a unique way of learning.

The brain tackles understanding, thinking and problem solving as follows:

- Each item processed for learning is compared to concepts that are stored in the brain until a match is found, the item is then added to that context.

- Misunderstandings or 'failures to understand' occur when words are unknown or have several meanings or are used out of context or an inference is not taken.

- There is a need for definitions, meanings and specialist jargon to be held in the brain related to each concept. For example, the word 'yellow' means that colour, which the brain can visualise, as if it sees it.

- Some people have fixed minds, some jump to conclusions; for some, their reasoning is flawed.

Experiential Learning and Acquiring a Skill as a Form of Learning

Experiential marketing uses experiential learning often through the acquisition of a skill. The acquisition of a skill arises through the interaction of the three component parts to any skill:

- *psycho-motor skill,* which is applied even when the skill is cerebral and parts of the body move;

- *perceptual skill,* making judgements and checking for correct performance such as singing a note; and

- *cognitive skill,* where, for example, patterns, plans, sequences and sheet music have to be understood and operated including reasons, safety rules and so on.

Learning a skill usually requires ensuring everyone has a clear view, pre-preparation of stages of the process – 'here is one I made earlier' – while the reasons and so on are explained.

The learner puts each part into practice as the session proceeds. If this does not happen then concentration may be lost. Experiential learning is active learning where the learner's attention and participation is required. Selling kitchen items alongside learning to cook, selling cars, offering a test drive (the same applies to other modes of transportation including leisure modes such as, for example, board sailing, skiing, parachuting and hang gliding). Experiential learning/marketing requires some counselling, managing experiences, reviews and types of assessment such as structured discussion and debriefing. The need to fully prepare and train experiential marketing staff should be recognised by the marketer.

Using Cognitive Dissonance as a Learning Technique

Where there is 'cognitive dissonance' – when the brain is faced with conflicting beliefs and is uncomfortable at having to find a solution – this will require effort. But as it aids long-term memory retention, so a learner should be challenged in this way. Marketers note this!

Modes of Learning

In addition to the five recognised routes to learning there are three modes of learning:

- **Follow me**
  'Follow me' is the simplest form of learning – the instructor demonstrates, the learners imitate the movements while the instructor watches them, corrects mistakes, comments and drills them in specific behaviours as needed.

  This kind of procedure is followed by athletics coaches, or military instructors and commanders exercising soldiers in the performance of specific skills such as assembling and dismantling weapons.

  It is also used when marketers employ demonstrators and in experiential marketing.

  This form of learning is appropriate for behaviours that are highly focused and specific and can be practised and replicated precisely. People as adults watch how others 'lead' and learn lessons from that.

- **Joint investigation**
  'Joint investigation' is a form of learning whereby an experienced person 'investigates' together with the learner the experiences that the latter undergoes, in order to arrive jointly at principles, concepts and 'actionable knowledge'. This is a form of coaching.

  Most marketing probably unknowingly uses this mode with the brand, supplier or retailer taking on the role of the 'experienced person'. Try this product, you will find it easier to use, it tastes nicer, it lasts longer, it does the job better.

- **Hall of mirrors**
  'Hall of mirrors' is a metaphor to express the idea of reflection from all possible sides, particularly reflection of sides that are not seen every day. A hall that is all mirrors naturally permits this type of reflection (known also as 360-degree feedback).

  Fashion items are sold using this mode of learning. What is the perception of others to the products on sale? How would I look and be perceived in this outfit or accessory? Clearly sales staff try to create the most favourable hall of mirrors.

Summary

If you have grasped how people communicate and how people learn it can but improve your capability as a marketer – a real and positive achievement.

How is that knowledge used? The key is first to decide what you want the shopper to do as a result of the message you send out – is it to educate, to learn to accept change, to embrace a new idea or to respond to a call to action? From that consider how best to communicate to the shopper – matching one or more of the marketing communication techniques available – and then, from Insights you have of your target shopper, that gives you their communication canvas; you match the message to that canvas for them, to best receive, learn from and then store the message.

The design and assembly of messages is crucially important. Through establishment of a good realm of understanding, messages can be created in such a way that they stand a far greater opportunity of building a dialogue between shopper and the brand, supplier or retailer. By appreciating the underlying emotions of the target shopper and the motivations which drive attitudes and purchase intentions, the balance and the pattern they assume can be shaped in such a way that they lead to effective message delivery.

A way to illustrate just how large or small the communication task is to use the 'Finding the stakeholders' communication canvas' diagram shown in Figure 2.3. Draw in for each stakeholder as a circle – the size depending on their importance/difficulty of the task – and then move the circle until the overlap indicates the scale of the communication task ahead of you as the marketer, in effect showing how large or small the realm of understanding is between you and the shopper.

The authors suggest that drawing the circles is the best way to illustrate the communication of messages as it rapidly illustrates where the greatest allocation of resource is required. As a concept, a communication canvas allows a better way of describing how best to put a message across – particularly when briefing others on how shoppers accept and handle messages.

The next chapter examines the reality of the shopper as customer.

Chapter 3
The Customer – Who Are They?

The Customer – An Overview

Marketers should always start with the customer. It is even more important now because technology has allowed the voice of the shopper as an individual customer to be heard. The key change over the last ten years is in the means and breadth of communication technology which has potentially transformed the customer into an 'all knowing and all seeing' person. However, from the marketers' point of view, research into the subconscious (reported in Chapter 1), the significance of ESOV advertising, the impact of social media, the significance of promotions and the delivery at the POS makes it even more relevant to *dissect* the customer in order to feed in appropriate messages to win the sale.

And what a change! The customer is taking charge, asserting their independence and communicating with ever more people – seeking other's views and advice on everything. The customer's search for knowledge includes recommendations as to what to buy, whom to buy it from, when and how to buy – and, of course, much of this comes from other customers. The scope of such change can make both supplier and retailer recoil from the seemingly enormous task of assessing the customer 'communication canvas' – but help is at hand. To anchor your evaluation of the customer activity, this book applies the 6Cs to define The Offer. The Offer is the customer view, broken down into its component parts, of the CVP made by the supplier, brand manager or retailer for each product or service.

But what are your customers like? What catches their eye? What messages persuade? How does the shopper gather and use information? The fact is that most decisions in-store are not purely rational, you have to accept there is a degree of randomness about the way a person shops – this shopping experience is basically about a creative process complicated by the 20 per cent of shoppers who are also unpersuaded and unconcerned about price. Yes, really! At the POS there is an involvement in purchase, dialogue, developing the customer relationship and 'nudging' the customer as a shopper to purchase – and MARI research (POPAI's Marketing at Retail Initiative) – has discovered what actually can and does make the difference to the purchase decision is the use of key words or a sales promotion. Research, remember, indicates that 70 per cent of brand purchase decisions are made in-store/on the web page. A number of models describe how people buy, one of which is the involvement model.

The involvement model for buying is increasingly seen as a realistic description of the way in which consumers buy products and services. The model extends well beyond marketing. The Church, for example, used to think that people started belonging to a church because they believed – often after a conversion experience. However, it is now understood that people belong before they believe. Studies in America have shown that people become involved in a church because of friends or family. It is often quite casual at first. Only after a period of years do they come to realise that they believe. The process of 'belonging before believing' is about 'behaviour before attitude'. The involvement model suggests that if you involve the shopper in your product or service sufficiently then they will believe in it and buy. The Ehrenburg model – Awareness–Trial–Reinforcement (ATR) – is based on the same 'early experience convinces' approach in the commercial world.

A sales promotion offering a sample or the deployment of experiential marketing can assist in a change in behaviour. Persuading someone to 'try' offers the chance to experience a product and the brand values that come with it. Once you have seen that the product or service matches or could match your preferred behaviour – then if the process continues – it is only a question of time before the attitude follows the behaviour and the shopper buys the product or purchases the service. It makes increasing sense in the light of evidence that behaviour precedes attitude to depend on it. Hence, for example, the importance of bounce backs in mobile marketing which stimulates further involvement. A bounce back is a second promotional offer when a shopper accepts a first promotional offer or responds to a requested action. It is a kind of thank you. Encouraging someone to try a product or service is often the best way to begin the process by which they become a long-term customer.

Behaviour and attitude have a complicated relationship. Surveys show that far more people think that regular exercise is a good thing (attitude) than actually practise it (behaviour). Surveys also show that people drink more alcohol (behaviour) than they are prepared to admit to (attitude). For years, the Government urged people to use seat belts (attitude), with only limited effect. They then passed a law making it illegal not to wear seat belts (behaviour). People grumbled at first but buckled up. Over time, people's attitude changed to accord with the behaviour they had become accustomed to. This suggests that marketing campaigns that directly impact on the behaviour of customers succeed and the desired attitude to the product or service will follow. A creative sales promotion can do this such as Nescafe, O2 or Orange. Post-Olympics, the distinctive symbols of success used by Mo Farah and Usain Bolt have been adopted by some brands. Advertising campaigns aimed primarily at creating awareness and attempting to change attitudes are less likely to succeed.

Is Loyalty an Extension of Attitude and Behaviour?

Loyalty is supposed to be based on attitude, though it is not necessarily a predictor of behaviour. Compromises do occur – behaviour beats attitude and loyalty when a customer is lured into buying a competitor product on price drop. Loyalty is also undermined by bulk buy discounts too, though the recent OFT intervention (November 2012) requiring the price of bulk purchases to be a genuine discount on the list price suggests that the customer is not as streetwise as they are supposed to be. Indeed the move to price everything at £1 has led to product price increases by some stores – with associated sales increases, as *The Grocer* pointed out as an example – in Asda supermarkets. There is clearly some loyalty as otherwise customers would simply buy supermarket own brand products and those branded products offering a discount. Forty-four per cent of all goods are now sold on promotion with 60 per cent of health and beauty products on a price promotion at any one time. There is a need to constantly promote products to maintain customer loyalty (and of course re-invigorate the engram). Errors in measuring loyalty can occur – dunnhumby tracking volume purchasing for Tesco recorded a particular product as 'low loyalty' and it was de-listed, whilst Morrison's customers loved the same product. dunnhumby were originally a market research company subsequently purchased by Tesco.

So what incentives are most influential in undermining customer loyalty to competitor products?

Table 3.1 A comparative survey indicating the relative impact of incentives

Have any of the following promotional routes tempted you to do any of the following?			
Please tick all that apply	**Buy product you would not have otherwise** %	**Switch brands during promo** %	**Permanently change brands** %
Coupon or voucher (however delivered)	55	32	4
In-store tasting	50	16	4
In-store money-saving promotion	48	34	4
In-store sample	47	20	5
Sample given with other product	41	21	5
Sample attached to other product	40	21	4
Door-dropped sample	39	20	4
Offer promoted in newspaper/ magazine and so on	37	21	4
On-pack offer	37	24	2
In-store demonstration	34	15	4
Magazine cover-mount sample	29	14	3
In-store TV presentation	24	11	3

Source: fast.MAP survey published by *Internet Retailing.*

The comparative survey by fast.MAP and *Promotional Marketing* magazine (Table 3.1) indicates how customers behave when offered different incentives (a coupon or voucher, 55 per cent positive response and to in-store TV presentation, a 24 per cent response).

Moneysupermarket.com estimated some 2.4 million vouchers are redeemed every day representing £30 billion in a year. The positive impact of a coupon on customer buying behaviour even works when the value of the coupon is small – research indicating that there is no difference in response between a 15p off or a 75p off coupon or voucher.

The Effect of a Brand for a Shopper

The power of a brand is immense. Seemingly a brand provides a shortcut to the brain – via an engram – triggering a range of perceptions and values. The brand response is usually triggered by a familiar logo that sets off a repeat of the messages in the brain, which are both reassuring and comforting. It makes decision taking easier when purchasing. There are some 1,300 brands of toothpaste – which to select at the POS? If there are no promotional offers then typically a buyer will select a brand with which they are familiar. There are of course other triggers beyond the visual, such as a sound – a particular jingle or sequence of sounds; smell – think coffee and perfume (the first exhibition of the power of smell, in that case brand perfumes, is on in New York as this book is written); or even vibrations for some niche shoppers, from the recognised powerful throb of top-end motors such as Ferrari or Porsche (and the vibrations of certain helicopters/aeroplanes is distinctive too – just think Chinook).

The Concept of Shopper Loyalty to a Brand

Brands are designed and built to secure loyalty and encourage purchase, generally at a higher or even premium price. Ehrenburg demonstrated that loyalty can be mapped as a statistical effect, resulting from the higher penetration that brands achieve with their higher marketing spend. If this is correct then something seems to be happening in the UK market at the moment. dunnhumby (remember – owned by Tesco) track loyalty through purchases at Tesco; as a result of this 'shopping basket research' they have indicated that loyalty – the tendency for people to buy on repeated occasions – is dropping very rapidly. The heavy trend to discounting is developing two types of consumer: the ones who are not driven by price alongside brand, and those that are. This suggests three different measures of loyalty: customers who are Loyal under all normal circumstances, those who are Loyal under discount – in particular, for example, when a shopper can 'larder fill' and those with no brand preference. There are, however, other trends of which dunnhumby cannot take account – for example, the increase in retailer 'disloyalty'. As an observation by the authors, the Tesco 'engram' itself may be in need of a major change – it seems that there is a resistance building up with the middle-class shopper to anything related to the name 'Tesco'. Another new development across all retailers is that research from many sources shows that if a retailer chooses, for one reason or another, to make a product unavailable, shoppers take charge, by buying what they want elsewhere.

Twitter research can indicate how shoppers rate supermarkets and predict the need to change the customer relationship. Categorising tweets in eight ways from Happiness to Disgust and examining each is revealing about the herd view. It allows analysts to predict the eventual outcome early, of the common view of shoppers, on brands, on retailers and on individual stores' service.

There are always those who buck any trend! Research by the Institute of Promotional Marketing (IPM) with fast.MAP showed that 20 per cent of people had hardly any percentage of their basket filled with a price discount option – although these people did report that they were open to other, non-discount, promotions.

Loyalty is to the Offer not the Offering

Retailers encourage loyalty to give people more than one reason to visit. Does this strategy have an impact? IPM research with the *Retail Bulletin* indicates that loyalty programmes are influential. If we take standard measures of loyalty used widely across the US and map this against the store performance of UK stores, there is a broad trend showing that loyalty cards have moved the two major users in the UK (Tesco and Boots) above their expected market position.

Myer of Australia has an extensive loyalty scheme described in the Introduction. Its main benefit for the stores is the data it provides on shoppers. Boots finds 68 per cent of sales are from holders of their Advantage card. Boots's 70,000 cardholders spend more than those without cards. Other surveys support the uplift finding and a retention improvement. The pressure is on Boots from its cardholders to do more for them and also to offer more – the need for such personalised service is proving to be incredibly powerful – but for Boots it is a ten-year project and they are proceeding cautiously. Fortunately the Boots Board are fully behind the loyalty card and Insights are discussed monthly for it is expected that it will be three years before there is any ROI (2012).

The Tesco experience would probably dictate that listening to the shopper with the card is actually at least as important as using it to promote with.

What about Technology – the Real Driver of Change for the Shopper?

Technology is enabling the customer to change the way they buy. The mobile telephone/tablet – presently emerging as a mix of computer, camera and phone – enables the customer to communicate with family, friends and colleagues through the Internet, giving access to anyone else or any website in the world. The technology is highly visual – pictorial and in writing – and aural (sound) – and is of high quality thanks to an increasingly available and affordable mobile and wireless network. Language is now less of a barrier online as website translation is frequently available whether the shopper is shopping across borders or a visitor to a country. Instant response is possible and at any time of day or night. That can be extended to the home or office through linked enabling software. Knowledge, and acquiring the methodology to apply it, is becoming widespread through the dissemination of apps, saving the customer the need to understand what happens in the background so they can concentrate on shopping. Typically a person uses a tablet at home and a mobile elsewhere. A survey found 63 per cent of consumers used a tablet while watching TV, with 28 per cent looking up products and services they had seen on TV and including 12 per cent who actually bought a product while watching TV. One billion tablets are forecast to be bought between now and the end of 2017. Typically, 22 per cent of tablet users in the US were spending $50 per month through a tablet and 9 per cent over $100 per month in 2012. Mobile/tablets, according to Deloitte, are influencing 5 per cent of total consumer purchases ($158 billion) in US in 2012.

Why do the retailer, brand and supplier need to bother with the new technology? Gartner stated in 2011 that '70 per cent of customer interactions will originate from a mobile device by 2013'. In other words, you cannot afford not to keep up with technology. The 'Mobile Outlook 2013' report on the post-PC era foresees the demise of many business models with agile marketers spending more on geo-targeting, augmented reality bar code scanning and location-reliant search. Mobile excellence is becoming a prerequisite of maintaining shopper loyalty, emphasising the need for brands and retailers to have a mobile strategy marrying online with mobile. It is possible to track shopper reaction discovering customer preference for a 'discount next purchase' rather than a free item.

Using electronic customer data is covered by data protection legislation in many countries. The marketer needs to build and maintain a database within the privacy laws and regulations of their host country. Offering transparent benefits to the customer to acquire their data is essential. For example, your customer agrees to location data being held if in return they receive local restaurant information.

The Effect of Technology on Brands – the Shopper View

In the US, 50 per cent smartphone ownership will arrive in 2013, while 50 per cent of the UK population own smartphones already. In the UK the growth trend is also for mobile TV interaction and social interaction. The shopper is using the web pages – on mobile, tablet and PC – both as a showroom and for actual purchase. The shopper seeks engagement with the brand, supplier and retailer. Personal recommendations, commentary and participation offer a great signal to those in one's sphere of influence, for, if delighted, shoppers are then given the opportunity to share their passions. Shoppers are accustomed to moving from one technology to another – they expect the brand or retailer to do the same.

Reacting to the Technology-Equipped Shopper

The future response for brands is to leverage both loyalty and established goodwill. Pinterest and Instagram are sites where their highly visual nature and social content will generate more favourable brand impressions. Using primarily Instagram, Hype (who sell T-shirts) has grown a business from zero to £8 million turnover in three years – Hype forecast in advance on Instagram their next designs and ask for comment; if favourable, they produce them. The marketer has to return to applying creativity to their communication. In a mobile environment – where sight, sound and motion are critical – then videos and gifs make content more interesting and engaging. Campaigns should tell a story and one that is relevant. Games are another way to support brand advertising – principally through in-app purchases or free-to-play (freemiums). Music apps should, when offered, be presented in a way that is both personalised and automated. Cross-channel campaigns should exploit the differences between mobile and tablet – making the message a holistic experience; that is the one message complements the other. Augmented reality – for example, where a shopper clicks on a view and computer-generated pop-ups add information or descriptions to the scene; geo-location – where the mobile or tablet using GPS produces messages related to the shopper's location (usually near the retail store or a brand outlet); and second screen – when something seen on TV can be accessed by the shopper on a mobile or tablet or through an app (it might even be downloading the app while watching the ad on TV) are strategies that should become more widely used cross-channel in 2013. 'Attract', 'engage' and 'delight' will be the marketers' watchwords. Make sure that any platforms you use work successfully in all of the regions and countries from which you draw your customers.

Measuring the effectiveness of all the above is a challenge and is covered in Part III. Real-time intelligence, where the brand and retailer pick up shopper reaction almost as it happens, is needed to turn the quantities of data into relevant and actionable Insight, transforming the end-user experience positively into purchases. The Kelloggs delivery overnight of on-pack gold medal winner naming, is an example of real-time action. (Yes, Kelloggs had the packs printed with winners' names, filled and delivered overnight to the shops!)

The Many Segmented Customer

Customers display many different shopping personalities according to the time, place or context of the purchase. The business executive may be buying top travel packages one moment and, the next, organising an economy family break. Within a few hours an office manager may be purchasing office materials, spending on entertainment at lunchtime with colleagues and then, after leaving work, he or she goes food and retail shopping with the children before returning home to shop online. The shopper is still one individual with a singular and distinct social, educational and cultural background but represents multiple customer personalities. The supplier or retailer that fails to recognise this duality is likely to fail the customer relationship test.

To segment by gender, demographic or socioeconomic station is no longer adequate. Ultimately, brand marketers must reach, engage, convert and amplify the user of the shopper – the one who will buy, share, post, tweet and participate in branded programmes and events. The shortest path to this shopper is through a well segmented, measured and well-messaged existing user base. The importance of well-planned and holistic Customer Relationship Management (CRM) practices has never been greater.

Myer (Australia), advised by Sarah Richardson of Global Loyalty Pty Ltd, (see the Appendix), segment their customers under five categories according to the way they shop as much as on the basis of what they buy: Busy Belinda – always in a hurry and often with kids; Premium Polly – who loves designer and high-end trends; Trendy TJ – would be and want to be Premium Polly's; Low Involvement Lou – who would rather not shop if they can help it; and Discount Dora – who loves to snag a bargain. This has helped their marketers and staff in assessing how to treat shoppers.

When surveying customers of financial services companies in the City of London, one author (Roddy Mullin) found that typically only a small percentage were of high value; that is, clients who generated substantial income for the financial services companies. Typically, in a small independent financial services company there are about 18 top revenue-generating clients, with some 75 quite high value out of a total of some 400 clients. By profiling these top-value clients and then matching their profile to prospective clients, many more potential high-value clients (some 14,000 typically) can be found. A small independent firm actually needs to acquire 20 new clients of this type per year to replace wastage, so these firms were advised to target 200 annually from the potential clients found. The financial services companies were also advised they could generate impressive turnover by moving more obviously to serve their client personal interests – that is, moving to fee-based rather than commission-based revenue generation (the latter seems to work against the client as customer from the 'shopper' view). For financial services firms this is the most profitable answer. The remainder of their customers (low return, for time spent on client servicing – about 320 clients) would then be encouraged to move to competitors. A similar experience was encountered with solicitors – here offering annual fee 'retainerships' to customers in exchange for immediate on-call personal service works well with customers, as well as providing an income stream. These 'segments' prove highly remunerative, once recognised by such niche service suppliers as solicitors and financial advisers.

Research (Autumn 2012) in the high fashion world has discovered that there exists a segment of fashionistas known as Digital Divas who are 'technically engaged' (typically using between three and four mobile technologies). They offer two-thirds of the purchasing power available in the sector (that is 34 per cent of all high fashion purchases in the US while influencing another 37 per cent (total 71 per cent) – and 24 per cent in Europe, influencing another 43 per cent (total 71 per cent)). Their influencing power comes from their social media network contacts. In consequence, such Digital Divas are the epicentres of a brand's success. They represent opinion leaders who spend time researching product information, especially customer reviews, while leveraging discounts. The level of retail service and quality of multi-channel experience decides where they shop. They use a mobile in-store to identify themselves as loyal customers (especially in the UK) and to ascertain that they are obtaining a value purchase (say, free delivery, in the US) but always to check for special offers – if not satisfied they use the shop visit to see and touch the product and then buy elsewhere.

The Varying Buying Process

The customer applies a different buying process to different purchases. Obviously acquiring a pair of socks may require no thought and allow an instant purchase – where the product subsequently can be rejected if the purchase is mistaken. There are not many parameters when considering a sock purchase. When buying a car, a rigorous examination of alternatives, consultations and research is undertaken (for example, the cost of insurance, tax and fuel consumption) in addition to performance, reliability and resale price. In fact, car salesman report that some shoppers know more about the car than they do – all the shopper is then looking for from the salesman is a better deal than a competitor car showroom. Factors affecting the shopper perception may be the cost of purchase in relation to shopper income or available cash or credit – but here the salesperson can invoke feelings that the shopper is worth it and overcome any price resistance. (The situation works in reverse – the salesperson must not assume anything about the shopper or whether they can, for example, afford to buy. Pity the Swiss sales girl who rejected Oprah Winfrey's capability to buy a handbag in 2013, the web and press column inches this simple act received may seem out of proportion to the slight. The learning is that the web could be expressly designed as a platform for complaint that can impact anywhere, at any time.) The shopper's emotional state at the time of purchase can encourage impulsiveness. Heightened emotion associated with a promotion, work, professional recognition, being on holiday or being in love can encourage us to bypass our normal caution and restraint. The status of products and services may also influence a purchase – some customers are heavily influenced by the signals a branded item portrays and their own perception of how people view others that own such branded goods. A customer attitude to purchase can be altered by the perception of an economic recession, the influence of green issues, medical disclosures, press speculation and whether they can be seen to shop in certain premises. The recent extended recession has made economy brand shopping quite chic for otherwise high net worth individuals; shopping at Lidl or Aldi with an Audi, BMW or Range Rover is no longer socially unacceptable.

The Customer Trigger and Stages on the Route to Purchase and How These Can Be Speeded Up by Shopper Interest in a Category

Normally triggers which kick start the shopper along the route to purchase can be almost anything – a comment by someone, reading a newspaper or magazine article, seeing something on TV or at the cinema or hearing something on the radio. A trigger may be one of the key words described later. The word 'new' is one of them. The trigger may be one related to time that starts the route to purchase and may in itself influence the route and the subsequent speed of advance along the route. A launch date for iPads or when Olympic tickets go on sale may be the start point. A particular interest of the shopper in a category – clothing, technology, music – may mean the shopper is easier to trigger and start their journey to purchase and – because they have been along the path before – they travel the route faster, particularly if the brand, supplier or retailer communicates appropriate messages (that match the stages – see below) along the way.

Once on the route to purchase, there are four generally acknowledged stages:

- taking in (*absorbing*) information – this is often subliminal;
- researching positively the proposed purchase by comparing alternatives (*planning*);
- setting out and completing the buying mission (*obtaining*); and
- assessing the merits and value of the purchase (*sharing* – passing information to other shoppers).

The Results of Encounters with Advertising

Brands used to rely on killer messages in their advertising (such as 'last day of sale', 'final reduction'). Shoppers are generally immune to messages that are unrelated to a category in which they are interested. Brands have tried to use killer messages with social media but the shopper no longer swallows the bait there either. Just 6 per cent of a brand's fans engage through Facebook via likes, comments and polls. The Facebook Edgerank algorithm decides which news feed items to put in front of a subscribing shopper. The algorithm considers the affinity (relevance to the shopper), weight (pictures and video carry more weight) and time decay of the news item. This means only a few will see a news feed. Until brands understand that social media are a network of influencers rather than a target, such advertising will be ineffective; the brand needs to embrace the empowered shopper encouraging the influencers to comment on the brand and favourably. For the shopper advertising has to be useful, building positive relevant experiences. In the future, those marketing brands need to engage, respecting the shopper while allowing him or her to participate in the brand experience. The key concept here is *experience* – something such as the opportunity to compete in an online game or contribute to a sport, activity or hobby. The impact of this activity depends on the stage the customer is at on their journey to purchase, the particular media and how the customer is connected to the media – the device they are using (whether it is capable of viewing items, whether it is GPS enabled) – a key element of their profile nowadays.

The Impact of Recession/Some Counter Actions and Reactions

The recession has changed the way shoppers buy. Clearly the need for frugality has meant shoppers have sought bargains and retailers have responded with 'essential' and 'value' ranges for what are commodity household and food items (an average person consumes 90,000 meals in a lifetime). There is a move to so-called cheaper stores as a result of recession. 'Habitual' becomes 'changeable' – loyalty is interpreted as 'its OK if I choose Asda/Lidl for some things rather than just Waitrose (M&S or Sainsburys)'. But there is also a revolutionary streak observable and some shoppers lash out and spend even in a recession justifying non-essential purchases with, 'I deserve a reward' or 'but I'm worth it'.

SHOWROOMING

This is a term that describes the shopper practice of using a store or its website to examine products which they later buy online from another source. JC Penney in the US and John Lewis in the UK both attract showrooming shoppers (John Lewis even provide in-store Internet access booths and the sales staff carry a tablet). Countering the practice of showrooming involves ensuring that prices are the same in-store and online, offering superior warranty or having a reputation (trust) for post-sales support and delivery with shipping options that are cheaper or more convenient. Immediacy can trump the appeal of a later, cheaper purchase online. Canadians will not buy in-store if the difference is $15 cheaper. In the US, MobileMarketer finds the researched figure is $5. Another tactic is to have in-store human contact – a salesperson, now practised by Homebase, or with the retailer providing the staff with a smartphone or tablet so they can check stock, product specifications and competitor offers and prices – Marks and Spencer (M&S) and Barker and Stonehouse (a furniture retailer) do this! Providing a retailer or brand app to the shopper can offer a promotion on the spot. Retailers now also offer home delivery from their own warehouse or another outlet should the item not be available in the outlet the shopper is visiting. Other internet click and collection methods are described later.

There are other approaches, of course, meeting this head on. China's *Global Times* newspaper reports that at Vera Wang's bridal boutique in Shanghai, customers must fork over about $482 (or 3,000 yuan) for a 90-minute time slot to try on dresses.

The store isn't alone. At a Brisbane, Australia, specialty food store, customers have to pay $5 for just looking, according to a post on Reddit.

'There has been high volume of people who use this store as a reference and then purchase goods elsewhere,' the company's sign said. 'These people are unaware our prices are almost the same as the other stores plus we have products simply not available anywhere else.'

Whether or not these will be long-term marketing successes or disasters remains to be seen. However, any attempt to charge people merely to shop is absolutely guaranteed to reduce the browser population, if that is the intention.

DAYPART MERCHANDISING (KNOWN IN THE US AS DYNAMIC STORE MERCHANDISING OR DSM)

Practised in Japan, daypart merchandising is customer centric, which means that the displays are changed throughout the day, matching shoppers' needs. This may be a solution for smaller retailers and in certain categories. The convenience stores (corner shop), for example, have different categories of buying by shoppers at different times of the day. The shopper can be assisted here by displaying stock matched to the pattern of purchases. Morning papers and breakfast snacks on the shelves first thing, products that are removed and replaced by lunch time favourites and impulse purchase items for the midday rush. Home goers look for ready meals and household and food commodity items and the shelves now reflect these products. A simple rotation of display stands can achieve this. The practice of DSM also means that a retailer can highlight goods that are perishable and on offer on their last sell-by date. This saves waste and throwing away any profit on discarded items – also saving disposal costs.

The 6Cs – The Offer – a Constant Base from Which to Evaluate the Customer – through Examining its Elements, the Brand, Supplier, Retailer Arrive at the Customer Value Proposition (CVP)

What has not changed in marketing terms is how the customer views a purchase. The study of marketing is reckoned to begin somewhere around the start of the twentieth century. Since the 1950s marketers have considered the 4Ps – Price, Place, Promotion and Product. Around 2008 the Chief Executive of Ogilvy stated the 4Ps to be dead (quoted by Roddy Mullin in his fifth edition *Sales Promotion* book). The flaw with the 4Ps was that they viewed the purchasing process from the perspective of the supplier, brand or retailer, rather than from that of the customer. The view today has to be that of the Customer, who views the purchase of a Product or Service by examining six elements which the marketer can then use to build the CVP: Cost (of lifetime purchase); Concept (product and service incorporated with brand values and now the engram); Convenience (of payment method, location, availability of item and ideally 24/7 purchase and delivery); Communication (the seamless arrival of appropriate and timely messages through preferred media and channels – what this book is mainly about); Customer Relationship (the customer expects to have a relationship and be recognised at any interface with the supplier or retailer – the involvement criteria); and Consistency (the same values of the brand and messages at all customer interfaces – research shows that inconsistency can lead to a loss of 30 per cent of sales).

Everyone needs a rock on which to apply leverage. The 6Cs provide that rock for marketers. This book touches on each of the 6Cs but deals principally with Communication –that is the seamless arrival of appropriate and timely messages through preferred media and channels – assisting the marketer to understand the customer's need for appropriate and timely messages: 'The Offer'.

The Offer is described in the language of your customers, using their perceptions. It is what an organisation has to consider when it is thinking of what to promote and what to sell to the customer – and all described from the buyer's or customer's perspective. Once that is established the brand supplier or retailer can construct the CVP.

THE OFFER

- *Cost* – a customer considers cost (and cost of ownership) within a value perception. That value perception is personal and includes a quality-of-life assessment. This perception is biased in that it is often based on brands with which the customer wishes to be associated for social, cultural or status reasons. A customer also adds to the equation the cost of time and travel to make a purchase. Future Foundation research indicates that for most of their activities and purchases UK consumers will travel within a 14-mile radius of their home.

- *Convenience* of buying – a mix of place/location, opening hours and cash/cheque/credit card acceptability. Customers are lazy. Exercising the brain requires effort and energy, so make it easy for them and convenient for them to buy. Location is part of convenience as is the ease of visiting – ease of travel and parking. Recent research confirms that it is the location of a store (or buying on the internet or mobile) rather than the prices it offers or the range of products for sale that wins every time. The rise of the mobile and using it to buy is simply the next generation application of the benefits already associated with the internet.

- *Concept* – a mix of product and service. The whole concept (the product and service together, as few products are sold without some sort of aftercare service) that you are offering as a supplier must match what customers need, want and perceive to be the solution to their need, offering greater benefit – that is, an advantage – over the concept of other suppliers, and it has to be provided at a cost and in a manner that the customer wants – known as value. The quality and fitness for purpose of the concept are assumed to be right. A warranty or return policy is taken for granted. A brand is principally a consolidation of the concept (though the other Cs come into it) into an easy-to-remember space in the mind of the customer – ideally concentrated in an engram.

- *Communication* – how well the product or service is communicated to the customer. This is where sales promotion may add a persuader; matching the communication of the feel of the brand at the POP. Customers will not buy if the communication is too complex or too dull or does not put the concept across in terms they commonly use. The mobile internet is the consumer technology of the future – certainly in the UK, where 86 per cent of the population own at least one mobile (which includes 96 per cent of 16–34-year-olds and 58 per cent of over-65s). It is always switched on. It is always with the consumer. And consumers are developing relationships – involvement – with their preferred brands; they look at the websites and register to receive e-mails. Alerts to brand experience opportunities will be the key using sales promotions – as has been achieved with the young with viral marketing text messaging in the drinks trade in the last few years. (Here a brand such as Diageo offers a free drinks voucher to a number of persons on their database who then forward the voucher to others – their friends and colleagues.) Mobile advertising is taking off especially where the mobile internet incorporates TV as well and 16 per cent of radio audiences listen through mobiles. The marketer also needs to be aware that the greatest users of the internet are the over-55s.

- *Customer relationship* – CRM principles apply. Customers expect to be treated with respect at all times and that all reasonable questions will be answered and problems resolved. Once they have made a purchase of any size or have signed up for a service, they expect to be recognised and remembered. For example, once customers have had their cars serviced at a garage, they expect the garage to know all the car's idiosyncrasies when they call. People like to build relationships – the retailer, supplier or service operator has to accept this. If customers get different answers from different people or departments within the same organisation they tend to trust the people and the organisation less. 'Integration' means making sure every part of your business delivers consistent answers.

- *Consistency* – the reassurance of ongoing quality and the reliability of the other five Cs – brand surety if you like. It is achieved through integration and comes from applying internal marketing within an organisation – so all aware of the brand values. Research shows an integrated approach is worth 30 per cent of sales (or a loss of 30 per cent if you do not practise it).

The Role of Influencers

Customers are influenced by others when making purchases and this influence must be understood. Viral marketing depends on this. You need to know how those around the customers, the people they follow and their perceived status can influence their attitude and their buying behaviour.

Managing the Brand – Influencing the Mind of the Customer

The bundle of characteristics – the six Cs – is the offer from which the CVP is constructed by a brand manager, retailer or supplier. It is their view of the Offer they make to the customer; the CVP is the 'brand' promise. Truly great brands achieve leadership in all dimensions, having superlative quality, unbeatable value and outstanding image in the six Cs offered. Making the most of 'brand equity' – the sum of quality, value and image as customers understand it – is one of the crucial jobs for any manager. As more businesses realise that a company is its brands, so more CEOs and MDs manage the brand. Evidence exists that customers ultimately bond with a brand (Tesco's loyals), not bothering to look elsewhere, as long as that brand delivers the brand promise. Bonding exceeds any loyalty. It has become a CEO deliverable. It gives a value far in excess of the bricks and mortar worth of a company. In fact, where bonding with a brand occurs it can be used as a measure for investment.

The most difficult element of a brand for any firm to manage is the 'brand psychology' – that is, achieving and retaining ownership of a piece of the customer's mind through the engram. Companies often talk about 'creating an image'. They may do so in the minds of the staff and agencies who work long and hard to devise it. They only do so in customers' minds when customers adapt, develop and absorb that image as their own. Companies can offer an image but they cannot control how the customer interprets the image or whether it sticks. If it is attractive and powerful and accords with customers' own experiences, it will form part of their image of the product or service. Thoughts and images in our own minds are, thankfully, beyond anyone else's total control.

Customers retain perceptions and images in their subconscious (the engram), and their own senses trigger the brand engram when a need or a suggestion relating to the engram occurs. If you can achieve this level of recall in a customer, your brand is secure. But beware that if the concept you are selling does not match the perception, image and experience of the customer, you are far less likely to make a sale. You need to nurture the engram continually to reinforce it favourably and secure its retention. Reducing brand support marketing in a recession is fraught with long-term risk. Guard against operational measures that destroy the brand's value. Recently in the King's Road, a very affluent shopping street in Chelsea, 75 per cent price discounting swept the street. Such a high level of discounting can be very damaging to a brand and a well-known branded store selling eclectic goods in the King's Road has gone out of business as a result. Research amongst its loyal shoppers showed they did not understand the discounting – they were happy to pay the full price. Had the retailer known or researched its customers it might still be in business today.

It is quite possible for customers in different parts of the globe, or even in different parts of one country, to have different perceptions of your brand. Guinness for a time advertised in Africa unwittingly using a symbol that implied that the drink improved virility and fertility. Brylcreem was thought to be a food delicacy in another African country. A failure of branding, you might think – unless of course you are happy to sell with that branding mismatch.

Business to Business Shoppers

Oracle (September 2012) reports cross-channel commerce has been a growing force in the consumer marketplace for the last decade, and is something that most B2B companies are finding they can no longer ignore. Because every B2B customer is likely to also be an online shopping consumer, B2B customers now expect their provider to be accessible online with a user-friendly, B2C-like experience that they are accustomed to in their personal life. But in B2B, the online user experience must go beyond just good looks and convenience. The B2B customer is performing their job often at a client site, and needs efficient and reliable support from suppliers. B2B organisations must deliver easy to use online or mobile commerce experiences that adopt proven tactics from the B2C world, while leveraging the necessary data to support B2B purchase decisions –for example, accepting text messages as purchase orders. Organisations that have employed this combination of using data and making the delivery business friendly reap the rewards. For example, investments in online (both web and mobile) provide new tools to enhance direct sales – Screwfix will take orders from builders directly and deliver to site. This is copying the just-in-time work practices of manufacturing – a proven cost-saving measure for the builder and enhancing the direct sales for Screwfix. In fact, Forrester Research reports that 'many B2B companies project that e-commerce will soon comprise 50 per cent of total sales'.

Investing in cross-channel commerce shouldn't be approached as experimenting with a nascent, siloed channel separate from the core business. The web and mobile channels bring an opportunity to scale in ways traditional direct or print catalogue selling methods simply cannot handle. Growing online should be treated as a strategic business decision that can increase the profitability and efficiency of the entire organisation.

A well-executed commerce site can assist your sales force when researching inventory, viewing customer order history and entering orders. The proliferation of mobile devices and tablets also brings new opportunities. These devices can replace large, outdated print catalogues, offer real-time inventory, order processing and order placement on-the-go, as well as serving as a compelling asset for showcasing demos and products while in the field. Investing in an enterprise-grade commerce platform that can support complex global deployments and transactions also forces enterprise-wide operations to be much more agile as the business grows. An example of agility is the ability to offer premium products with messages relating to sponsored sporting event success the day after an event – such as Kelloggs printing and distributing the names of Olympic gold medalists on packs. Connecting and centralising the disparate systems and sales channels required to scale a meaningful online commerce initiative has numerous internal and customer benefits, ranging from real-time custom catalogue views and logistics reporting, simplified support of different languages and currencies and a more complete understanding of the customer lifecycle and customer behaviours that are difficult to measure in the offline world. With a functional online commerce environment, organisations can better serve and understand their customers, reduce operational costs and identify new opportunities. In summary: B2B should follow B2C practice.

Place the Customer at the Centre of Your Business

IBM now advocates the simple strategy of putting the customer in the centre of its business through IBM's vision described in its document 'Portraits of a Smarter Planet'. In essence the future chief marketing officer is seen by IBM as achieving three things: harnessing data about the shopper to paint a predictive picture of each shopper as an individual (from social media, transaction data and other information); creating systems of engagement so that the business protects and shapes desire (upgraded CRM); and designing the culture and brand so that they are seamless (reputation, trust building and delighting customers). The seemingly overwhelming task is entirely possible through technology –'listening' to social media, 'engaging' with customers for life and predicting the future.

Summary

Start with the customer as shopper, Identify your customer, Think from the customer viewpoint.

Chapter 4

Communicating with the Shopper/Customer

In Chapter 2 we looked at the mechanics of communication and learning and how the subconscious works (with engrams, initially described in Chapter 1). In Chapter 3 we identified the Customer/Shopper. The key purpose of this book is to examine communicating with the shopper. It is therefore important to discover the preferred communication of people described in previous chapters. What makes an impact? To what do shoppers respond?

When that is achieved, we can then look at the marketing communication dimension – retailers/brands/suppliers communicating to people as shoppers – discovering what is available in Chapter 5 and in the later parts of this book on how marketing communications are used to make shoppers aware, then lead them to the purchase and finally sell to the shopper!

Do Shoppers Know Everything? No, But They Are Beginning To Discover They Can Find Out

A Bronto survey (May 2013) found that today, consumers do not walk into a store and say to a sales associate, 'I need a dishwasher. I don't know anything about them: what have you got?' with the expectation of buying in that store. Instead, the store visit may well be part of a research process leading to a sale that might be remote from a physical site. They may also visit a retailer's site to learn what brands they carry, then visit those manufacturers' own sites. Or they may employ their mobile device while at the store to scan a barcode, then use a price comparison app to find the best deal across any number of channels. They may also enlist any number of their friends' opinions and experiences via a social site. The paths to a purchase have grown exponentially in recent years, and retailers' first priority should be to understand better what their customers are doing before they make a purchase.

Growing Dominance of Mobile and Tablet

So what and how are customers communicating? A few facts! The mobile is proving to be addictive – users spending nearly two hours per day (of which 15 per cent is on gaming) on calls, internet access and social media in a ratio of 1:2:1.2 (figures from O2). A half of smartphone users (more than 50 per cent have smartphones in US, 70 per cent of 18 to 35 year olds and those in households with more than $75,000 annual income) have used a mobile to compare prices in-store (Source: Gartner). A third have scanned a QR code to reach a website. Mobile-optimised sites have attracted 60 per cent more viewers than traditional websites. The mobile is proving to be the search tool and is used especially while second screening to check on products or search information. The PC is replaced by the tablet, the land line by the mobile phone – which is never far from a person and soon the two will combine – a tablet mobile? (The Asus Fone pad has just arrived.) Unsurprisingly, consumers are spending 5 per cent a year more on technology each year ($2.1 trillion in the US in 2012), of which spend on mobiles is half. Predictions are that in 2016 80 per cent of searches will be by mobile (by some three billion mobile users (Source: BCG and Google)) attracting revenues well in excess of $10 billion on eBay (the figure achieved in 2012). What is suffering is, of course, retail (bricks and mortar) outlets, print (newspapers and magazines) and TV (watched while using the mobile). Retail solutions are discussed in other chapters – how to use mobile to drive traffic back to store. The corollary is that marketers simply must change to spending their budgets on mobile internet-related marketing. The opportunity is now there for brands to influence shoppers at every stage of the shopper journey – in a personal and direct, two-way, one-on-one communication, albeit accepting that the shopper can privately seek third-party opinions, even at the POP, while the shopper can, if so minded, instantly inform potentially a huge audience through social media of their treatment (good or bad) of the retailer and brand (52 per cent of US reviewers do so on mobile, Source: Empathica survey). An example of mobile marketing is Amazon in the US: during Christmas 2012, via the Amazon app, Amazon offered a US $5 voucher for anything scanned in Walmart but bought online immediately at Amazon.

How Good Customer Communication Developed

Historically, the only way to communicate was person to person – a very personal communication. The ancients invented the theatre and amphitheatre with excellent acoustics. If you did not have either to rouse a crowd (Henry V before Agincourt, Elizabeth I before the Spanish Armada) you gathered the people round and sat on a horse or stood on a cart. Tales of events past were usually given by storytellers who embellished 'history' to suit their listeners. News was through runners and later riders. Even in France in the eighteenth century the peasants in villages only knew they were at war when the requisitions for horses (and men) arrived. Church bells were used for alarms. A kind of mass media arrived with the invention of printing, but it was only 'one way', from publisher to reader. Letters to the editor could be selective, not reflecting the majority. The church and a few professions initially learnt book reading. The telegraph system next passed on urgent items. The telephone and the radio were just alternates to voice channels. It was not until after the internet arrived that individual response and feedback was possible. But truly mass instantaneous response only came about with social media. This is 'people-centric' communicating. By putting one person talking to others into a single pot actually emphasises the flight back from the impersonal to the personal. So, within the virtual mass, it is perceived as one-to-one by the individual – and that seems to be the ongoing expressed preference.

A Good Communication Dissected

What makes a good communication? What makes people listen? For listening is a voluntary occupation (see Chapter 2). The recipient can switch off. Some people can bore, while others have the 'gift of the gab'. The storytellers of old wove word pictures, exemplified by tales such as 'The Arabian Nights'. Good communication needs to be interesting and informative – and even tell a story. The Shakespearean crowds used rotten vegetables if they thought the play was rubbish. No change to twenty-first century persons, so a communication has to be interesting, exciting, informative, challenging, beneficial or alarming to make its mark. It has to be at a level that overcomes the noise. And it has to match the receiver's communication canvas (see Chapter 2).

The Cocktail Party Phenomenon

A cocktail of media reaches people from all around. At any one time a person may be texting, picking up texts or e-mails and location-based messages; viewing posters or the television; or reading a magazine.

The cocktail party phenomenon – selective attention – is the phenomenon of being able to focus one's auditory or visual attention on a particular stimulus while filtering out a range of other stimuli, much the same way that a partygoer can focus on a single conversation in a noisy room. This effect is what allows most people to tune in to a single voice and tune out all others. It also describes a similar phenomenon that occurs when one can immediately detect words of importance originating from unattended stimuli, for instance hearing one's name in another conversation.

Gaining attention increasingly requires relevance, as well as an understanding of context. In high distraction environments only simple messaging cuts through. (Here the authors have work showing that cut through of more complex messaging is best where people are moderately, positively aroused.)

Marketing Communications – Development for the Shopper

What elements stand out that persuade the shopper to participate in the sale at the point of decision?

Over the past 100 years, opinions have varied as to the way that advertising works before a shopper enters the store. They have similarly varied as to the way that shoppers choose from the options placed in front of them. It is important to understand the way that the shopper responds to what you say, in order to understand where and how you say it.

In the early part of the twentieth century, the prevailing wisdom was that a purchaser needed to go down a pathway before they took the decision to buy. A typical model was AIDA – Awareness, Interest, Desire and Action. The natural assumption was that a purchase decision was something that required a conscious decision, and that this conscious decision happened in definable stages. Advertising was there to smooth the passage to a purchase.

The assumption was, of course, that you needed to know about what you were going to buy, before you bought it. In this regard, then, the first role of advertising was seen to be 'to inform'. This may have been possible before the age of materialism. But now a very large selection of alternatives is presented to the shopper. The 'noise' from competing products and their advertising is immense.

The growing influence of social media, along with multi-channel possibilities, is here and now. It is a form of mass media, but individual! How does a retailer or supplier cut through and deliver their message? Whichever media or channel should a retailer or supplier use? How can a supplier or retailer get a message to cut through everyone elses' soundbites or straplines? Does the new media succeed?

Research has found, advocacy through social media by customers, delivered 23 per cent of new triallists for products persuade by remarks they read (Source: IGD 2010). Impressive! Try to estimate the cost of doing that through conventional communication.

The Importance of Multiple Media to the Shopper

Numerous studies have suggested the importance of dominating a single channel as giving predictable brand share. However, a recent, influential report by the IPA (see Table 4.1) was based on all of their award winners. They unpicked the elements and suggested that the magic number was three channels for success. Three channels are better than one for getting hard results state the IPA. (These are results in such terms as profit and of market share – see next paragraph for definitions.) They do suggest using as many channels as you like if 'softer' results, such as brand fame or reputation, are sought.

Table 4.1 Effectiveness success rate by number of advertising channels

Number of Channels	1	2	3	4	5
Any hard business effect	67%	64%	78%	74%	77%
Any soft business effect	51%	57%	63%	72%	85%

Source: IPA (pub WARC 'New Models of Marketing Effectiveness 2011').

The authors here disagree with IPA and advocate more than three channels for both hard and soft results – probably six channels – and six are developed in Part II and Part III of this book in order to generate Path to Purchase impact.

The IPA Findings: Synergy Matters for the Shopper

The IPA conducted a major review of all of their 256 award winners (2004 to 2010) to see whether Multi-channel Campaigns are more effective than single channel ones and to see what individual or mixed elements contributed most to success. In their report, (pub WARC 'New Models of Marketing Effectiveness 2011') they concluded the following:

- Multi-channel campaigns are more effective than single channel ones.
- TV is still the most effective medium at driving hard and soft measures (see below for definitions).
- Three is the most effective number of media-driving hard measures, but the more the merrier for intermediate ones.
- Advertising coupled with a sales conversion channel such as direct marketing or sales promotion is the most effective combination to drive hard business success.
- Advertising coupled with sponsorship or PR are the most effective combinations to drive intermediate metrics such as brand affinity.

The IPA publish their definition of business objectives, which they divide into hard and soft:

Hard measures reflect what shoppers 'want to buy' and measures of this success would include:

- sales/profit gain;
- reduced price sensitivity;
- market share defence/gain;
- customer acquisition/retention.

Soft measures make people feel better about the brand – they can also be regarded as intermediate measures on the way to developing harder metrics. Measures of success here would include:

- brand values/trust;
- brand differentiation;
- brand awareness;
- brand commitment/loyalty;
- interpersonal communication as media.

The Shopper View of Face to Face?

People talking to friends, colleagues and relatives has always been important. Now, with sites such as mumsnet, it is possible to meet virtual friends right across the globe with much in common.

Does this mean that face to face has been relegated down the list? Not if a research report in 2011 as part of the Marketing Gap is correct, which shows that in the UK, face to face was still important. The shopper prefers experiential marketing – road shows, exhibitions and demonstrations giving the opportunity to try, test and sample. As long as the correct message is delivered through the shopper's preferred channel, media or format, a nudge, journey prompt or last-minute prompt can be effective. The plethora of communication could be overcome using the average vocabulary, with the correct regional variations and meanings.

There may well be a real benefit in not biting off more people than you can chew. Martin Glenn, Marketing Director of Walkers Crisps in the UK put it this way:

> *It would be nice to say that Walkers went from business plan to megabrand in one cunning and brilliantly executed leap; but it didn't. It was built patiently, from the bottom up over a generation and more. In recent years, we refined our brand philosophies into one, built around three cores: advertising, sales promotion and in-store merchandising ... But I made sure we never forget those three cores were rooted in solid bedrock: the unimpeachable quality of the Walkers product. If making quality products were cheap and easy, everybody would do it. But quality costs money and it's all too tempting for businesses to view it as something they can skimp on or trade off for other product attributes such as image, style or price. At Walkers we never saw quality that way. From the very start, I knew we had to be prepared to go to seemingly unreasonable lengths to achieve consistently excellent quality.*
>
> *The reason for the obsession was simple: crisps taste much better when they're fresh. Given the number of packets the average Brit consumes in a week, we had to meet challenge of selling to the world's most discerning connoisseur of the potato crisp. So we had to be sure our crisps tasted good – every bag, every bite.*

What Shoppers Like by Way of Communication

However, though, social media works – the best social media influencers are real friends and family, not social media friends or 'contacts' (Source: British Consumer Index (BCI) April 2013 – data provided by Data Talk Research Limited) backing up the earlier IGD finding. The survey (Table 4.2) found that past experience of brand or retailer was the next most influential (the engram again), then discounts, vouchers or offers through the door.

Table 4.2 Ranking of influence when making a purchase

Advice from friends and family
Past experience of brand or retailer
In-store sales discounts
Offers or vouchers through the door
Price comparison websites
Seen on TV
E-mail offers/vouchers
Online customer reviews
Magazine newspaper reviews
Internet offers (for example, vouchers.co.uk, groupon.co.uk)
Salesperson advice
On-pack promotions
Professional advisor
Newspaper offers or vouchers
Offers by post
Leaflets while shopping
Recommendations on social networks (Facebook, Twitter and so on)
Competitions
Brands on Facebook, Twitter and so on
Mobile phone offers while shopping
Celebrity endorsement
Prize draws

Source: BCI.

The ranking demonstrates the importance of the engram and word of mouth. Endorsements by celebs and competitions do not work as well as offers and discounts. Door to door (D2D) leaflets are better than handouts. Both online and offline reviews matter and TV is still influential (ASOS!).

Core stores – those with the highest proportion of target market in their area – have the highest demand pressure and run out of stock first as discounts increase. Other stores cope better. Therefore maintaining stock in core stores is a joint sales and marketing objective. Between discounts, promotion-sensitive shoppers can be attracted with efficient smarter promotions.

Buy One Get One Free (BOGOF) and Half Price – Is There a Difference in the Message from the Shopper Viewpoint?

The shopper does not seem to be greatly affected if they can consume more of the product or if it can be put away in a larder, but if neither applies then the category may not be 'expandable', in which case single pack deals may be more attractive than multibuy promotions. Otherwise it is the retailer that seems to hold the cards on the success or failure of a BOGOF or half-price promotion which depends on in-store execution. This means that for each product or retailer research and analysis is the answer to find the difference. As a side lesson of this study it was found that, in practice, store managers ignore head office guidelines and have a great influence on display and hence the success of the promotion (a corollary of this is that head offices should accept this and delegate more to managers – see Chapter 15). This means that the promotional management team must be aware that though they can establish the price, mechanic, POS and in-store displays and gondola end allocation for the promotion, the in-store manager can change the actual promotional space and gondola end display, off-shelf displays and promotional stock levels from whatever head office decide.

Many companies use promotions to beat the shopper into submission. Research shows much smaller incentives move the shopper in the right direction. Here is a flavour (see more on all the below in Chapter 10).

Selecting the right shopper matched incentive. The incentive must be proportionate, appeal to the target market, be well presented and able to offer exceptional standout. (Did the shopper respond and then react?) For the retailer: What do the best promotions campaigns do? Hold sales from competitors while on discount, build sales between discount periods. Geo-demographics research shows that people react differently to promotions and there is a correlation with postcodes but this can be profiled. Multicultural areas respond best to multiple buys and cash incentives and discounts. Modern couponing can be tightly targeted to a specified store. Demand can be met responsibly to respond. Incentive levels do not need to be high to be persuasive. Couponing further improves response to a TV ad.

What Makes an Impact on a Shopper?

Eye tracking shoppers, observing pupil dilation and blink rate, shows that correctly delivered graphics make a huge difference to how the same offering is viewed.

DON'T SPOIL THE ENGRAM

Tropicana lost 20 per cent of sales on a re-designed pack which was then withdrawn after seven weeks, costing £20 million in sales. 'We underestimated the deep emotional bond customers had with the original pack.' In fact Tropicana had removed the image embedded in the minds of shoppers – the Tropicana engram. They could not find what their subconscious mind had stored.

WHAT IS THE RESULT OF USING THE SHOPPER'S FAVOURITE WORD 'FREE'?

Kingsmill found that a 'free' promotion increased the emotional activation engagement from 3.4 to 4.1 which, converting to purchases, meant effectiveness rose from 19 to 31 per cent. A Marmite jar with a 'free' offer raised emotional activation to 5.8 (normally associated with top-shelf magazines) and increased purchases.

AND HIGHLIGHTING THE PRICE?

A Baltsen chocolate wafer bar with 'only 99p' beat another chocolate bar with a promotion – albeit complex. Just putting the price on the pack beat typical promotions.

Do Shoppers Like Direct Mail Messaging?

Seventy-eight per cent of households open mail delivered to their door especially if it is from a brand they know and 47 per cent open a letter if they believe there is a coupon inside. Between 60 to 70 per cent of households redeem coupons – 40 per cent a 20p coupon, 47 per cent a 50p coupon, 52 per cent a £1 or £5 coupon.

Surveys of marketers show that only 3 per cent are aware of the impact of coupons. Mis- and mal-redemption stories may affect that view. In fact 55 per cent of shoppers do not mis-redeem with a further 38 per cent only occasionally mis-redeeming. So 93 per cent receive the message of a coupon.

The advantage of couponing or using vouchers is that they can supply valuable information about the shopper who completes the coupon. A coupon within a campaign reaches new targets.

Distributing coupons at a 20 per cent uplift per week rate, optimises the store response capability.

A Glimpse of the Future

Carphone Warehouse is working on developing a consistent experience for the mobile telephone where the dialogue between the shopper and the salesperson will be treated as: 'It's a conversation.' It can be taken up and dropped at any point in time. It is not a 'hard sell'. One sales colleague can pass information on to the next about the shopper journey. It retains the order in which the shopper searched so the salesperson can see the priority placed on any parameter as the shopper moves around the online shop. Should the shopper move from mobile to tablet or PC then the 'conversation' accommodates any alternative channel. The corollary is that the data can also track the salesperson performance when dealing with the shopper. More on the future in Chapter 21.

Summary

Shoppers seek communications, which are available more than ever. This means, on the one hand, where the purchase does not matter much they increasingly rely on a set of shopping engrams to shortcut the time they spend, your own engram, or known power words such as 'new' and 'free'.

On the other hand, shopping expeditions can easily become part of a research process, rather than a part of the direct purchase process.

Brands need to take advantage of the additional shortcut engrams that shoppers will look for as part of this research process (for example, QR codes and interactive media), and make sure they don't fall behind. Keeping the way the engram reaches the shopper, wherever they may be, is vital. In this regard, multiple media can be much more effective than a single approach.

The actual POP, when you can define where this is, is a very important place to get your message across!

Chapter 5
Getting the Message Across

This chapter examines the plethora of ways with which to communicate with the customer/shopper through a wide variety of marketing communications. Even standing on a street corner holding a placard counts as a marketing communication – particularly if a shopper is a tourist looking for somewhere to eat and the food outlet is not situated on the main drag!

For the experienced marketer, use this chapter as a reminder of what is available – skip if you know it all – included here are some researched and tabled facts and opinions about effectiveness you may not have seen.

The Media Both the Shopper and Brand Manager Face

Today's media ecosystem has clear characteristics that are radically different from just ten years ago:

- abundant;
- cheap to buy – and sometimes free;
- cheap to populate with content;
- but more expensive to reach mass audiences due to fragmentation;
- blurred … where once a channel had one platform, now it has many;
- a shift of advertising away from mass media towards personalised forms of marketing including, for example, direct mail, the internet, mobile, retail media, word-of-mouth;

- but all media are under pressure because of issues of accountability and ROI. Financial auditors and CEOs now expect to see measurement of the effectiveness of any media activity.

Before this chapter looks at who uses what media and channels and what each can do – it would seem a no brainer to find out if the money is being spent to any useful effect. This is not as a generality carried out by most retailers – the first paragraphs below cover measurement and using data – a further neglected available source of Insight about the shopper.

Measuring Effectiveness – the Majority Haven't a Clue!

Of course, those overseeing the marketing communications budget will need to know that they are getting value for money and they have some measure of effectiveness.

Staggeringly, relatively few people measure the effectiveness of the marketing that they pay for. *The Grocer* reported in May 2012 that 61 per cent of retailers do not measure anything. In addition to knowing whether marketing communication works or not, making a comparison between media and channels is also important. Only a business can make such comparisons and just for their particular customer segments. Note that measuring marketing effectiveness is relatively easy to do and is covered in a separate book by Roddy Mullin (*Value for Money Marketing* – a new version is on the stocks for 2014) the main requirement is the intent – the will to do it. It is of course the only way to find out what works for the customers you target, with the marketing communications you pay for. A summary of the book is in Chapter 16.

Good News on Those Who Use Data In-Store and Online at All Stages of the Path to Purchase – the Few!

A Bronto survey (May 2013) finds that, as consumers steadily integrate more online activities into their overall shopping behaviours, retailers are aggressively pursuing new means to not only understand the new consumer's online behaviour in the countless paths to purchase that now exist, but to also communicate that understanding back to the consumer. Moreover, they are trying to do so in a truly meaningful manner; to market to the consumer with what matters most to him/her – and, at the moment that it most matters. Gone are the days when a retailer could simply 'sell' an item to a blank-page consumer;

today's shoppers are educated, empowered and quite simply demand more than that. They want a relationship with their chosen brands and relationships are built on communication. Chapter 9 describes relationship building.

Bronto surveyed retailers under three categories (May 2013); store-focused (only 20 per cent revenue from online), online-focused (more than 50 per cent) and e-mail-driven (40 per cent of their business from e-mail) retailers took differing actions pre-purchase, in purchase and after purchase.

A retailer's pre-purchase communications are based on activities that signal that a consumer is shopping but has not necessarily made a selection or is ready to purchase. This is a critical part of the purchase process because, when done well, retailers have the maximum opportunity to influence consumer shopping behaviour.

That 53 per cent of retailers who do collect product-level browsing data, however, are already leaps-and-bounds ahead of their competitors – they collect a large number of data points. Of those who do collect product-level data (product category and specific product, price, product details, ratings or reviews, quantity, image URL), more than 80 per cent of respondents leverage product category and Stock Keeping Unit (SKU) information when using browsing data to target e-mail communications. What is interesting is how few retailers are leveraging product images: only 59 per cent. This is a vastly missed opportunity as market research has continually shown that images have far greater suggestive impact on consumers than text. Eighty-four per cent then send an automated e-mail response.

In-purchase activities move shopping behaviour from browsing to the transaction itself. For retailers looking to build repeat business, an important point of continuity is in using the transaction as a bridge to driving the next sale. Of those retailers who send transactional messages, most only send order and shipping confirmations. Fewer than one in four retailers are taking advantage of the revenue-driving potential and customer service engagement opportunities of a multi-e-mail post-purchase series. Even though 75 per cent of respondents automate data exchange between their e-commerce platform and their e-mail service provider, 34 per cent of respondents are not able to use that information to market to shoppers in the purchase cycle. For those who can leverage the data, they are nearly evenly split between the ability to use only e-mail-related purchase data (32 per cent) and data attributed to both e-mail and non-e-mail related purchases (34 per cent). While possessing the data is a first step, actually using the data can be a challenge. Of those who collect purchase-related data, nearly half (42 per cent) have not actually used the data in e-mail communications.

Once the purchase is completed, retailers should begin enticing that consumer to make their next purchase and become a loyal customer. What we see instead is that while retailers are interested in continuing the dialogue with a hopefully happy customer, those communications tend to not be very imaginative – focusing primarily on inactive purchasers (versus recent purchasers) and doing basic segmentation of past purchasers. Only 24 per cent will customise campaigns to active purchasers beyond their transactional communications of order and/or shipping confirmations (Figure 5.1). The percentage is slightly higher, 31 per cent, among online-focused retailers, showing again that retailers who conduct the majority of their business online are more willing to experiment with communications that go beyond 'standard operating procedure'. It would seem the scope for retailers to make shed-loads of more sales is enormous.

So Who Uses What Online?

By way of example of what a media channel can do, take a look at social media, a so-called 'new channel'. A recent analysis of McDonalds social media activity by EConsultancy (March 2013) found McDonalds had not touched its Google account. IKEA and Walmart have done the same; while ASOS and John Lewis are active with daily updates. On Pinterest, McDonalds has one single account but runs no competitions and, because it operates in 119 countries and the rules vary in each country, it is not very active and simply copies content from Flickr on to Pinterest – it only has 2,000 followers there. By contrast, Red Bull and Walmart are very active on Pinterest. McDonalds is active on Twitter in some countries but not others. It posts a lot but only responds to about 20 complaints daily in the US. Facebook is the social media where McDonalds is most active but only locally (500,000 fans in the UK), globally there are only about five posts a month. McDonalds does record a high 'liked' ranking – possibly because it is a global corporate. If the intention is to maintain a presence in peoples' minds (see the earlier Chapter 1 on engrams) then its wide coverage has maintained that.

What Can Each Media Do?

What each form of media can do is perhaps best shown Table 5.1. Some media are good for coverage, some are liked by the trade, some are intrusive and, as for duration – it is said that a cinema ad is impactful, but that the impact only lasts for about 15 minutes.

Table 5.1 Illustrative effectiveness of media

	TV	Cinema	Radio	Print	Outdoor	Internet	Mobile
Visual colour sound movement	√√	√√	√	√	√->√√	√->√√√	√->√√√
Intrusive	√√	√√√	√?	√	√		√?
Detail				√√		√√√	√
Interactive	√?		?			√√√	√√?
Time flexible	√?		√√			√√√	√√
Duration			?	√		√√?	√?
Coverage	√		√	√	√	√√	√?
Profile	√?	√	√	√√		√√	√√
Less Cost/'000			√	√	√	√√-√√√	√√√
Trade affinity	√√	√	√	√√	√	->√	->√
Customise message				√		√√√	√√

Source: Based on a Saatchi and Saatchi idea.

The persuasiveness of the different media will of course vary by each customer – depending on a number of social and cultural factors. How well developed a media is in any country will also have an impact, along with the legal environment in which the marketing communications operate. There are enormous variations between urban and rural media in any country.

Again there are general principles that apply and some media are better at making customers aware of brands, their products and services than others. Such awareness, if effective, is stored away by a customer until some need prompts a search of the knowledge stored in the brain and the media is recalled. How this works is explained through engrams (see Chapter 1). Experience is a powerful re-enforcer of memory and so those retailers that allow customers to test or try a brand may really benefit long term.

This applies to intangibles such as software too. 74 per cent of digital businesses according to Econsultancy now recognise that user experience improves sales.

The customer, however, will look at the total Offer and the 6Cs will feature in the customer assessment of any purchase (see Chapter 3). Table 5.2 illustrates the way that the alternative media impact on the customer.

Table 5.2 What the media can do illustrative

	Awareness	Acceptance	Preference	Insistence	Reassurance
TV	√√	√?			
Radio	√	√?			
Cinema	√√	√?			
Outdoor	√√	√?			
Press	√√	√	√?		
PR	√√	√	√		
House literature		√	√√	√	√
Direct mail	√√	√√	√√		
Door to door	√	√√	√√		
Website		√?	√√	√	√
E-mail	√√	√√?	√√	√	√√
Mobile	√√√?	√√?	√√	√√	√√
Experiential sales	√√	√√√	√√√	√√√	√√√
After sales service					√√√

Source: Based on an Admap idea.

The Media and Channels Themselves

The following paragraphs examine each of the media in turn, starting with across the board message techniques such as QR codes and sales promotions, then direct marketing, PR and advertising, looking at the adverse as well as the positive features.

The key, by way of comparison of different media and channels, may be to use 'Share of Voice' and here the report from the IPA showing how advertising is improved with the addition of other approaches is helpful. There are some really important new research papers covered in this chapter; the authors find the IPA research showing the magic number three (that three media is the best number to get hard results according to the IPA) is a good start but insufficient in the holistic overview of the shopper's journey to purchase.

Outdoor (see next after advertising) and some research done by the British Population Survey (BPS) shows the importance of local media. The authors venture to suggest that the shopper perspective should be paramount. It is a no brainer really, examine the shoppers' environment, as only there will be presented messages that are effective in the shopper's journey to purchase.

Synergy Works

The IPA Report 'Models of Marketing Effectiveness' looked at the lead medium – the medium the authors identify as the primary channel with the highest spend or focus. This analysis was restricted to TV, press and outdoor as there were too few cases in the IPA Databank where other communications channels were noted as the lead. Using press as the lead medium demonstrates the biggest hard business effects, whereas outdoor drives the biggest intermediate effects such as brand fame or awareness. However, synergy delivered the best overall results (Table 5.3).

Table 5.3 Hard and soft business effects

Channel Combinations	Advertising Only	Advertising and Web	Advertising and DM	Advertising and Sales Promotion	Advertising and Sponsorship	Advertising and PR
Very large hard business effect	71%	71%	77%	84%	74%	70%
Very large soft business effect	57%	65%	61%	68%	72%	70%

Three proved to be the most effective number of advertising media to drive hard business measures but 'the more the merrier' for intermediate measures. See Chapter 4 for more on this.

Advertising coupled with a sales conversion channel, such as direct marketing or sales promotion, was the most effective combination to drive hard business success such as sales or market share.

Advertising coupled with sponsorship or PR were the two most effective combinations to drive intermediate metrics such as brand fame.

Across the Board (Apply to All Media and Channels) Techniques for Message Placing

Sales promotions (a vast subject in itself) and QR codes apply across all media, as do creativity and innovation. Marketers select promotions above all other communications.

SALES PROMOTION

Sales promotion can be and is used across all marketing including direct, online and mobile, PR and advertising. A sales promotion uses any one or more of five types – that is, off-the-shelf promotions, price discounts, joint promotions, prize promotions and premium promotions. For a full description of each and how they work see Roddy Mullin's book *Sales Promotion – Fifth Edition* available on Amazon. The book is translated into many languages and is the core text of the Diploma in the UK and Australia. It is not an academic book but one written for practitioners. Its replacement *Promotional Marketing* is published in September 2014.

How does a sales promotion work? In this world of choice, a good sales promotion will stop customers for a moment, cause them to think about a brand and product and, if it has the right impact, move them to make a decision to follow up the sales promotion – purchasing the product or service. A good sales promotion leaves the shopper feeling rewarded and adds fun to the shopping experience. There are hidden benefits – if customers take up your 'three for the price of two' offer they will not be purchasing a competitor product while using yours, and their experience of enjoying a product or service is a great influencer on future purchases. Indeed, a second sales promotion delivered with the product or service when the customer takes up the first sales promotion can entice them to make their next purchase of that product or service. In mobile marketing parlance – use a bounce back or even two.

For the customer as consumer at the POS, there are now too many choices. Careful placement can influence purchase from the shelves, to ensure your customer finds and buys your product. You can pay for specific positioning and check it with Field Marketing (FM). But there are, for example, around 1,200 brands of hair shampoo to choose from. What do consumers do? Excluding the engram effect! They are generally busy people who make their buying decisions and choice of brand from the offers available. This is not new. People have always looked for what is 'in season', what is a bargain, what is familiar (the engram!) and has met their need before. Shopkeepers and stallholders in previous centuries would make an 'on-the-spot offer' to help persuade people to make a purchase – sales promotion is the modern equivalent, when no salesperson (field marketer) is there. The Apprentice programme on TV frequently requires some bargaining – a rare experience?

Philip Kotler, the US marketing academic, estimates that 20 years ago the advertising to sales promotion ratio was about 60:40. In 1997, he calculated that, in many consumer goods companies, sales promotion accounted for 65 to 75 per cent of expenditure and had been growing annually for the previous two decades. More is now spent in all companies on sales promotion than on all other advertising including direct marketing. In 2002, from figures given by the ISP, the AA and DMIS, the ratio had reversed to become 40:60. In the UK alone in 2010 the spend on sales promotions was estimated at £47 billion. In a nutshell if that much is spent – exceeding all other categories of marketing/ sales expenditure – a retailer or brand or supplier should join them, they cannot all be wrong. You should note that price promotions – a large part of sales promotion – may not always be counted as expenditure, but as 'lost income'. Expenditure on altering packs and products for a promotion may also not be counted as promotional expenditure. Also check the basis for comparisons – it used to be only the media spend was used in comparisons; be aware that, to boost its figure, advertising now adds agencies costs, rather than just the billed value of advertising.

Sales promotions use vouchers, coupons and discount codes for shoppers to present at the time of purchase. Their effectiveness is covered in reports by Valassis (who manage 86 per cent of UK coupons) showing a 14 per cent rise in redemptions year on year (2011 versus 2012) with retailer issues beating manufacturers redemptions.

In March 2013, Research by Atom reports that Unilever have confirmed that they are reappraising their approach, as Unilever have found in-store promotions beat social media ROI, delivering a 50 per cent higher ROI. Unilever had shifted large parts of brand budgets to social media but a recent evaluation has shown that Unilever are undertaking more in-store promotional activity too!

There is more on promotions in Part III describing implementation (see Chapter 11).

USE OF QR CODES

Figure 5.1 Example of a QR code

The QR code is another across-all-media message deliverer (Figure 5.1). A QR code (quick response code) is a type of 2D bar code that is used to provide easy access to information through a smartphone. The QR code is offered on any photographically available media – print is the most common form – on packaging and on posters in magazines and newspapers. It can also be produced on a dynamic media – the only requirement is that it can be photographed by a smartphone.

In this process, known as mobile tagging, the smartphone's owner points the phone at a QR code and opens a barcode reader app which works in conjunction with the phone's camera. The reader app interprets the code, which typically contains a call to action such as an invitation to download a mobile application, a link to view a video or an SMS message inviting the viewer to respond to a poll. The phone's owner can choose to act upon the call to action or click cancel and ignore the invitation.

Static QR codes, the most common type, are used to disseminate information to the general public. They are often displayed in advertising materials in the environment (such as billboards and posters), on television and in newspapers and magazines. The code's creator can track information about the number of times a code was scanned and its associated action taken, along with the times of scans and the operating system of the devices that scanned it. Note that in US markets they are finding QR codes take up valuable space and affect creativity, while on the shopper 'minus side' the app has to be loaded before the shopper can use the QR code. Activating a QR code should be engaging for the shopper but many are not (Source: Mobile Marketer April 2013).

Dynamic QR codes (sometimes referred to as unique QR codes) offer more functionality. The owner can edit the code at any time and can target a specific individual for personalised marketing. Such codes can track more specific information, including the scanners names and e-mail address, how many times they scanned the code and, in conjunction with tracking codes on a website, conversion rates.

CREATIVITY

In the marketing sense it generally means visual design but it also applies to an overall campaign and its delivery. The Chapter 1 revelation relating to engrams shows design has a great part to play with the shopper. Creativity means generating the most effective concept possible to market a brand, product or service. It applies across all media and as the shopper expects consistency, it needs to be considered and applied strategically. As Chaucer used the word so should the marketer; creativity imparts the sense of a wonder. 'Wonder' should be in the minds of the target shopper. Truly great ideas withstand the test of time. Shell's make money promotion of the 1960s created wonder as shoppers searched for the other halves of banknotes. Osram, selling long-life light bulb,s albeit costing more, only found sales took off after they sent a locked box to finance directors telling them the key with the contents had been sent to the director responsible for maintenance. When the box was opened they could see the offer – light bulbs lasting four times as long but for only a little more than existing light bulbs. Previously finance had only sanctioned maintenance with purchasing the cheapest. This was a creative way to get the two to discuss the matter.

Targeted creativity in marketing usually only comes with answering the question – whom do I want to do what? There is a need to involve all those involved or participating – including suppliers and retailers. Golden Wonder once offered 'Wombles' patches for jeans just as the fad for wearing patches on jeans started and the Wombles were being acclaimed. The sales of their crisps soared. Simple elegance is the key to successful creativity. There are five well-established techniques for brainstorming for creative ideas: listing, using mind maps, thought showering (old brain storming), the village and 'being someone else'. These techniques are fully covered in other books such as *Sales Promotion* by Roddy Mullin.

INNOVATION

Literally means doing something new. It can also be inventing a totally new use for an existing product. Lucozade was originally an expensive drink for invalids. It was said that when a mother bought Lucozade for a child you knew they were really ill. In a Dublin bar the marketing manager found Lucozade was being used as a mixer. Realising there was no limit to what he could sell Lucozade as, he then had the idea of rebranding Lucozade as an energy drink for athletes – sales took off. Innovation usually occurs from 'thinking out of the box'. Strategic thinking is covered in Chapter 20 in Part III. Clearly anything innovative must have a potential market. Strategic consideration in the light of the market and subsequent planning to achieve the change is required.

INDIVIDUALLY OR NEAR INDIVIDUALLY TARGETED MESSAGE CHANNELS

Direct marketing is a communication between seller and buyer directly. Direct marketing is the generic term. No intermediary media is used. It is visual and sometimes auditory (telemarketing). It is also to an extent sensual and olfactory. The thickness, embossing and smell of paper can deliver a perception of quality. It is most often in print or text format – originally using just the post – but now encompassing the internet, telemarketing and mobile marketing. Direct marketing is targeted towards an individual, though not always by name – it is enabled by the customer choosing to open or to activate the message. The original purpose of direct marketing was to get the shopper to buy through the post or ask for a catalogue, to request a demonstration, or to persuade the shopper to physically visit a bricks and mortar establishment (for example, a store, restaurant or personal service establishment such as a spa or hairdresser) or to take part in some action.

Direct mail is the original form of direct marketing. This is when a personally addressed letter is sent making an offer to the individual. Software programmes now allow the letter to be personalised using data held on the individual. A sample can often be added to a direct mailing in addition to or instead of a sales promotion. A direct mail should give clear benefit to the recipient and be persuasive and appropriate. The response of the shopper to the direct mail varies by the attractiveness and creativity of the message and the offer it conveys. Rates are published by organisations such as Central Mailing Services, British Market Research Bureau, Royal Mail and others for the success of such mailshots. Nine out of ten people open direct mail. Seventy-five per cent like to receive a voucher or offer. A third of the UK population responded to direct mail in 2011 and as a result 6.2 million went online and 7.3 million went to a store. The response rate stands at 3.42 per cent. 17.7 million people ordered from catalogues received through direct mail in 2010.

Door-to-door delivery is when the message, still usually in letter or leaflet format, is delivered to a house but not addressed to the householder by name. The service is offered by the postal service or by other organisations that deliver door to door (D2D) such as local newspapers or specialist firms that deliver to houses. Samples and sales promotions are again used to make the unaddressed message of greater interest to the receiver. Again success of a D2D depends as for direct mail but the rates of response are usually lower with people assessing such material as junk mail.

Inserts are included in magazines or newspapers delivered to the door – though also they are available when the magazine or newspaper is purchased in a shop (for example, supermarket or newsagents). They are similar to leaflets and handouts (see below) but the delivery mechanism is different and depends on the shopper noticing the material and taking action. Inserts can also be glued on to the advert or to a front cover. These are known as tip-ons.

Telemarketing/telesales. Telemarketing is the outbound activity of a call centre. Experience shows that telemarketing is more effective with B2B messages as long as the offer is both relevant and beneficial. It is even more effective if the telemarketing call is preceded by a letter. Telesales is where an existing customer is contacted. The call centre can be used to acquire data about the shopper being called. Codes of practice exist for telemarketing and 'cold calling' is often not appreciated by shoppers. It has been extensively used in the UK for PPI claims calls, energy companies and telecommunications companies seeking householders who are prepared to change their supplier or service provider.

Leaflets/handouts. These are normally sheets of paper left in places where people can pick up information, typically about holiday and tourist venues (available in tourist information centres, hotel and B&B lobbies) and activities or cards that are offered by persons standing in the street or in places where there is a high footfall, usually advertising an event such as a store or restaurant opening. Local councils, concerned about litter, often have by-laws about what may be handed out when and where and marketers may need to check and obtain permission – certainly this applies on station concourses too. A person holding a placard can be a temporary solution to market communication near the POS.

FIELD MARKETING (FM) AND PERSON-TO-PERSON ONE-ON-ONE SALES

FM has many sub-disciplines which is where, as a means of putting a message across, the specific interest lies in this book. Some 34 companies operate within the sector in the UK; it is a £1 billion a year business. There is some misunderstanding about the term FM. Technically it is outsourcing the sales function. How to outsource FM is described in *The Handbook of Field Marketing* by Alison Williams and Roddy Mullin. What is outsourced in detail is sales, experiential marketing, demonstrating, sampling, merchandising, audit and mystery shopping.

Sales: experiential, road show, events, exhibitions. It was Confucius who said, 'Tell me and I will hear, show me and I will see, involve me and I will believe.' In the past few years there has been more involvement of the audience by the introduction of theatre and creativity to gain the audience's buy-in to the brand through emotional and sensory involvement. This has become known as live brand experience or experiential marketing. Although this FM discipline is not new, it is an interactive development of the events discipline and it is becoming increasingly recognised as such as more companies choose to specialise in it.

The Experiential Marketing Committee (part of the DMA) has stated that:

> *Experiential marketing is a live and interactive marketing discipline, which builds positive emotional sensory engagement between a brand and its consumers.*

A road show is when a promotional activity is created, which then moves around the country, for example when a radio station has promotional trips to different seaside resorts in the summer. An event is an activity that does not move. This might be promotional activity in a shopping centre, at an exhibition, in a car park or at a county show for example, although of course events can be conducted at more than one venue across the country, thus the difference between a road show and an event is blurred.

Road shows and events can be truly experiential when they appeal to the consumer's senses and involve them in the brand and the activity.

Experiential marketing, road shows and events are designed to meet the consumers of the brand, and through trial, sampling and interactive involvement to develop an affinity with the brand, which will generate positive awareness and drive sales. Clearly it has an impact on a brand's engram.

The purpose of experiential marketing, road shows and events is to generate brand awareness and brand loyalty in a lively and engaging manner that reflects the brand image and values and it is an entertaining way of putting a product or service in the public eye. Part of the development of this brand awareness is to engage the public with the product by running an event or a road show. This can also be a lively part of any integrated campaign, and events are becoming one of the key methods of attracting the consumer to participate with the brand and associate it with enjoyment and, through this pleasurable experience, develop an affinity with the brand that will lead to purchase. Interestingly, many venues that have been used for years by field marketers are now actively looking for interactive, lively activity on their premises. They wish to see their visitors entertained (and not hassled) as part of the pleasurable experience in the venue, for example at a shopping centre. This discipline involves putting on a show that involves the product and the potential consumers, so that the sampling of the product is an experience for the consumer, who has an opportunity to interact with the product, have fun and thus develop an identity with the brand.

Experiential marketing at its best is a very creative event that will reflect the brand being experienced. It is creative in every sense of the word – in conception, visually, emotionally and in its execution. It is designed to win the hearts and minds of consumers and to get them to develop an involvement with the brand. Obviously a balance has to be found between the impact and excitement of the activity and the logistics and safety aspects that must be in place before it goes live. Location, location – the venue is key to successful shopper participation.

Where to hold the event? Whether the event is termed a road show or a live brand experience, it must be held where the target consumer market is prolific, so that there are many positive experiences. For example, events held at music festivals and rock concerts will target young people, events at popular seaside resorts are held to meet families, events on railway concourses target commuters. Car dealers use a new car launch event to offer test drives to existing customers of previous versions of the marque – adding excitement by arranging the event held at a racing circuit.

Sales: sampling and demonstrating. Sampling and demonstrating as an FM discipline are always face to face; that is, in the presence of an FM staff member, who guides the customer through the sampling or demonstrating process and notes any customer reaction and responds to it. Sampling is straightforward and often is a simple taste or smell opportunity, whereas demonstrating can be a more complex exercise where the consumer is shown how a product operates. While carrying out sampling or demonstrating, the FM staff will be communicating – describing the product or service, its features and benefits – while informing and educating the listener. The FM staff person is the brand ambassador. A key difference between sampling and experiential marketing is that the latter uses the five senses to involve the customer, who is frequently a hands-on participant. Sampling is when the consumer is offered the opportunity to try a product in the presence of an FM person who explains, influences and presents the product in a positive light, often by focusing on taste or smell of a product. Food and drink, perfumes and aftershaves fit this sampling category. Samples may be handed out for later consumption, such as shampoos, newspapers, printed materials or software on disk. There is a cross-over with sampling and experiential marketing.

Demonstrating is when the product or service is shown, explained and demonstrated to consumers: the consumer observes and sometimes operates the product as demonstrated. These are typically demonstrations of small domestic items related to the kitchen or for cleaning the house, or mobile phones and other technology.

The value is that people who have sampled or been demonstrated to now understand the product. People will always talk about a product and use it when they understand it, and feel comfortable with it.

Sampling. As outlined above, sampling is the use of field personnel to present potential users with a product or service. It is an important part of brand awareness, as it allows the consumer to trial the product or service. This could apply to a variety of products from a chocolate bar or a cup of coffee to shampoo or a newspaper – and with 85 per cent of the business in the UK coming from the service rather than the manufacturing base, many services also use sampling as an effective means of trial; for example, companies providing internet services and mobile phones. The brand ambassadors will introduce the product to the customer by giving or showing them the sample, explain the benefits of the product and its USP, offer trials and raise brand visibility. During the sampling a short brand message can be delivered and a leaflet can accompany samples where appropriate. The more memorable, lively and involving the activity is that surrounds the trial, the better the product recall and the greater the affinity between the consumer and the brand (see also Chapter 8). By sampling the product, end users are not only made aware of the product but they also know that they like it. They have a knowledge of that product and this understanding will translate into future purchases.

Merchandising. If a brand is not on the shelf, or not visible, it cannot be bought; which makes merchandising a crucial part of proclaiming product or service presence, and in ensuring good placement, correct pricing and product availability in sufficient quantity to meet demand and drive sales. Merchandising is also a very important part of brand awareness and the purchasing environment for the consumer – after all, 70 per cent of purchasing decisions are made in-store. It involves making sure that the brand is obvious and available – it will generate sales by:

- placing POP or POS material in an outlet to promote the product;
- stacking the shelves to the correct number of products or varieties and number of facings so that availability is obvious;
- placing self-talkers advertising the product;
- building a secondary display, for example a free-standing display in an aisle, or a display on a gondola end in-store;
- installing a special promotion and placing all the communication for the activity;
- meeting with the staff in-store and promoting the brand to them, checking their ordering procedures and ensuring that systems are in place to avoid running out of stock.

The amount by which sales will be uplifted by merchandising activity will vary according to the product, position and environment, but, as a guideline only, a secondary display in a grocery multiple can lead to a minimum of 25 per cent uplift in sales and frequently much more, depending on the product. Merchandising can be a tactical or a strategic ongoing activity with regular POP materials replaced and updated, and this ensures that promotions and products are communicated with impact.

If you have followed the process so far, you will understand the crucial ingredients in devising a well-considered merchandising campaign and its value in the sales process.

However, the FM merchandising discipline has extended, becoming somewhat of a hybrid, borrowing parts of the elements from other disciplines, to include:

- visiting a retail outlet, establishing a rapport with the retailer (CRM);

- discussing the retailer's stocks of the brand, the presentation of the brand and discussing the profit the retailer can expect from the brand (sales);
- selling some of the product to the retailer, either from the merchandiser's car or by taking a transfer order (sales);
- merchandising the product on the retailer's shelves (merchandising);
- conducting an audit to highlight the status of the brand in that outlet on entry and exit defining the achievements of the call (auditing).

If merchandising calls of the hybrid type are conducted with the same retailer on an ongoing basis as part of a strategic contract, the rapport becomes stronger and more brands or product variants can be sold in to the retailer, extending the reach of the brand. By including so many steps in the visit, the outputs from the visit are maximised, which makes the best use of the merchandiser's time and, therefore, the budget.

Face-to-face sales by a salesperson. This is more than just 'order taking' which is when a person just takes payment and perhaps packs the item purchased. 'Sales' is selling, when a salesperson engages with the shopper to obtain their trust and confidence in the knowledge held by the salesperson. A trained salesperson will qualify the shopper and fact find. They will also discover where the shopper is in the buying process to match the sales process to the shopper. Only when the salesperson is assured that the shopper is ready will a 'sales close' be attempted.

After sales service. A follow-up to a sale will discover useful feedback on the product or service and allow an opportunity to sell in more associated products and services and accessories. It builds the relationship and reinforces the engram.

INTERNET AND MOBILE DIRECT MARKETING

Table 5.4 shows online retail media predicted spend. It shows that actually marketers seem to change their budget little, year on year. A survey for Kingston Smith on web spend and trends (2008) actually found that marketers left media spend to agencies year on year and often did not control the web spend, which came from a different budget.

Table 5.4 UK source trending

Marketing Budget for Online Retail Media	Two Years Out	Five Years Out
The same budget	53.2%	43.3%
A different existing budget	21.3%	22.1%
A mixture	20.2%	21.7%
A new budget	5.3%	12.9%

Hopefully a survey now would find that marketers control internet and mobile budgets and each year would re-evaluate this increasingly key area of communication.

The spend on media in 2010 in the UK was: about £8 billion on advertising, £14 billion on direct marketing, £4 billion on PR, £12 billion on promotions with £36 billion on price promotions. (In 2014 the figures are £14 billion on promotions and £41 billion on price promotions. Source: IPM and University of Westminster.)

INTERNET

Website and search. The search engines are now remarkably responsive to search. Shoppers rapidly access websites. There is now enough professional support for a website to become an excellent marketing and sales site and it not intended to describe in this book the setting up of a website. The messages they should carry, however, is covered in later parts of this book. In addition search engines such as Google take advertisements on a pay per click basis that appear alongside the results of search and alongside web pages. As an aside, research by Sponge (April 2013), finds 78 per cent of UK retailers do not offer wi-fi free in-store to shoppers. Half of the shops that do are collecting valuable information and benefitting from the opportunity to engage with shoppers while offering something of value to the shopper. The best experiences the survey finds come from John Lewis and Warehouse, with Debenhams and Pret A Manger providing a more involved experience. According to EpiServer, Debenhams meets shoppers' demands in terms of speed, key functionality and ease of use. One in ten log on to free wi-fi at restaurants and cafes daily – so the shopper demand is there.

E-mail. Advertising can also be placed alongside e-mail messages when e-mails are accessed. If the shopper/customer has agreed then they can be sent marketing and sales material and messages by e-mail. Usually this is after registration with the originator.

Social media. A dedicated team is required to be able to respond in near real time – both to pick up and use plaudits and correct misunderstandings or misinformation. Kellogg's reported at the 2013 Industry Insights Summit how they, as traditional partnership marketers, use real-time marketing to drive results. Kellogg's maximised their 2012 Olympic partnership, producing an on-pack overnight when Gabby Douglas won gold, she appeared on the front of a Corn Flakes box and the image garnered one million tweets in one day.

Why is social media useful? Booz (May 2013) reports that understanding social sentiment which differentiates between positive and negative feedback helps marketers establish the shoppers' pulse, but also allows the marketer to harvest and to use the shoppers' language in subsequent messages.

Social media consists of many alternatives, the principal ones in 2013 being Facebook, Twitter, Pinterest and Instagram. Google and Youtube have featured. Pinterest is now offering an app which can be integrated with supplier and retailer software packages offering a smooth transfer to websites. This allows the shopper to move to make a purchase from the non-purchase Pinterest site. Instagram is probably overtaking the others for marketers as, according to *Mobile Marketer* in March 2013, it offers to cross-fertilise a brand's most loyal fans visually enhancing through genuine real-time content material all of which is more relevant to shoppers. Instagram was not intended originally for commercial use but offers lifestyle Insights of other shoppers and can be linked both to a brand website and to Facebook. Mobile social is another increasingly popular way to communicate with a mobile audience. Soon, there will also be HTML5 push notifications, giving marketers a way to message users who are on their mobile websites. In May 2013, *Mobile Marketer* reports that Facebook is another victim of the battle to secure the homepage for mobile suggesting it may not survive if it is not mobile compatible. The potential for advertising revenues when some social media firm succeeds in achieving a mobile home page will be significant.

Sir Martin Sorrell in 2013 commented in an interview with the *Harvard Business Review* that he thinks Facebook and Twitter are for PR, not advertising. He believes they are a branding medium and about developing the brand over the long term. Someone saying something nice on Facebook about your brand is probably not going to drive an instant purchase! As consumers, there is only so much room for communication from brands in our lives. Do we really want to receive tweets and Facebook posts from every brand we buy, including toilet roll, milk and frozen peas?

The impact of social media on shoppers is immense and marketers need to somehow direct shoppers to social media sites.

MOBILE MARKETING

Marketers are almost overwhelmed just trying to decide which to use and when with a staggering number of options when it comes to messaging mobile users – SMS, push notifications, in-app alerts and mobile e-mail. Mobile is an important way to send a message to consumers who increasingly have their smartphones and tablets within arm's reach 24-hours a day. However, it is easy for marketers to fall into the trap of sending too many messages and annoying users, especially when the same message is being delivered across mobile's multiple messaging platforms.

The challenge for marketers is, that because mobile is such a personal medium, users have a high expectation that messages be relevant and add value to their lives. There are ways for marketers to address these issues, including increasingly sophisticated user analytics that provide customer context alongside traditional methods used in advertising such as A/B split testing (where two versions (A and B) are compared which are identical, except for one variation that might impact a user's behaviour. Typically version A might be that currently used (control), while version B is modified in some respect). As with any direct marketing strategy, testing and learning is key. One of the challenges for marketers is aligning the channel with the target user experience on mobile. Marketers need to think about mobile as being interactive. Gen X, Y is hugely driven by instant gratification and the fastest way to reach them with an interactive message is SMS – they send something and get it back right away. *Text message (SMS) and with pictures (MMS).* SMS is a widely popular method for reaching mobile users and is expected to remain relevant for some time. However, mobile users are also increasingly using their devices to check for e-mail messages, making it imperative for marketers to ensure their e-mails are optimised for mobile.

Then there are push notifications, which are becoming a popular way to reach users who have downloaded a brand's app. These can include local push notifications, app-originated notifications and in-app alerts. But the choices do not stop there.

- Proactive. The mobile user is required to register to receive messages. These usually make offers. When an offer is taken up a further offer (bounce back) should be made to retain involvement. Registration can be achieved through the offer of a game or app.

- Reactive. Responding to shopper queries without the need for registration.

PUBLIC RELATIONS (PR)

The Chartered Institute of Public Relations (CIPR) defines it as: 'Public relations is the discipline which looks after reputation, with the aim of earning understanding and support and influencing opinion and behaviour. It is the planned and sustained effort to establish and maintain goodwill and mutual understanding between an organisation and its publics.' PR is the opposite of advertising. In PR, the article that features your company is not paid for. The reporter, whether broadcast or print, writes about or films your company as a result of information he or she received and researched.

Publicity is more effective than advertising, for several reasons. First, publicity is far more cost-effective than advertising. Even if it is not free, your only expenses are generally phone calls and mailings to the media. Second, publicity has greater longevity than advertising. An article about your business will be remembered far longer than an ad.

Publicity also reaches a far wider audience than advertising generally does. Sometimes, your story might even be picked up by the national media, spreading the word about your business all over the country.

Finally, and most important, publicity has greater credibility with the public than does advertising. Readers feel that if an objective third party – a magazine, newspaper or radio reporter – is featuring your company, you must be doing something worthwhile.

Sponsorship. This is a very broad subject and is particularly useful to indicate a brand dimension. It is a part of PR. Support for a charity (for example, the name of the charity appearing on their website, stands or vehicles) can show a caring dimension of a brand. Even Police vehicles may now be sponsored in UK. Football strips, however, need to have the sanction of their team's supporters! The Charities Aid Foundation (CAF) has a website that can advise on local charities by category. Contacting the CAF may be helpful as they can align the objective of the sponsorship to a specific charity (see the Appendix).

NON-DIRECT COMMUNICATION

Advertising. Advertising is not an individually targeted medium. In advertising, you pay to have your message placed in a newspaper, TV or radio spot or outdoor on billboards, both static and digital.

Advertising embraces many sub-disciplines. The classic mechanisms are posters, print (newspapers and magazines), broadcast media (radio television and cinema) – where typically a 30-second audio/video message is put across– and also packaging and POS.

Outdoor advertising. Such as posters, including digital posters which change or video posters which show a video clip. The Outdoor Media Centre (OMC) approach to the customer journey is the four-stage process – absorbing (the shopper becomes aware of the message); planning (considering what to do about the message); obtaining (purchasing a product or service); and sharing (telling others about the message/purchase). Categories variations researched are for a static (typically 48-sheet poster) and the dynamic phase posters which scroll or are electronic. Static results show it is rated higher for absorbing.

Dynamic results indicate 70 per cent remain in the absorbing stage, though two-thirds generated 'feel' or 'do' response. There is some evidence to support that advertising does move people onwards on the journey to purchase.

By way of comparison using the OMC approach, TV is best at the absorbing stage, Online is best for planning, whereas radio and press communicate detail better at the obtaining stage, but TV and outdoor can assist if there is a driver here giving a call to action.

Outdoor advertising is best used on routes to venues, shops, outlets and events.

Transport advertising. Can be considered as a part of outdoor advertising, however when displayed on external surfaces of the transport it is in effect a moving billboard. Posters on walls, walls opposite platforms, escalators, steps (all of which can now be dynamic) have a time measured in seconds for people to view. Small posters are also placed on the inside of buses, tubes, trains and trams.

MESSAGE SITUATION

As discussed elsewhere, the location of a message has an impact on the way that it is received – 'The medium is the message' is a phrase coined by Marshall McLuhan, meaning that the form of a medium embeds itself in the message, creating a symbiotic relationship by which the medium influences how the message is perceived. This is certainly the case for messaging in venues.

Research by the IPM for the British Council of Shopping Centres showed that visitors in shopping centres and pedestrianised city centres were in a much better frame of mind to receive complex messages. Those in high streets with traffic were concerned with safety. Meanwhile, venues such as train stations left people more stressed (too many other messages to concentrate on or ones which use unfamiliar language such as Latin plant names). Meanwhile garden centres actually *under* stress people. You need to be engaged properly with your surroundings to be able to take in everything new coming your way. So always consider the surroundings at the same time as the message.

TV advertising. Thirty-second slots are usually sold alongside appropriate programmes. Some programmes of a certain type or genre can be sponsored, meaning that the advertisements are more suitably linked to target audiences. These advertisements can also be interactive where the customer can feedback a response using the buttons on the remote controller (direct response).

Note that TV advertising with sales promotions show a greater response rate than without.

Booz reports that alongside filmed comedy, the Target Corporation offers shoppable content (they run outlets similar to Walmart) providing the chance to buy clothes and other items as shown or worn by the characters in the film. The shoppers were linked to the website but also to social media for product reviews by other shoppers. Marketers, in areas including consumer electronics, clothing/apparel and consumer packaged goods (CPG), are investing in direct-to-consumer relationships to drive value across the Path to Purchase and close the loop between engagement and sales. Nike with its Fuelband mobile fitness experience links with the shopper's personal fitness profile, introducing shoppers to other Nike products that supplement the fitness experience.

Local radio advertising. Slots are offered alongside commercial radio broadcasts.

Cinema. National and local only advertisements can be placed on screen before feature films.

Print. Magazines and newspapers – both take advertisements.

Advertorial. Where the advertisement is written in the magazine or newspaper style, appearing to be an editorial, inserts – printed loose leaf pages inserted into a magazine or newspaper, tip-ons which are stuck onto the relevant page.

House literature. When a retailer offers such it is usually free. Supermarkets and department stores, hotel chains often use publishers (such as River Publishing) to produce a free monthly magazine offered through outlets.

PACKAGING

A key placement for the engram – the product package itself may be the engram.

POINT OF SALE (POS) MATERIAL

Alongside the product or service, POS that draws attention to the product may be hung from the ceiling, stuck onto the floor, on the shelf (adjacencies), in a special dispenser or arrangement (ensembles).In-store video can give advice on using products that help people to buy while on their shopping mission.

HELP TO SELECT MEDIA

Econsultancy have produced *Marketing Attribution 2013 A Buyers Guide* which is described in Part III suggesting which media to use. The guide describes which firms undertake analytic work.

Summary

The way you stack media does, to an extent, influence the outcome that you get. If you stack hard (sales promotion) on top of softer lead media such as advertising, media or outdoor, you are much more likely to get hard outcomes. So if profit is your goal, this is the route to start with. Remember that media also includes elements that you might not normally consider, such as POP, as part of the marketing budget.

If, however, you are seeking brand fame, image or reputation, then opt for other partners.

Chapter 6

The Barriers to Purchase

In the Introduction we suggest that it is a better metaphor to see a shopper as a little like a random particle with many options as to where to go and what to buy. Some of these location options may not stock the product, some may not sell it. Very few products are destinations. Part of the role of marketing is to remove obstacles to purchase.

Why Might People Not Buy?

Working with fast.MAP and *Promotional Marketing* magazine, the IPM polled 1,154 people carefully matched to the UK population. Seventy-seven per cent of these shoppers reported that they had arrived at a store to buy an advertised offer, only to find that it was out of stock. In June 2013, by way of a further example, Waitrose had three separate three for £5 specialist bottled beer offers; only one beer was available for each of the three promotions. Store staff explained that the promotional labels were prepared and circulated centrally and the stock delivered never matched the labels. One beer had never been seen in the store, another had not been stocked for some time, another of the beers had run out of stock – the history of the three other 'no-show' products was not available; so the promotion was in effect a lie due to the central control applied. Carphone Warehouse in Oxford Street (June 2013) on a central gondola offered a brand new ASUS tablet phone – and though they had the stock, the sales staff had a 'stop' on selling the product – no reason given; the gondola and its display should have been removed. Of course suppliers may be being conned by retailers – the suppliers have presumably provided the products (and the discounts?) and even seen the promotional shelf labels and gondolas, but there are no products available to sell. The result is the shoppers being unhappy with brand, supplier and retailer. FM companies really help brands and suppliers here as they undertake to merchandise and audit retailers. (See *Field Marketing* by Roddy Mullin for more information.)

The Shopper Now Demands Value and Service

Seventeen per cent of shoppers are 'not satisfied' with the frequency that promoted products are not in stock when they want to buy them (Shoppertrack survey). *The Grocer* found that availability was 92.9 per cent, which is a major difference in a £120 billion market. Store systems base supply on historic sales not on demand that is going to be generated by the promotional offer. Shoppers also say that when they are frustrated in trying to buy a product on offer, a significant proportion are left with a bias against the product and, being forced to trial the competition, may leave a brand permanently. The IGD in 2003 found 37 per cent of shoppers would go to another store and 6 per cent would not buy at all – leading to a loss of 43 per cent of intended purchases for retailers; 19 per cent of shoppers would switch to a rival brand which leads to a loss of 25 per cent of intended purchases for manufacturers. In 2009, a survey found that if products are out of stock two or three times this leads to nearly 50 per cent switching to another supermarket and 50 per cent buying an alternative brand. The trend is a retrograde step for both retailers and brands. On-shelf availability, for 33 per cent of the grocery and FMCG sector, is not a key business objective. Interestingly, if promotion stock management is right – the product is available – a retailer gets post-promotion sales benefits.

WHAT MAKES THE DIFFERENCE?

Promotion stock management, particularly for the first day, and smaller stores is key along with matching the discount offered. Calculation of the necessary stock level is complicated and depends on the product, price sensitivity, the retailer, the shelf space, the length of the promotion, the store's customer profile and whether the store is smaller (where it is possible to manage promotional stock demand). Typically, by way of example, for a half price or BOGOF, what appears to be an uplift of six times (looking at sales) is a demand lift of 14 times, that all stores could reach but over half fail to because they are not prepared. In effect sales could be 1.8 times what they currently are – or the same uplift of six times could be delivered for much less discount. This is where it is possible to find an optimisation of the discount level and the store systems' capability to meet the uplift demand. The key is to concentrate on customer satisfaction such that the secondary benefits come into play and a happy shopper returns to the same retail outlet. The shopper profile of the store itself makes a difference – those with wealthy executives or struggling families in their catchment area can do much better or much worse if the products are suited or unsuited. Shelf space too should be optimised and matched to shelf filling with promotional stock management.

WHAT CAN A RETAILER DO?

Establish a strong promotional management team, develop a promotional strategy that produces a framework for timely promotions that optimise promotions to demand and supply, and identify the core stores, products and shopper profiles at the stores selected for promotions. A prerequisite is an understanding of how the brand and products (and product variations) sell: that is understanding shopper buying patterns – the RFM, their consumption patterns, the pricing and value perception by the shopper, brand values, what promotional activity (on-pack, advertising, POS) there has been hitherto – with what mechanics, display, shelf display, facings, space and what were the results of the promotion (volume, profit, analysis by time) and any post-promotional feedback. As a general observation, many retailers will hold the raw data; nobody will have analysed it. Direct and indirect competitor dealings within category would also be helpful if they can be established. The view and a benefit analysis of each of the stakeholders follows; looking at shopper, retailer, supplier and internally management, sales, marketing, supply chain, finance priorities, focus and targets.

Bait Pricing

The Office of Fair Trading (OFT) has published papers in support of their review of unfair pricing policies at retail. Advertised price discounting, also known as 'bait pricing', is making an offer without enough stock to support the demand that this creates – and is described as unfair practice by the OFT. This excerpt is from a report commissioned by them: 'Details of price framing experiments' completed by London Economics with Steffen Huck and Brian Wallace.

'They (the shoppers) choose the store based on the deal they are being offered in the advertisement. This choice raises their willingness to pay because they expect to get a deal and again envisage owning the good. Subjects (shoppers) reported that this frame enticed them to go quickly to the shop with the best deal so as not to miss out. They reported anger and frustration if they missed out on the offer in the experiment, however, they reported they may buy any' – so few immediate downsides for the store. The first store that their testers visited benefited very strongly from the offer, selling more product. However, over time, the research reported that shoppers learned (became cynical?) about these offers. Bait pricing in action delivers badly for stores but also for the brands, in terms of destroying their brand values over time. This was confirmed in the IPM survey.

The IPM survey in detail explored other shopper reactions:

- 84 per cent of the panel regularly shopped at the same supermarket, however only 35 per cent of them do not make special trips to take advantage of advertised offers, 26 per cent do so often and 38per cent do so occasionally.

- 77 per cent of these bargain hunters arrived only to discover the item in question was out of stock.

For the retailer, it is important to note that a quarter of these disappointed people said they would actively try to shop elsewhere and half (51 per cent) reported that they would be less likely to respond to that retailer's price promotions in future. But almost half, 49 per cent, say it will not affect where they do their shopping.

Manufacturers are by no means unscathed: 14 per cent of the consumers surveyed said they would be quite or very likely to buy from the competition in future. That's enough to take the edge off any upcoming marketing campaign. Meanwhile a third (34 per cent) said they will be less likely to respond to that manufacturer's price discounts in future.

Of course, the one effect not reported at all by the above research is the impact on long-term loyalty given that 77 per cent of people were forced to a competitive product. In the OFT research most people did not leave empty handed.

What Do Shoppers Actually Do if They Can't Find a Product They Are Seeking?

Some previous research has already been done in this area, by the IGD in 2003. Clearly the impact will be different depending on the product area. As an example, a staple product, with no alternative (such as perhaps bread or milk) would have a different profile from a more discretionary product. Table 6.1 gives an indication of where shoppers place the blame.

Table 6.1 What do shoppers do if they cannot find the product they are seeking?

'Thinking about occasions when the product has been out of stock, please indicate how much you agree or disagree with the statements below.'					
	Strongly Agree	**Agree**	**Neither Agree nor Disagree**	**Disagree**	**Strongly Disagree**
I blame the retailer	26%	38%	22%	8%	5%
It will not affect which brands I buy	14%	37%	37%	10%	3%
I am less likely to respond to that retailer's price promotion in the future	15%	36%	33%	14%	2%
It will not affect where I do my shopping	13%	36%	36%	13%	3%
I am less likely to respond to price discount promotions for that manufacturer's brands in the future	7%	27%	38%	20%	8%
I will actively try to shop elsewhere	7%	18%	47%	27%	6%
I will actively try to buy rival brands	4%	11%	46%	31%	8%
I blame the manufacturer	6%	9%	38%	40%	9%

Source: fast.MAP 29 July 2010.

A study commissioned by SCALA Consulting, the supply chain consultants, in 2009, found almost half of those questioned said they would only tolerate products being out of stock two or three times before switching to another supermarket. Nearly half of those quizzed said that if they could not find their favourite brand they would simply buy an alternative. This represents a retrograde step from 2003 for brands. Yet many brands seem unconcerned. SCALA Consulting also commissioned a survey of some of the biggest global brands and over a quarter of those questioned (26 per cent) – representing a cross-section from the FMCG and grocery sector –did not view On-Shelf Availability as a key success factor for their company. What is more, a third of retailers (33 per cent) didn't have On-Shelf Availability as a key business objective.

So not getting availability right is a 'lose–lose' for retailers and for brands. There is the immediate loss of revenue, followed by the immediate loss of loyalty to both the retailer *and* the brand by the shopper. While brands might argue that it is not their responsibility if products go out of stock – that is not the way that shoppers see it. Blame attaches to both for not getting it right. This is one area where key brands and retailers can work together to improve their mutual loyalty.

UK – Link between Satisfaction and Profits

Following the *Retail Week* report (see page 264), the IPM asked fast.MAP to ask 1,000 representative members of the UK shopper universe how each of the key retailers across the whole spectrum of the UK retailer universe measured up against the *Retail Week* published measures. The *Retail Bulletin* then placed these results against the companies published performance.

The result proved very illuminating when taken (2010) when the line between financial results and shopper satisfaction was quite easy to spot. Two standouts doing better than the average were Boots and Tesco – both with expensive loyalty schemes as an alternative to getting their basics right! On the other hand, stores that were clearly performing badly, such as the Focus Group, subsequently disappeared.

Shoppers Speak Out over Easter 2013

Previously, only surveys of customers produced answers. Now social media can be interrogated on satisfaction or anger and disgust (there is a range of eight states of the shopper).

There was a great deal of publicity about the fact that all of the major UK fmcg retailers ran out of Easter eggs by Easter 2013, while there were plenty to be had the previous Christmas.

How do we know how people feel about this? In the current climate people are addicted to continual online communication. Twitter feeds, Facebook and Google searches all add up to an instant research poll of the health of the Nation. Spectruminsight.co.uk trawl through all of these to reveal what people are saying and the emotion underlying this (see the Appendix for Spectruminsight contact details).

Shoppers clearly believe the duty of retailers is to have in stock what they need, when they need it. There is the sense that they see retailers as being there to actually sell; as opposed to being there to make money. They get really upset when they cannot buy what they set out to get.

The Spectruminsight research reveals a huge emotional reaction to not being able to find what they really needed in their local of choice with a scale of eight emotions. Sainsbury's proved to be the retailer that got it most wrong (adjusted for market share), and 17 per cent of shoppers attached emotions to their comments. However, the position is not quite as clear cut as this. While Sainsbury's was the biggest offender, however, Waitrose – which was only beaten by Tesco in being the best performer – had the greatest percentage (20 per cent) of emotive comments. Moreover, whereas the rest were a mix of mainly anger, surprise and sorrow, for Waitrose, there was no surprise, but a very considerable (25 per cent) of people expressed disgust. Disgust is the worse emotion of the eight categories assessed.

If you set yourself up to be the best, you need to be so much better than the rest.

Tesco and Asda shoppers were not disgusted, nor were they surprised, they were angry. In Tesco and Asda head office, I am sure surprise would have been what they wanted to hear. However, availability has been so poor in these outlets that it would be futile to expect better. At least Morrisons and Sainsbury's can be pleased that their customers expressed a healthy measure of surprise. Surprise is not a derogatory emotion.

The position is an outcome of the current focus on discounted product, which makes holding excess product after an event extremely expensive. When you combine this with inadequate space in-store to keep discounted product in stock, you have a recipe for disloyalty that increasingly forces retailers to spend more to attract new customers than satisfy their existing ones.

A Mutual Focus for Growth

Of course, if the preceding findings are accurate, a simple test would be to see if improved availability really did result in improved sales at a subsequent non-promoted period. This analysis has been done by Storecheck Marketing Ltd reported in the IPM white paper – 'In Place of Price'. This research covered promotions across a broad range of over 10,000 products for a period covering five years. The research separated stores into good, poor and average performers based on their uplift multiplies from the period before.

Here the benchmark was the same for every promotion and each store. Sales two weeks before are averaged out. The promotion could then be evaluated by comparison with this position.

Key measures are:

- the average uplift for all the stores – representing the strength of the offer;
- the uplift of individual stores compared to the average – representing the local impact of the offer, combined with the way it is presented;
- the sales after the activity, both overall and compared to promotion uplift individually;
- key measurable factors impacting on performance that can be measured.

There is no such thing as a representative average. The actual uplifts for a shopper discount level vary very widely, by category and brand. Similarly, within a promotion for a brand, stores also separate into good, average and poor performers.

If you select a good performer as having an uplift of 20 per cent or better than the average and a poor performer as 20 per cent or less than the average, average is then within a 20 per cent band either side of it.

Interestingly, for many brands, there were very few stores actually average, the bulk being either good (above average) or bad (below average).

Of vital importance though is the knowledge that, as the level of shopper discount increases, the uplift performance of good performers increase markedly, while the other two hardly move. Simply stated, give a better offer to your core buyers and they will buy considerably more than the average. Put this way, not, perhaps a surprise.

However, there is a sting in the tail, so to speak. It would perhaps have been expected that the best performing stores would have had a greater level of depressed sales after a promotion than the poor performers. Why? Simply because much of the explanation for uplifts depends on stock cupboard filling or buying forward. Both of which would impact more on the better performers.

This was also substantially untrue. The above average stores also recovered much more rapidly.

This effect, of course, explains why the average in the immediate post-promotion period is a dip. However, it seems that getting promotion availability right is a win–win, bringing better immediate sales as well as post-promotion performance for the brand and the retailer.

The linking factor here is that the above average stores promotionally are typically synonymous with stores that are core, that is to say they have a higher proportion of the target market in their catchment area.

Third Party Associated Factors

The factor most associated with discount success was the stock cover the week the promotion starts. Stock availability allows the stock system to swing into action immediately, reducing orders as the promotion wears down. It also empowers core stores to build additional shelf stock so that the increased numbers of shoppers over the average are not disappointed.

As a final benefit, the fact that the supply chain has started high also means that it can respond to the downturn at the end of the promotion immediately. Stores with high stock at the start end up with lower stock at the end than those that were always struggling to keep pace. In these stores demand always seems to increase, and never quite keep pace. Until, of course, the promotion ends.

The Issue of Stock Management is Really Important

Just in Time (JIT) supply has evolved because excessive inventory is wasted capital. Ideally products should arrive just as the shelves empty. This means too that you need little space for stock and sales space can be increased, so design of retail outlets is changing. Fashion retailers, such as Zara, because they only introduce new stock, only discount to clear slow movers. However JIT has a down side in that cannot tolerate fluctuations in demand larger than 10 per cent.

Store systems base supply on historic sales, not on demand that is going to be generated by a promotional offer. As an example, a failure to stock in 68 per cent of 300 stores, found by a FM audit, reversed a decision that would have led to the abandonment of a product on trial, which subsequently became a 'must stock' item.

It is, of course, not necessary to actually see a product is not selling with access to store by store Electronic Point of Sale (EPOS) data. This is usually revealing. Colin Harper from Storecheck points out that they have never come across a brand that is selling in all the stores they are listed for. In some cases the gap can be as much as £500,000 per annum.

The Impact of Non-Availability on Retailer Profits in the UK and US

Non-availability is a feature of the US market as well as in the UK. A recent (March 2013) Bloomberg report isolated Walmart as being significantly poor. The article 'Customers Flee Walmart Empty Shelves for Target, Costco' commented that, 'Last month, Walmart placed last among department and discount stores in the American Customer Satisfaction Index, the sixth year in a row the company had either tied or taken the last spot.' The reason given for this was the lack of product on the shelves – the critical measure for shoppers of retail satisfaction. The article quoted a Walmart spokesman, Brooke Buchanan:

> *In-stock levels are up significantly in the last few years, so the premise of this story, which is based on the comments of a handful of people, is inaccurate and not representative of what is happening in our stores across the country. Two-thirds of Americans shop in our stores each month because they know they can find the products they are looking for at low price.*

The facts support Walmart's spokesman. Walmart's re-stocking challenge coincides with slowing sales growth. Zeynep Ton, a retail researcher and Associate Professor of Operations Management at the MIT Sloan School of Management in Cambridge, Massachusetts, whose research examines how retailers benefit from offering good wages and benefits to all employees, published an article in the *Harvard Business Review*, which stated:

> *When times were good and people were still shopping, the lack of excellence was OK. Their view has been that they have the lowest prices so customers keep coming anyway. You don't see that so much anymore. Shoppers are so sick of this. They're mad about the way they were treated or how much time they wasted looking for items that aren't there.*

So re-stocking matters to the shopper and shoppers are angry if the product they seek is not there. Ton added that retailers consider labour – usually their largest controllable expense – an easy cost-cutting target. That's what happened at Home Depot Inc. (HD) in the early 2000s, when Robert Nardelli, then Chief Executive Officer, cut staffing levels and increased the percentage of part-time workers to trim expenses and boost profit. Eventually, customer service and customer satisfaction deteriorated and same-store sales growth dropped.

So What are the Barriers?

Barriers occur in-store because of operational failures – stock control and delivery, shelf stocking and 'silos', where in-house rivalry and contrary instructions hinder the shopper/customer. Barriers also occur through a failure to develop a relationship with the customer, losing their trust, contradicting their mindset and muddling their view of the brand. Organisational structure can effect this where businesses operate through a silo structure.

There are many seemingly basic shop errors that can occur relating to stock/ display:

- Not maintaining the shelf stock – nothing for customer to buy or levels reduced that are not conducive to purchase (research shows shoppers tend not to buy from low stock levels).
- Failure to check stock levels – nothing on-shelf or in-store or on order.
- Errors in placing – wrong part of store – wrong shelf. Hidden behind other goods.
- Failure to anticipate demand – this frequently occurs with promotions. (Waitrose's heavily promoted half-price prawns and smoked salmon had all gone despite the advertisements still running in November 2012. M&S ran out of half-price hot cross buns, though promoted with vouchers in full page ads in 2011. Sainsbury's ran out of Easter eggs in 2013 though these were ordinary stock.)

The silo mentality of some businesses (banks, financial services, the professions and charities) can affect sales. Virgin One Account had some 75,000 customers but, seeking more, ran a series of advertisements commissioned by their marketing 'silo'. Unusually accountants (not normally assessed as eager shoppers) found the complex sales pitch attractive – linking bank account, credit card and mortgage into one. The marketing offer had not been notified to any other 'silo' within the business. In consequence, the call centre staff (mostly younger than the target market and probably unaware of accountancy as a profession) did not understand the potential customers' questions – in any case they were motivated (that is, paid) only by the number of computer applications they sent on to 'fulfilment', the next silo, so they entered anything into the boxes. In 'fulfilment' they could not understand why there were so many errors in the computer forms and they also had to delude the applicants, unaware of marketing's offers. Thirty-four per cent of potential customers had fallen by the way within 13 weeks of initial enquiry. A brilliant concept – loved by accountants – but because of the silo structure barriers, the 'volunteer' applicants fell by the way. They are not alone. Virgin Media silo problems are recounted in Chapter 15.

Getting the Price Right is Key

Too large a price discount just eats into profit, eventually converting products into commodities – all in the interest of retaining retailer volume rather than maximising the return benefit. And of course retailers are aware that if you are discounting your margin to give you a competitive edge against other retailers, the speed with which you can turn your capital employed (that is, your stock) is what makes the difference between success and failure. However, going too far on price promotions can be terminal. In 1996, the electrical retailer Comet made an offer for its competitor Norweb. Norweb held out for more, which was refused, and then began an extensive campaign of 0 per cent finance offers. Comet decided not to match them. Instead, whenever customers asked about finance, it directed them to Norweb. Comet's margins went up, and Norweb was crippled by the cost of its promotion. Soon afterwards, Comet was able to buy Norweb at a lower price than it had offered before.

Using Price Discounting Wisely

Price discounting is a valuable tool for many manufacturers. It represents an opportunity for minor brands and new brand entrants to gain a foothold. However, it carries with it the requirement for manufacturers to take responsibility for shopper availability. Brands enter into an arrangement with retailers to run discounts, and put pressure on retailers for deeper discounts. They need to be aware that, over a certain point, unless additional space and stock is available in core areas and the stores serving them, the net result will be long-term loss of loyalty both for the brand and the retailer.

The best mutual positioning is, therefore, to understand and manage both supply and demand together. Research has gone into many aspects of discounting – see Chapter 11. Managing availability is covered in Chapter 10. However, a few guidelines are available from the following published results. Of necessity, these are only guidelines, and results will vary by product type, and branded/non-branded. However, any guidelines are better than none at all.

Single-Unit/Multiple-Unit Discounts

Research by Wansink et al. (1998) found that, on average, the sales volume increased by 125 per cent with single-unit promotions, compared to 165 per cent with multiple-unit promotions. Research by Manning and Sprott (2007) studied specifically the effects of multiple-unit price promotions on purchasing behaviour. The uplift in quantity purchased as a result of multiple-unit price promotions was found to be dependent upon the magnitude of the quantity specified in the offer and the rate of product consumption for the specific product category.

How Long Should I Discount For?

Both the length and the frequency of promotions can affect how responsive the consumer will be. The longer a promotion lasts, the less effective it will be, because over time the effect of the promotion upon sales will be reduced (for example, Rao and Thomas 1973, Blattberg and Wisniewski 1987). The explanation for this may be that after a promotion has run for a certain length of time, consumers will come to expect that they can buy the product at the offer price and so will stockpile less and increase their inter-purchase time. Martínez-Ruiz et al. (2006a) advised that promotions for non-perishable storable products should not exceed ten days, otherwise profitability will be reduced. The frequency of promotions will affect the consumer's reference price (Kalwani and Yim 1992, Mayhew and Winer 1992) and hence can lower the height of the promotional spike in sales (Raju 1992). If a brand is discounted often, consumers will come to anticipate the promotion and will expect to always pay a lower price for the product.

Individual Product Differences

Factors related specifically to individual product categories such as brand share (Bemmaor and Mouchoux 1991), perishability and bulkiness (Bell et al. 1999, Manning and Sprott 2007, Wansink and Deshpandé 1994), and the occasion for which the product will be used (Meat and Livestock Commission 2002) can all influence the shoppers' response to promotions. For example Bemmaor and Mouchoux (1991) found that, as a result of price cuts, smaller brands experience a larger relative increase in sales compared with larger more established brands. It was found that consumers will increase their usage for products which are perishable, as a result of promotions (Bell et al. 1999). However, in categories of more staple items, such as toilet paper and detergent, stockpiling takes place, increasing the inter-purchase time, meaning that unsurprisingly (research confirming common sense) the consumers move their purchasing forward, but do not increase their overall consumption (Wansink and Deshpandé 1994). Most, if not all, product categories have a variety of brands and products suited to different uses or occasions and this can influence how the shopper responds to promotions within a category.

If a lower-tier brand is promoted it does not attract customers from high-tier brands, but the promotion of higher-quality, premium-priced brands impacts significantly upon weaker brands (see, for example, Kumar and Leone 1988, Krishnamurthi and Raj 1991, Mulhern and Leone 1991, Martínez-Ruiz et al. 2006a).

Shopper Differences

Characteristics related specifically to the shopper and their household can also influence the effectiveness of promotions, such as the household size, presence of children, age and income. The larger the family, the further the budget needs to stretch and the more likely they will be to buy into promotions (Bawa and Gosh 1999, Urbany et al. 1996). There is conflict in the literature as to the effect age has on promotional response. Some believe younger shoppers are more likely to purchase products on promotion, either because they are more price sensitive than older shoppers (Ainslie and Rossi 1998) or because they are more likely to be influenced by stimuli such as displays and advertising and hence make decisions on impulse at the POP than older shoppers (Inman and Winer 1998). However, it has also been suggested that older shoppers have more time to shop and therefore may be more likely to take advantage of promotions (Raju 1992). In reality it is quite likely that the response by different age groups will depend upon other factors such as the product being promoted and the mechanism used.

Promotions

Promotions by branded goods manufacturers totalled £25.6 billion (in 2010) with an additional in-house spend by retailers bringing the total to £36 billion. Price promotions damage brands in the long term despite being loved by retailers. Value added promotions (where some other benefit is added rather than a price cut – see *Sales Promotion* by Roddy Mullin) are best, building brand value and real customer loyalty. Promotions are not just about sales but are also a call to action – such as cutting back on consumption of unhealthy foods and taking more exercise. The IPM is studying how promotional marketing affects people, the way they behave and how it changes their purchasing patterns – the results are included in Chapter 11.

The retailer now (the big boys, the other grocery retailers, the non-grocery) finds the pressures, the statistics – and the increasing crossovers between competing products – mean matching the C for convenience is more important.

Core stores – those with the highest proportion of target market in their area – have the highest demand pressure and run out of stock first as discounts increase. Other stores cope better. Therefore maintaining stock in core stores is a joint sales and marketing objective. Between discounts, 'promotion sensitive' as opposed to 'price sensitive' shoppers can be attracted with efficient smarter value added promotions.

What Can a Retailer Do?

A retailer can establish a strong promotional management team, develop a promotional strategy that produces a framework for timely promotions that optimise promotions to demand and supply, and identify the core stores, products and shopper profiles at the stores selected for promotions. A prerequisite is an understanding of how the brand and products (and product variations) sell; that is, shopper buying patterns, consumption patterns, pricing and value perception by the shopper, brand values, what promotional activity (for example on-pack, advertising, POS) there has been hitherto with what mechanics, display, shelf display, facings, space and what were the results of the promotion (volume, profit, analysis by time) and any post-promotional feedback. As a general observation, many retailers will hold the raw data and nobody will have analysed it. Direct and indirect competitor dealings within category would also be helpful if they can be established. The view and a benefit analysis of each of the stakeholders should follow, looking at shopper, retailer and supplier and, internally, management, sales, marketing, supply chain, finance priorities, focus and targets.

The supplier, brand and retailer today need to monitor social media to ensure they are not losing sight or trust of the customer both in grocery (for example, Tesco) and non-grocery. The failure to build a real relationship with customers requires all shopper facing persons – including those in call centres – to implicitly trust the customer. It is no good saying – 'you are a valued customer' – and then not trusting the shopper (an example of this practice is Virgin Media).

Clearly the failure to market is final: If customers and sales staff are unaware of a product or service they cannot buy. As a supplier it is worth spending time training sales and call centre staff on new products, but as an observation the authors find it rarely happens. One author went on behalf of a client to a Birmingham call centre with a new product; they said it was the first time anyone had done that. Seeing the product and having it explained rather than just seeing the literature made a huge difference to their ability to respond to shoppers (in this case purchasing through a promotion). Other clients of the author always train John Lewis staff as new products are launched because they are eager to learn and the sales return is better.

Choice – the Great Divide(r) – Pressure on the Shopper is a Barrier to Purchase

Many companies with a successful line immediately turn to brand variants as a way of adding incrementally to their sales, as well as increasing their space in-store (in itself often a guarantee of increased sales).

Botti and Iyengar (AMA 2006) reviewed the importance of choice on an eventual purchase. They considered the everyday grocery shopping experience of a typical US consumer. An ordinary supermarket contains 285 varieties of cookies, including 21 chocolate chip options alone; 20 different types of Goldfish crackers; a dozen varieties of Pringles potato chips; 80 pain relievers; 40 lipstick shades; 16 varieties of instant mashed potatoes; 75 different instant gravies; 120 different pasta sauces; 175 different salad dressings; and a whopping 275 types of cereal.

Obviously a fantastic range that must guarantee something for everyone, you would think. Not so, in fact. Iyengar and Lepper (2000) observe that though consumers state they prefer contexts that offer them more rather than fewer options – too much choice actually deters purchase. They set up a tasting booth in an upscale grocery store, Draeger's, located in Menlo Park, California, that displayed either six different flavours of jam or 24 different flavours. They monitored the traffic at the tasting booth, discovering that whereas 60 per cent of the passersby stopped to sample one of the displayed jams when there were 24 flavours, only 40 per cent stopped when there were six flavours. However, comparisons of purchase behaviour revealed that of the customers attracted to the jam in the extensive choice condition, only 3 per cent purchased a jar of jam, whereas 30 per cent of the customers who encountered the limited display bought a jar.

Indeed, subsequent studies conducted across a variety of contexts reveal further unfavourable pernicious consequences of offering choosers more rather than fewer options. First, the presence of more rather than fewer options makes decision makers more likely to decide against choosing, even when the choice of opting out has negative consequences for their future well-being (Iyengar, Jiang and Kamenica 2006).

Second, the presence of more choices has been associated with lower chooser confidence and greater experiences of negative affect; that is, people choosing from more extensive choice sets are less satisfied with their decision outcomes (for example, chocolate choice) and pay more for purchases that make them less happy (for example, car choice). Even when more choices yield seemingly better objective outcomes (that is, higher salaries for job seekers), they yield worse subjective outcomes. For example, job seekers who pursued more rather than fewer job opportunities were less satisfied.

It seems that, although people like to have the freedom to choose what they consume and are attracted to larger product assortments, they are more likely to make a purchase and be satisfied with it when the choice is made from a limited number of alternatives. This may explain the popularity of stores such as Lidl and Aldi where the stock on display is limited. (Aldi won grocer of the year award June 2013.)

Similar results have been found by researchers studying the optimal number of product features. Advances in technology have not only allowed retailers to offer consumers an ever-increasing number of products, they have also allowed manufacturers to load products with a growing number of features.

Take, for example, today's mobile phones that include the capabilities of a gaming console, text messaging device, wireless internet, calendar, contact organiser, digital camera, global positioning system and MP3 player in addition to its multiple telephone functions. Although each of these features are individually useful, when combined in large numbers they can result in an effect known as 'feature fatigue' (Rust et al. 2006, Thompson et al. 2005). When consumers are deciding which product to buy, they tend to focus on the capabilities of the product (that is, what it can do); however, their satisfaction with the product, once it has been purchased, is driven mostly by how easy it is to use (Thompson et al. 2005).

Ironically, consumers prefer to buy products that have many features and, as a result, they are less satisfied with their choices. Consequently, this dissatisfaction decreases the vendor's long-term profitability (Rust et al. 2006).

The Shopping Experience Impacting on Product Experience

Many commentators have concluded that shoppers would like choice but need help to decide what to buy. Here the web is able to help with Interactive Consumer Decision Aids (ICDA) tools. These help by narrowing choice down to a few items. The items presented could be recommendations based on tracking a particular consumer preference or by picking up preferences from other consumers that are similar (Murray and Haubl – Too much choice for consumers).

So How Can the Issue of Barriers be Addressed?

Part III covers organisation and strategy. Chapters 10 and 11 cover the in-store problem area, along with correctly managing stock especially for promotions.

Finally: Measuring Your Improvement Incorrectly Can Affect Sales to Shoppers

Many companies use second-remove measures to divine success in activity. The problem with associated change, that is not financial, is well illustrated in The Rosser Reeves Fallacy described below.

'Follow your audience' is the fundamental mantra of media planning. Today, that audience is spread increasingly wide and thin, and the fact that an audience is present on a media platform does not necessarily mean that advertising there is effective. The evaluation of media's effectiveness is the single biggest issue for planners today (or at least advertisers hope it is) and there are a variety of effects that contribute to the confusion surrounding it. Here is one common mistake.

Confusing cause and effect is a specific example of the Questionable Cause Fallacy (QCF). The QCF has the general form:

- A and B occur together.
- Therefore A is the cause of B or vice versa.

In fact, there may be no common cause that links A and B.

This fallacy is made when it is assumed that one event must cause another just because the events occur together: the conclusion is drawn, without adequate justification, that A is the cause of B simply because A and B are in concurrence. It is possible that cause and effect are both present but the mistake is in choosing which is which, or it is possible that both are caused by a third event? When people put up umbrellas cars generally get wet, but putting up umbrellas does not cause cars to become wet, the rain causes both. A typical mistaken causal effect might be:

- People wear shorts when it is sunny.
- People wearing shorts causes sunny weather. (A totally implausible concept, but illustrates reverse logic.)

To bring this closer to the reality of media, Rosser Reeves, who 50 years ago was head of the Bates advertising agency in the US, demonstrated what became known as the 'Rosser Reeves Fallacy'. He showed that consumers aware of his client's ads were more favourably disposed towards those clients' brands across a range of measures, including likelihood to buy. Did this mean his advertising was more effective?

No. Generally, brand purchasers have a higher awareness of a brand's advertising than non-purchasers. We tend to remember better those things we like or are familiar with. So rather than those aware of the ads being more likely to buy the brand, it is actually those who buy the brand being more aware of the ads. The effect of the engram creeps in here. The subconscious mind draws attention to the familiar.

Is there a direct lesson for media here? Yes. All media suffers the same plight: namely that more often than not, proxy measures such as brand and advertising awareness are used to measure effectiveness. There is not one single piece of proof that demonstrates that increased awareness is a measure of advertising's ability to build sales. Indeed the only measure of success for media that has any validity is the ability of adverts on that media to build sales. Measuring and linking exposure to advertising to consumer behaviour is the Holy Grail for all media owners, from Google to the Puddlewick Gazette.

The authors believe that measurement, as described in Chapter 16, is the answer and analysing data to obtain Insights is the solution.

Summary

Correcting/removing the barriers to purchase would seem relatively simple to enact.

In the modern era, national averaging is not enough. Targeting shopper incentives and support at the stores and the areas they are in is necessary. A case of increasing demand and supply in parallel, and linked, not separated.

Any Board should establish their own business parameters on failures to stock, promotional management, measurement and Insights, and consider the effect on shoppers of choice if the range of products in any category is too large – then make the strategic decisions that arise.

In ranging, at least, more is not necessarily better.

PART II
Communicating with the Shopper in the Future

Part I has concentrated on the customer and communicating with both the conscious and subconscious mind of the shopper, covering the importance of placing and then encouraging the engram, how people learn and communicate, what matters to the customer – as defined by the 6Cs, what the customer looks for in communications, what is available to the supplier and retailer as the means to communicate with the customer and the barriers to purchase the supplier and retailer unwittingly provide to put off the shopper.

However, there is a considerable volume of researched facts that are available to the brand, retailer and supplier on how the shopper reacts to the shopping messages experienced along the route to purchase. Part II produces the facts from that research and suggests what the messages you send out at the different stages of the shoppers' journey should contain, as a result of that research, ever mindful of the budget limitations.

Chapter 7 is all about shopping as a task and the messages to the shopper in general. Chapters 8 to 12 cover specific messages along and after the route to purchase. Chapter 13 draws out the conclusions that come from this research urging retailers to both consider the long *and* the short-term relationship with the shopper – to dare to be different, before Part III suggests what has to be done by the retailer and supplier to get the shopper to buy their product or service over the competition.

Chapter 7

The Shopping Mission

This chapter is all about shopping as a task and the messages to the shopper in general. On the subject of the shopper, here are some facts and figures to be going on with – which you may or may not be aware of.

Online or In a Store

- 70 per cent of all purchase decisions are taken at the facing – looking at the product (Source: Mintel).
- 0.9 seconds – the time marketers have to convince shoppers to see their display (Source: MARI).
- Between 60 and 120 seconds – the time taken for a shopper to purchase an item (less in convenience outlets).

In a Store

- 3,700 – the average number of POP items passed by a shopper in Tesco stores during a main shopping mission.
- 20,000 – the maximum number of POP items actually found in a large store. POPAI comment in their Grocery Effectiveness study (2012) that 'you can have the best POP in the world, but if it is located at the back of the store, with low traffic flow, next to the toilets, then you will only get a response from the elderly and incontinent'.
- Between 0.5 to 1.5 mph – the average speed range of shoppers walking down an aisle.

- 4 per cent is the impact ratio of POP located above head height – shoppers rarely look up! The impact ratio as defined by POPAI is a measure on the number of shoppers who look at a display, as a ratio of the total number of shoppers who have an opportunity to pass and 'see' it. (The definition of look is more than merely a glance, requiring shoppers to make eye contact with a display for a sufficient period of time –typically just under a second – for them to drop out of 'autoshop' mode, Type 1 thinking (see description below) and think about change.)

Online/Mobile

Internet Retailing reported (May 2013) that total e-commerce revenues were up by almost a fifth (19 per cent) on 2011 to €311.6bn in 2012 dominated by the UK (€96bn in sales), Germany (€50bn) and France (€45bn). This leads the US where the figure is €294bn. The mcommerce market accounted for 5.5 per cent of total sales in 2012, and the share was expected to jump during 2013 as smartphone and tablet ownership rises. IMRG and CapGemini (June 2013) confirmed that more than one in five ecommerce purchases were made by mobile in Q1 of 2013.

This is the decade of the mobile, states Chris Webster of CapGemini, when tickets, boarding passes, keys, payment, loyalty cards and even passports (details held on the mobile in future) will become objects of intrigue and amusement, just as typewriters were before. In the UK, mcommerce reached 12 per cent of total online sales in 2012, against just 5 per cent at the end of 2011. In Scandinavia the share is currently 8 per cent and in France 2 per cent. In the US, meanwhile, m-commerce is estimated to have reached close to 10 per cent – almost double the size of 2011. Resource Nation forecasts m-commerce sales in the US will rise from $8.8 billion in 2012 to $28.7 billion in 2015.

SLI Systems develop websites to move shoppers to a sale based on the premise that shoppers, when selecting a gift, often do not know what they want so need assistance, which SLI Systems provide though a 'Gift Finder' tool. This narrows down item-related questions, such as what event or occasion is the gift for, establishing price ranges, product availability and offering product reviews. Sitecore's recipe for a website includes recognising the importance of the brand (engram) on the homepage, keeping text on that page to a minimum, offering a usable intuitive navigation; all items should be pictured and allow for enlargement with text available and accurate, with links to reviews (a video is beneficial), as is information about whether it is a best seller and availability.

Personalisation improves sales and is achieved through analysis of data. At the checkout have no more than four steps and emphasise the security of the transaction.

The marketer has to realise from this that a shopper is really pushed to take in any information. KISS your message (Keep it Simple Stupid). What can you do in 0.9 of a second?

Thinking Your Way to a Purchase

Psychologists identify two types of decision making:

Type 1 Thinking

This type of thinking operates automatically, and quickly, without conscious control or interference. It is the subconscious taking over.

Type 2 Thinking

This is thoughtful decision making, the one where you weigh up the options. Do you want a blue or a black car?

Most people think that they weigh up the options before they buy. However, many conclusions reached are based on things that are subconsciously known. Examples of this would be:

- What's 2x2?
- Car driving on an empty road.
- Read simple words and sentences.
- Detect hostility in a voice.
- Complete the phrase bread and ...

However the two systems are not actually independent, Type 1, which is used most, hands across to Type 2 the moment it hits an issue. These systems can conflict in an area where, on the face of it, you don't need to think, but in reality you do.

Here is an example of using Type 2. Go down each column calling out whether each word is printed in lower case or upper case. Then go down each column saying whether a word is printed to the left, or the right. You may find this more difficult than you imagine.

LEFT	upper
Left	lower
Right	LOWER
RIGHT	upper
RIGHT	UPPER
Left	lower
LEFT	LOWER
Right	upper

If a decision is not important,or is, on the face of it, simple, Type 1 will kick straight in. It delivers an easy way to get through the day. You can think about other things while the Type 1 part of the brain makes the key decisions that keep you walking, talking, and yes, buying.

The Shopper Mindset

The way a shopper tackles the task depends on their shopping mode and the mission they set for themselves.

The amount of time shoppers spend shopping, their mindset and familiarity with the website or store, unsurprisingly affects the way they shop. However, modes can change during shopping especially when presented with a promotion. Research shows (Source: JC Decaux and the BCSC) that the state of mind of a shopper varies depending on the location. The information they can take in depends on the state of mind they are in at the time. Some environments are more stressful than others. The JC Decaux study compared and contrasted the high street with shopping centres. The message that comes out loud and clear is that a person under pressure has half a mind on environmental problems (cars, people with trollies) and the remaining half does not leave much for posters and POP. So again for brands, suppliers and retailers – simple messaging only please.

Shopper Modes

Research by Phillip Adcock (who writes supporting literature to make consumers better shoppers) suggests there are five modes of shopping. These relate very firmly to the type of product and its immediate importance to the shopper.

- *Unfamiliar or inexperienced* with product or service. (Examples are – electronics, health foods, DIY, household, or where young and old are put together.) Need is for information, advice. Phillip Adcock advises shoppers to always find staff and ask. Labelling does not accommodate the many who do not wear glasses to shop.

- *Experiential* where 'need to try' exists. (Examples are clothing, perfumes, health and beauty products.) Shoppers also like to test for freshness and fullness of packets, some shoppers need to feel or 'weigh' products. Shoppers need to compare products openly.

- *Considered.* (Examples are buying presents, birthday cards.) A need to assess a range of products on display.

- *Grab and Go.* Commodities (examples are bread, milk and newspapers) and replenishment purchases. Changes in layout or shortages are only ways to distract this mode.

- *Impulse.* (Examples are chocolate bars alongside queues at the checkout.) Men buy more on impulse than women.

Phillip Adcock gives the shopper rather complicated advice on preparing for shopping (the summary is more than four pages long) which includes: establishing the reason why the shopper is shopping; making a shopping list; examining what is thrown away; keeping receipts and routinely comparing them over time; making brand comparisons; not shopping if hungry, thirsty or tired; realising that emotion drives purchases; listing the outcomes and benefits of purchases; and always paying cash.

The Five Types of 'Shopping Mission', Off and Online

Offline customers do not shop in a homogenous way, they shop for different purposes, and different outlets tend to serve different needs. dunnhumby, who collect data internationally, identify six core missions that account for over 90 per cent of shopping value.

OFFLINE MISSIONS – BY VALUE (SOURCE: DUNNHUMBY 2005)

- Full shop – accounts for 20 per cent of total visits, and 63 per cent of total spend.
- Top up – 38 per cent and 13 per cent.
- Immediate – 29 per cent and 8 per cent.
- Non-food visit – 2 per cent and 3 per cent.
- Eat tonight non-convenience – 3 per cent and 1 per cent.
- Eat tonight convenience – 1 per cent and <1 per cent.

ONLINE MISSIONS – BY VALUE (SOURCE: KEY WAY 2009)

- The predominant mission is 'full shop' (as above), but with a significantly bigger basket spend than offline (typical food retailer £52 offline, £94 online).
- Special occasion when the shopping is being driven by a home event (for example, party, barbecue).
- Eat tonight, non-convenience (as above).
- There is also a full shop on behalf of an elderly relative or student son or daughter.

The needs of these shopping missions drive the type of messaging and signage a retailer needs.

Key Messages to the Shopper Online and In-Store

There is a limit to the number of messages the shopper can take in (George Miller established in 1956 that this is between five and nine); hence the importance of signage to them online and offline. Price and information about any one item while shopping is stored for no longer than about 18 seconds and rapidly erased (Source: Oxford Professor Greenfield in her book *The Private Life of the Brain*). Hence shoppers, when researchers ask questions, respond with 'don't know', or make a guess or resort to a rationalised response.

This cognitive load of five to nine messages varies between individuals, and after a time the messages are 'chunked' to make the memory load manageable. Similarly, brand information is chunked into an engram and placed in the subconscious – the long-term memory. Phillip Adcock notes that such long-term memory fades at the slow rate of 3 per cent per annum which explains why childhood 'emotional' memories last – such as smells. A visit to the Museum of Brands, Packaging and Advertising in London's Notting Hill is salutary: after following the displays chronologically year by year, it is fascinating, as suddenly you are shocked to discover the familiar as you are faced with a plethora of strongly recalled childhood brands.

For the marketer, there is nothing more important than the interface between the product and the shopper, whether this is in the online website or the offline shop.

Perhaps, surprisingly for the marketing person, the shopper is not as interested in an individual product as the marketing expert is. So an understanding of the mind, and approach of the shopper to the shop or website, is actually vital to understanding how change can be implemented – persuading a shopper to buy their brand rather than a competitors. As a result marketers often try to say too much in the wrong place and at the wrong time, to have an impact on the shopper journey.

What Does This All Mean?

The odds of getting a message across is low, which makes the prospect really daunting. Indeed, you can overlay more barriers to communication for the shopper by presenting too much information. And as for the words used; the French tested in a Carrefour supermarket the number of different words used on packaging – it was around 89,000. The average vocabulary of a French person is some 4,000 words. A real mismatch.

Tilting the Odds in Your Favour

The way a shopper reacts to a shopping situation is often 'scripted' in the mind. 'When at the garage I buy cigarettes.' 'In a CTN (Confectioners, Tobacconist and Newsagent – the corner shop), I know I have to state the bar of chocolate I want.' Once a person has cooked a meal several times, the ingredients for that particular recipe will be embedded in the mind and the ingredients will be sought often in the order of use in cooking. Habits or scripted behaviour governs near mindless shopper action. To break the script is not easy.

So first the engram needs to be implanted in the mind of the shopper. Next an innovative or unexpected message and media intervention is required both on the way to the shop and near the POS. An incentive such as a promotion offer (see Chapter 11) is required on-pack or at the POS. ESOV (defined in Chapter 1) is beneficial and quite achievable at a garage or in-store with more advertising than market share of the product deserves. The decision to buy will have been helped by favourable social media comment too. More of this in Chapters 8 to 12.

In a separate survey shoppers also report that trial (that is, testing the product or service) for them is the most effective way of getting them to switch brands (fast.MAP for *Promotional Marketing* magazine). This is confirmed again by the IGD in 2009. IGD found 37 per cent of shoppers said in-store promotions, such as 'reduced price' and BOGOFs (see Chapter 11) prompted them to buy a new product when they were food shopping, compared to 29 per cent who said advertising on TV or in magazines encouraged them to try something new.

The Messages Shoppers Need

Whether online or offline, shopper needs are the same. In 2005, Egg Research suggested that there are four distinct needs that signage/messages need to address:

- Tell me about new brands and products – open information and advice.
- What's on offer, so I don't miss out.

- Help me choose – ensure the customer gets to the right aisle and shelf or website and page and can find the product they want. Navigation on and offline needs to be clear, simple and correct!

- Inspire me to make purchases outside of my everyday essentials.

A brand manager, supplier or retailer should ask: Do your products deliver against these really simple requirements? Is there anything you could do to improve?

Getting the Message Across

Shoppers are not normal people. Or to be more precise, shoppers do not behave like normal people.

You are reading this book. You understand, we hope, both the words and the meaning behind them. You will, I am sure, weigh this up and consider the implications for you as you go on. You may consider that the reading process is constant and universal. This is not the case with the shopper; in the broad sense (that is to say, out and about with a general objective of buying) or the narrow sense, which is online, or in the physical store with the intention of making a purchase shortly. The shopper/buyer applies different processes at different times depending on the shopping purpose, their mood, their perception of the messages received and the environment.

Building a brand, through its engram, gives you standout and you change it at your peril. Behavioural economists have preached for a long time the fact that people learn to use very simple cues to react to unimportant decisions. This is Type 1 thinking (see above). *Thinking Fast and Slow* by Daniel Kahneman identifies the subconscious nature of some purchase decisions What this, of course, means is that a decision that you have not consciously made, cannot consciously be explained, and needs to be understood by looking at the impact on behaviour change.

For example, the decision to buy a fmcg product would typically be Type 1 thinking, although in radically new areas, with a potential high degree of interest for the shopper (perhaps a new gluten-free product for people with sensitivity) Type 2 thinking might be engaged. In this case, more information available at the facing would be absolutely vital. The shopper is open to many messages before they get to the store as the next few chapters explain.

Understanding the needs of a shopper for information in-store (see Chapter 10) has to be considered in the context of:

- the store environment
- the aisle
- the category
- the shelf
- the product.

The objective of any Shopper Marketing, as has been stated elsewhere, is to increase the actual or virtual availability of a product. Each of the above touch points have an impact on bringing the product closer to the top of mind when you finally achieve an active purchaser in front of the shelf or web page on which your product is placed.

While 70 per cent of decisions may well be taken at the facing, if the shopper has a written list from which they shop, on average they buy 46 products. If they do not have a physical list, research (POPAI) shows that they actually buy 48. Not much of a difference.

In practice shoppers all have a list. This could be real, one they hold in their hand, or a virtual one in their mind. That is to say, to make sense of a complex environment, they use cues that they recognise so that they can shop nearly as fast as those on a pre-planned mission.

Much Shopper Marketing needs to concern itself with activity that will bring a product further up the recognition structures on the way to the purchase. Brands do this by generating simple shapes –which may be the engram – that can be easily recognised from quite a long way away. Think of the Heinz shield, the Coca Cola bottle, the Apple symbol or the Red Bull logo, and colours (think easyjet) as good examples. In reality it is this instant communication that makes a brand valuable. The power of the engram!

Consistency of communication builds the image in people's minds, and a simple image that can be recognised and flagged on the way to a purchase is the way to build awareness and sales at the same time.

However, if your brand cannot be appreciated at a glance, you will waste your time displaying any message in a stressed 0.9 seconds environment.

I Don't Have a Brand Yet – How Can I Get Noticed?

There are certain cues that will gain attention more than others, and what they are may surprise you.

Here we draw not from what shoppers say, but on what they do. Two companies have issued reports in this area and they both agree on some key elements. The research looks at what shoppers have actually looked at and also at what they subsequently do.

It is important here to understand that if you asked people after the event if they recalled seeing the message, they may well be unlikely to be able to tell you. Phillip Adcock's company's research confirms this. What we are seeing here is the shopper programmed to notice something that is important to them. This may not be consciously read, just absorbed.

There are of course, two types of change you can get from this subliminal impression. One is that it stops people in their tracks as they walk down the aisle (at between 0.5 and 1.5 mph). The next is that they consider the pack by picking it up.

Lastly, of course is the objective, they convert interest to a purchase.

If you choose letters or colour combinations that need to be looked at, then they will not be absorbed.

There is something to be learned from the messages that impact most on the shopper, that is, get them engaged to read the message. POPAI listed the core messages they found in order of their appeal. Interestingly, over half of them are compound – they make two offers, not just one. 'New and Price Reduction' in the same category as 'Competition and General Information'. Alongside these are 'Extra Product Free' and 'Ex-Display'. At the base of the engagement list is 'Quantity Discount with Multibuy'.

However, when you turn to look at what happens when they do engage, 'Quantity Discount with Multibuy' comes very much higher up. 'Extra Product Free' comes second down the list for conversion to sale – and as a result should come very high up the list of messaging you really would want to reach the shopper. Headed in the list only by 'Price Reduction/New Lower Price', it is interesting the value that extra free has for changing a looker into a purchaser.

The Words That Make the Difference – 'Big', 'New', 'Free' (Cheap)

There has, for many years, been an old saw circulated around the industry that 'big', 'new' and 'free' are the messages you need to put across to get noticed on a pack. Surprise! Surprise! This turns out to be the case (or nearly).

Not a great deal has changed for many years, although the prevalence of discount offers has increased. No surprise, then, that a price reduction on its own is down the list of what stops people in their tracks (literally).

Non-Price Messaging

It will surprise many retailers that shoppers actually respond very well to other messages than discount. In fact 20 per cent of shoppers (Source: fast.MAP 2011) had very little that was discounted in their shopping basket. These 'aberrant' shoppers in the view of the standard EDLP or HiLo retailer were keener on non-price promotions. The shoppers tended to be more upmarket and have a greater disposable income. (Note: EDLP stands for Every Day Low Price, and offers the lowest possible price – here there would be no theoretical room for additional promotion discounts. HiLo is based on advertising great offers – perhaps even loss making – to bring in the shoppers, while the other products are at a higher price to recoup the lost margin.)

On-Pack Messaging

The ultimate tool that brands have is their pack. Research by iMotions shows that on-pack messaging can bring a pack alive.

Working with iMotions, the IPM examined the credentials of a range of award-winning promotions for their impact on the shopper. This whole area is to be further examined in a future white paper, which is to look at measures of forecasting demand from the messages received by the shopper – whether on the pack, in the store or online.

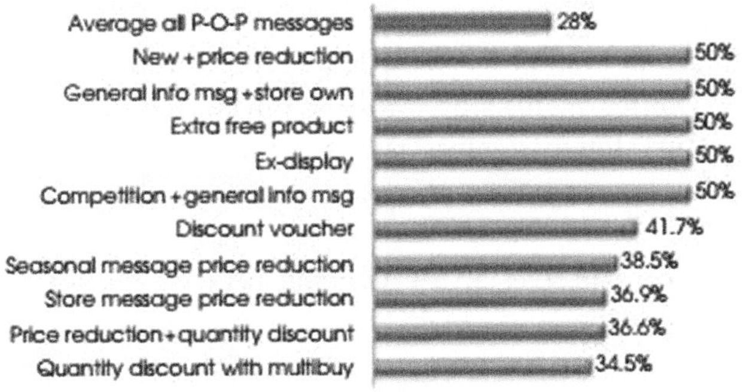

Figure 7.1 Engagement ratios for the top 10 POP messages for all shoppers

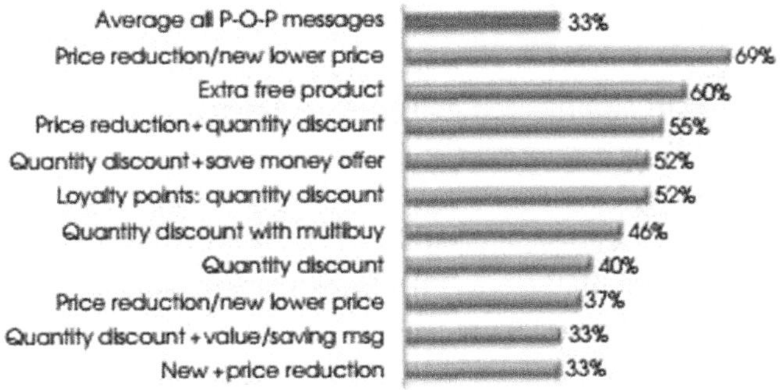

Figure 7.2 Conversion ratios for the top 10 POP messages for all shoppers

People respond to sights of interest by changing their blink rate, as well as their pupils expanding, both of which are externally measurable. iMotions has validated its approach on a scale of one to ten. In August 2010 the IPM put standard packs and promotions in front of consumers and measured the impact. The incentive varied from the very strong, such as 'free', to the weak, such as competitions.

The Kingsmill Bread promotion which demonstrates the eye-grabbing appeal of a 'free' on-pack offer was analysed by iMotions. The resulting engagement rose from 3.5 to 4.1.

The ultimate in 'eye candy' from the last award-winning promotions belonged to Marmite – not perhaps the brand you would first have nominated for the honour – after analysis by iMoions. But in the eyes of the shopper a reading of 5.8 from iMotions analysis puts it up there with eye-grabbing pictures for male shoppers you would more commonly expect in top-shelf magazines.

The authors were puzzled by the amazing attractiveness of Marmite. With the help of Shopper Behaviour Xplained (SBXL) they commissioned an engram. The result is shown in the final chapter of this book. The non-prompted view of the shopper about Marmite contains words such as 'Mum' and 'Love'. This engram fully explains why Marmite has achieved this result. A real lesson for brand managers and what you can achieve!

The Online Shopper

Sitecore's six steps to empowered ecommerce describes what a retailer needs to do:

1. *Engage in a consistent dialogue across channels.* Even as you optimise for different platforms and devices, make sure that your voice and look remain consistent.

2. *Guide the shopper with contextual offers at exactly the right time.* A well-timed, personalised offer can translate into an instant cross-sell or upsell.

3. *Prompt their route with suggested next steps.* A gentle nudge here or there can help reduce cart abandonment – and increase Average Order Value.

4. *Identify and overcome customer interaction challenges.* This applies particularly to user-generated content. If a loyal customer writes a negative review of your product, how will you engage, if at all? Know your engagement strategy and stick to it.

5. *Understand customer experience at an individual and segment level.* Who is the individual customer, and how has he or she engaged with you in the past? What does he or she have in common with other customers? The more quickly and accurately you can answer those questions, the better you'll be at effective personalisation.

6. *Regularly test and refine offers and promotions.* With more targeted offers, you can attract and engage more shoppers across more channels.

Summary

The shopping mission is in large part pre-defined and is an activity in which the subconscious (engrams) plays a large part, along with the list, whether actual or virtual, the shopper holds. To make the shopper stop and take notice is difficult and requires impact.

Key words are: 'big', 'new',' free' (cheap), but also indicators such as 'Find Me Here', or something *inspirational* – these core messages need to be passed across at the POS to get people buying into a product.

Remember KISS – KEEP IT SIMPLE ... as you have little time to get the message across and it needs to be related to the shopping mission and the venue.

Chapter 8
Out of Store

So What Happens in the Very Beginning?

The shopper discovers a need, or comes across a mention of something that might be useful to them. Is that the true start of the journey? No, a shopper journey is nothing special. When a shopper sets out to shop for anything the attitude to the process is firmly based on a shopper's reality. What they have learned since the last shop. How the consumers report their experience, what they have seen and who they have talked to. Subconsciously the mind is making a note and storing information all the time for future needs. When a need arises the mind puts forward potential solutions – garnered from the subconscious – and an engram will then be a part of what is offered to the shopper from their own subconscious, if the mind thinks it is relevant. The 'mention of something that might be useful' – usually of which the shopper is unaware – may alternatively indeed be a true start and a real trigger for search. The search will of course be directed by the source of the mention, but the mind will refer to any seemingly similarly categorised engrams that the mind holds, presenting those to the shopper.

In-store magazine reports (June 2013) that online trading of high-end brands are opening luxury fashion products to a wider community of shoppers who, for example, care less about having the latest Mulberry bag than they do about the social status of just owning one Mulberry bag. The same applies to top-end shoes such as Manolo Blahnik or Jimmy Choos. The importance of creating a retail environment for luxury brands is also noted. And this is why the engram is so important – for all brands, suppliers and retailers. You are storing engrams in the mind for a later day use, even by persons outside your normally expected shopper profiles.

So the true start then is the embedding in the subconscious of your brand's engrams – and this will equally apply to items outside the normal economic range of the shopper – a Ferrari say, or a Rolex or a Gucci item, or if the products and services relate to matters of no concern to the shopper – such as medical and health issues which are at the time irrelevant to the shopper. Similarly, if the shopper has no garden, any garden products or services are irrelevant (until they decide that a need for a relative or friend deserves a garden-related purchase and the subconscious mind suggests a few engrams it has stored). Engrams are embedded in the subconscious whether they are relevant now or not. If the shopper is totally unaware – say of an innovative service or product – then there is a need to educate and make aware and in doing so it will also implant the engram. Particularly for any new customer, for the latter awareness and educational input will be required or a shopper will not store the engram unless it can be categorised.

This chapter describes planting the engram (how it came about is described in Chapter 1) in the subconscious, which is the task of brand managers. So messages here must describe products fully and their use, benefits and features as well as offering a mind storable logo/symbol or something that is different from other engrams.

Getting a buzz about the brand is also part of this stage – to start brand excitement and obtain feedback – clarifying shopper queries and correcting misunderstandings early. However to avoid mind overload for the reader, these matters are covered in the next chapter.

Your Engram

A creative eye-catching memorable different design is required – either in the packaging or the logo or the container, or the message (think 'durchsprung') – this becomes the engram. 'Eye catching' relates to shape, colour or pattern that the eye can register. It must be memorable. It must be different. It can be associated with senses other than visual; audio (a jingle/piece of music, a sound), olfactory (a distinctive smell – perfumes, roasting coffee, hot bread), it might have a certain feel to the touch (tongue as well as fingers) or have to be held in a certain way. Ideally it should intrinsically relate to the product or service.

The messages to support it must meet the Chapter 7 requirement for information; they should also inspire the shopper.

Reinforcing Engrams

These messages should continue to display the engram but also persuade that a purchase is truly beneficial in every way – socially acceptable, status enhancing, valuable, intellectually supportable and universally recognised.

Creating the Buzz

The product (with engram clearly visible) should be shown in stimulating situations that are memorable and cause comment or discussion.

Where Engrams Can be Placed – Which Media – in What Order

Chapter 5 covers what is available. But as an engram is probably visual, a place to consider first is the visual media. 'As seen on screen' is a good place to start. In programmes or in advertising in the breaks, a story can be put across about the benefits of the product or service coupled with the engram – see the message section below. Experiential marketing should be of primary consideration for non-audio or visual engrams: olefactory and taste would certainly qualify – with sites placed where high footfall is expected of the target markets. (Hence drinks targeted at youth offered as samples in clubs and bars.) When new foods are offered in supermarkets the point of sampling should have the engram everywhere – on the salesperson, visually displayed, in order that while the shopper is eating the sample the engram can be registered. In fact, an extra engram packaged sample to take away might actually assist the shopper to implant the engram when they return home and show it and share it with relatives and friends. Think of how often you have digested a sample and later cannot recall what the brand or engram was. Engram branded items handed out should be given away in quantities of more than one per head. One to try – and one to keep for later perusal when the engram will embed.

In the US, the number one TV show in 1970 was 'All in the Family', watched regularly by 60 per cent of households. In 2007 it was American Idol watched by 17 per cent of households (Source: OMD).

Highlights from a recent US Nielsen study concluded:

- In 2006, the average US home received 104.2 channels, an increase of almost eight channels since the previous year and a record level.
- As the number of channels available to a household increases, so does the number of channels tuned into. In 2006, the average household tuned to 15.7, or 15.1 per cent of the 104.2 channels available for at least ten minutes per week.

- The 30-second commercial is still the television advertising standard in prime time, accounting for 57 per cent of all commercial units.

In the UK, BRAD's database has over 13,500 media platforms (from newspapers to hot-air balloons as they describe it) where advertising can be bought; and BARB currently measures 227 TV channels.

It has been estimated that it was possible to reach 85 per cent of the UK population with three TV spots in the late 1980s. Now it takes 180 spots (Source: *Campaign* 2005).

This fragmentation of media and audiences has led to an undermining of the traditional, mass media-based advertising model but this should not be over exaggerated. TV is still dominant. TV can still work effectively at building brands as can print and radio. And in times of economic uncertainty, marketers will even more err towards the familiar, as we have seen in 2008 and since.

Whatever media choices arc made, consumers are estimated to be exposed daily to over 3,000 advertising messages (Source: *The Guardian*). It is possibly more, indeed numbers of up to 6,000 can be found quoted – though rarely with any attribution. None the less, experience, if we only stop to think about it, would lead us to believe that whatever the actual number, there are a lot.

POPAI described 50 or more different types of in-store communication. Their research indicated that shoppers pass 1.6 items every second. In a 30-minute shop that would mean they pass 2,592 pieces of communication. And then think that each brand's packaging itself is a piece of communication too.

However, despite this seemingly over-powering dominance and confusion of commercial messages, marketing does work. (It is just that, in its old form, it's not as effective as it should be.) This might well be due to our ability to absorb information with only a fleeting need to experience it. Dr Robert Heath of Bath University has used neuroscience to demonstrate the brain's capacity to absorb certain types of brand information even when we pay virtually no attention to it. His research has shown that we routinely scan press ads in under one second yet we can still recall the salient message. In his opinion and experience, advertising is most often about fleeting glances and that we can build high levels of awareness and interest without ever being consciously aware that we have seen an ad. He has dubbed this Low Attention Processing (Source: http://www.lowattentionprocessing.com/).

This leads to the belief that much of what we do is subconscious and intuitive – including deciding what we purchase – hence the importance of the subconscious mind and the engram to brand, supplier and retailer managers.

The Rosser Reeves Fallacy is discussed in Chapter 6. This is the claim that shoppers once aware of a brand, supplier or retailers advertisements are favourably influenced by all their communications spread across the media and across all products. This was of course before the role of the engram was understood. The engram, the authors believe, now takes precedence. How many consumers are aware of which brands are Unilever or Procter and Gamble? Actually it does not matter to the shopper.

After the Discovery of the Need By the Shopper!

The shopper, as described in Chapter 3, will have alternative mindsets. When on holiday, for example, they may override normal reluctances and prejudices as to what they might buy. They may have been given a pay rise, found a new partner, been sacked or are facing divorce. It is up to the marketer to consider all the potential scenarios that might affect a shopper as they start their journey to purchase. A need is a strong motivation and should be encouraged. So encourage the shopper!

Observing How the Shopper Reacts to the Engram

It is, of course, possible to observe the shopper in the moments after establishing the need using an eye tracker. A case study and results of an eye tracker in the home are given in Chapter 18.

What Happens Immediately after the Mind Starts Work on the Need?

Initial research by the shopper can be active or passive: picking up a tablet, smartphone, PC or laptop and using words to start a search – proceeding to follow up one or more search pages; purchasing relevant niche magazines or looking at the same online; websites may have advertisements alongside; there are telephone numbers giving access to call centres; using online forums or social media or e-mails can bring in advice from colleagues, relatives and friends to participate in discussions of how best to meet the need. 'Passive research' can be found in the home or office, acting as triggers to search – brands, labels, on-pack information, specialist books, magazines, newspapers; promotional items that the shopper has acquired now sitting on desks or walls– such as pens, pen holders, desk furniture, calendars and business cards.

How Can a Brand, Supplier or Retailer Take Action Here?

Random timely communication is required – both general and with the individual on mobile, to home or office:

- For both the individual and general use try D2D, direct mail, e-mail, call centres.
- The messages need to promote awareness/be educational, stimulate trial (sales promotion? Or offer a demonstration or sample with a bounce back – voucher or coupon) and include a call to action.
- And, of course, include the engram trigger.

But More Than Just the Engram is Needed

So let us have a look in the chapters that follow at approaches that have actually worked in delivering change on the way to the stores, showing the necessity for message influence at various levels, on the way to a purchase.

Summary

The shopper journey does not have a definite start. The next shopper journey is based on the experience from the last. In the same way a shopper does not take a defined path to a purchase.

However, there is media that you can place on the route. This includes, of course, the home, with positive feedback from the family, mobile media, POP from the store entrance onwards, and, of course, the pack itself. This latter has a dual life on the shelf in the supermarket, or on the screen on the web, and again when the product is consumed.

Chapter 9
On the Way to the Store

The shopper has now identified a need and started the journey to purchase. The engram has made inputs to the shopper that the mind considers relevant. There are three further identified opportunities for messages to be put to the shopper before they enter the shop or go online.

This chapter describes how brands, suppliers and retailers can obtain Excess Share of Voice (ESOV), support the advice coming from others – peer groups, relatives and friends, while establishing and building a relationship with the shopper.

WPP ShopperMarketing research finds that 75 per cent of shoppers research the store and the product before they enter – for women it is 86 per cent, for men it is 47 per cent.

As an aside – there is a need for brands, suppliers and retailers to facilitate communication by being accessible on a mobile platform and offering apps. Shoppers need to see your messages – especially on mobile. To mark 40 years since the introduction of the first mobile, Auros surveyed (between 8 and 10 April 2013) and found that – in a world where by the end of 2013 mobile devices will exceed the number of people on earth, where 20–25 per cent of UK and US shoppers only access the web through their mobile – while 83 per cent of retailers had a responsive website, 38 per cent of retailers are not directing mobile traffic to their mobile site and, of those who had apps (80 per cent), 46 per cent were only for Apple platforms and 40 per cent of app providers did not prompt a download of their app. Only 30 per cent of retailers use geo-location to find the nearest store for the shopper nor was it possible to resize text on any of the retail sites. Auros concludes that 'being serious about mobile is about more than just hosting a token website for iPhone users: it's about taking advantage of a rapidly growing market, leveraging the things that make mobile great, understanding the platform, building trust with users and delivering a superb user experience'. The Appendix gives the link to the Auros report, which lists the retailers (and public sector) sites examined. In the context of this book, there will be no overlap of communication canvas if the shopper and retailer are not on the same media or channel. A Juniper research report, also in June 2013, noted that a number of hurdles still needed to be overcome if mcommerce were to achieve its potential in the coming years. According to report author Dr Windsor Holden, 'A significant minority of retailers have yet to optimise their sites for mobile. Unless retailers ensure a seamless, user-friendly mobile shopping experience, they will fall behind competitors who are already using mobile channels to enhance customer relationships.' The report observed that the introduction of mobile wallet services was providing first time financial access in many emerging markets where the proportion of unbanked adults exceeded 50 per cent. In the same markets, partnerships between OTT (broadband and internet delivery of video and audio) storefronts and network operators – enabling payment via carrier billing – were enabling greater access to the digital economy. The message is crystal clear – everyone needs to be on mobile.

Excess Share of Voice (ESOV)

ESOV is when advertising messages to the shopper exceed the market share of the category in which the brand exists.

For most offline outlets, achieving ESOV nationally is prohibitively expensive, so the solution – which can be applied by all – is to target a store and its shopper customers. A website can operate in just the same way as a single store. Brands, retailers and suppliers would need to work together to do the same online as in a local-to-shop area – pointing shoppers to a web page or pages.

The same collaboration is also needed to establish a promotion (see Chapter 11) that creates interest, stimulates existing and new shopper customers to enhance the ESOV success – a reason perhaps for the additional media impact on shoppers to be understood by the shoppers (that is, the promotion could be the reason for the ESOV advertising campaign).

Finally, the store or website has to deliver at the POS – this is the subject of the Chapter 10, and here the store or web must be stocked to match the shopper demand, especially for a promotion. The store has an advantage over the website in that shopper gratification is instant, whereas there is a delivery delay for the website purchase. Bricks and mortar outlets should capitalise on this benefit more than they do.

Research first needs to select the appropriate store or website, then establish that the profile of the local or niche shoppers matches the target for the promotion and finally apply the advertising to achieve the ESOV. The promoted product needs to match the shoppers and be something they would normally purchase. The means – the media and channels to communicate with the target shoppers – must also be researched and match the shoppers' communication canvas (Chapter 2) and perhaps even tested first on a small proportion of the shopper targets. Brands, suppliers and retailers should insist that the research results prove the basis for the ESOV promotion when deciding to go ahead with the campaign. If they are satisfied they may well want to join in the Share of Voice advertising. The research should indicate the media and channels to use. The messages to put across should be in a format and language the shoppers prefer.

Online, a shopper will be influenced by the regularity of contact and offers made in e-mails by one supplier over a number of similar providers. Online shirt sales provide an example – it is easy for one supplier to achieve ESOV. A niche model railway supplier such as On Tracks achieves more e-mails that are interesting and stimulating with promotions than their competitors, even though punching way above its actual market share.

On communication, the research should describe what is available locally – from cinema, local papers, free newspaper, local radio, local TV if available, outdoor sites, transport possibilities, door-to-door delivery. Insight should describe the preferred media and channels of the targeted shoppers. Local to store reinforcement is possible – through banners, placards and handouts. Escalators at stations offer both static and dynamic advertisements. Signage may be allowed through obtaining local council planning consent. For example, brown 'Superstore' signs may be placed by councils at nearby junctions. Local transport and all moving media can be used. Bus stops now have dynamic outdoor signs – even with NFC (Near Field Communication) and QR codes (see Chapter 5) alongside. Platforms at stations on the London Underground show advertising videos. This research alongside matching shopper preferences will enable a decision on how to achieve ESOV.

Thinking outside the box, another local possibility is to use the window display, available 24/7 – communicating through the glass – shoppers receive information through WiFi, QR code or a Proximity Infra Red (PIR) detector activating playing of an audio tape when a shopper is looking at a displayed product and inviting a response. (Note that some Pilkington glass may defeat infra red!)

The message content should use the engram. The message should create excitement: it is usually easiest to offer some sales promotion or event (charity road run!) or road show, to create interest and excitement at a local promotion.

Encouraging Social Media

In addition to the engram and the ESOV, the brand, the supplier or retailer should facilitate the shopper's access to social media as well as garnering the feedback.

The shopper values the advice from peer groups, friends, colleagues and family social media contact. A link to seeing the product in use on YouTube, supplied by another shopper, is a simple solution through links on a website. Linking the promotion to a local event may provide the answer, for example, recognising the success of the Kelloggs partnership marketing, with the Olympics described in Chapter 5. A retailer can ascertain from local sources whether there are any local events occurring. A local marathon might have winners' names or pictures displayed in-store – even on-pack the following day alongside the promotion. A charity may be happy to have a promotion alongside a fundraising charity event. Schools and hospitals are other linking causes to approach.

Social media – there will be local social media groups – should be revealed by research. It may be necessary to establish a local mobile or e-mail network for the store – helpful in any case. Niche outlets will certainly need to capture data on potential and interested enthusiasts.

Relationship Building

Once the engram, ESOV and the links to social media are established, the brand, supplier or retailer should work on building a relationship with each shopper.

For any store, both bricks and mortar and online, the location and e-mail of shoppers expressing interest in a purchase should be followed up. After shopping in your outlet, the shopper should be captured for future store or web outlet use and contacted as often as they wish. This is important when planning relationship campaigns. The shopper can be asked for their preferred frequency and also the subjects on which they wish to be contacted. Online abandoned baskets should be queried. In-store the offer of joining loyalty schemes or taking up a store card or somehow noting purchase details alongside the shopper data should be captured. Shopper e-mail addresses and mobile numbers (permission-based) data should be preserved for future online campaigns.

To record the success of any relationship marketing, the shopper should be provided with a code that they can present in-store or online so the retailer is able to record the purchase against that marketing activity.

An example of relationship building is dressipi.com (see case study) who provide women shoppers who sign up with fashion outlet information (dress styles, colours, prices, sizes) matching the preferences of the shoppers from the data they provide.

DRESSIPI CASE STUDY

The Challenge: How do you personalise recommendations for emotional purchases like fashion?

The Solution: Dressipi

Dressipi is revolutionising the way women shop and dress, offering an effortless experience where everyone has free access to the digital equivalent of the personal stylist they have always dreamed of.

By combining proprietary technology with the know-how of a team of expert stylists, Dressipi allows women to discover and put together the clothes, accessories and brands that fit their shape, style and personal preferences perfectly – so they can look their best every day, whatever the occasion. It works when customers are purchasing new products and/or wanting to better utilise their existing wardrobe.

The service is easy to use. Customers simply create their personal Fashion Fingerprint © (no measurements or scans necessary), which identifies their body shape, style, size, colour and brand preferences and which areas of the body they would prefer to reveal and conceal. Our recommender then searches the universe of clothes to identify the perfect products and combinations of products (outfits) that best match the individual's Fashion Fingerprint and the occasion for which they are dressing.

Then, at POP, for those wanting to find the right fit for their style and shape, the Dressipi Size Finder determines their best size for each individual brand and style of clothing – ensuring they never have to purchase the wrong size again.

From Banana Republic to Balenciaga, the Dressipi Size Finder app is also available to download as a Smartphone app, so customers can always find the right size, wherever they may be shopping.

Whether customers want to build their perfect capsule wardrobe, change their style, discover new brands or learn their dressing must haves and must avoids – Dressipi allows all women to achieve their shopping and dressing goals with helpful tools and personal advice from stylists.

How we do it

We believe that to succeed in the fashion industry and be genuinely disruptive, a service needs to understand and deliver on the nuances of a consumers relationship with clothes – this means true personalisation and a service that can change and evolve with a customer's life and situations. This requires more than a crowd-sourcing, taste making or general search solution. One person, for example, may love what their best friend or a celebrity is wearing but they understand that they are unable to wear similar clothes because they are too tall, short, thin, large and so on. Additionally fashion is not static – and a customer's preference for a particular pattern or material one month, may not be reflective of their preference the following.

For that reason, we have worked with some of the industry's most renown stylists and world leading technologists to deliver a solution that is genuinely unique to each customer and delivers real value to all women when they are shopping or getting dressed – building their confidence and ensuring that they look and feel fabulous at all times.

With no consistent data in the industry, we have created our own taxonomy of necessary features (and labeling system to ensure scale). Dressipi now assigns between 30 and 50 consistent features/meta data to each garment of clothing (with varying levels of automation). For each customer we have approximately 70 data points and for each brand we have about 30.

With ten simple and fun questions we capture 90 per cent of a woman's fashion preferences, including context and emotion, which matter most to women when it comes to buying clothes or getting dressed.

Using a number of algorithms, Dressipi then narrows down the hundreds of thousands of products available to a smaller unique set that is more or less a perfect match to what the shopper is looking for.

The final 10 per cent of preferences – which statistically are the most valuable – are then captured through a variety of features that include natural language search, liking and disliking garments, advice on how to build their capsule wardrobe and adding clothes that they currently own to get access to our outfit builder. Everything personalised to them.

And finally we capture the emotion of the buying process, knowing that people generally shop with a purpose in mind (wanting to look confident for a new job, look appropriate for a wedding, glamorous for a date and so on) and through the 'Style Ambassadors' we understand who their real influencers are.

Does it work?

It is clear that the Dressipi solution (combined with its data insights) is greatly improving the core metrics of the industry – delivering both efficiencies and real margin improvement (Table 9.1).

The Dressipi advantage

	Dressipi Average	Industry Average
Conversion rate	5%	1%–3%
Average garment return rate	10%–15%	30%
Average e-mail open rate	45%	18%
Average basket value	£91	£35.09
Sell-through	N/A	60%

Another example is model railway/railroad shoppers who have few bricks and mortar outlets and inevitably search online. Each shopper for this category has a special interest in a limited range of products which need to be discovered, and messages tailored to those interests are needed when campaign promotions are considered. An example of a supplier to such a niche mentioned previously is www.OnTracks.co.uk who routinely e-mail special offers both for new enthusiasts and existing hobbyists. One OnTracks mailer invited modellers from across the country to the National Exhibition Centre (NEC) for a scenery training day – scenery techniques are universally applied across the hobby. These established relationships can (and have) continue for many years. The long-term benefit to OnTracks is repeat customers who return time and time again.

In Finland, 22 stores operate under the Hong Kong Department Stores banner. The stores decided to open up with online retail as well and chose a niche section (fishing) for its first online store (next niche is DIY). Fishing is popular in Finland and the online store is set up on an IBM WebSphere commerce solution (provided by IBM's local business partner Descom) with access to social media reviews. IBM Coremetrics provided analytics. The result has been that the website has outsold the stores, but the stores' sales have increased too – and the customer relationships have benefitted along with the ongoing opportunity to market to this niche's shoppers. Win–win all round.

HONG KONG DEPARTMENT STORES BUILDS AN ONLINE E-COMMERCE COMMUNITY

Harnessing social networks to provide a richer consumer experience

Founded in 1989, Oy Hong Kong Import Ltd owns and operates 22 Hong Kong Department Stores across southern Finland. Its stores sell a vast range of local, international and own-brand merchandise – gardening, tools, outdoor equipment, homeware, electronics and appliances, accessories and toys. It employs more than 600 people.

A targeted online strategy

To complement its physical department stores, Hong Kong wanted to introduce a new online sales channel. However, instead of creating a single online store that would mimic the physical stores, the company decided to take a more targeted approach.

'One of the most important elements of online sales is creating a reputation for being a specialist supplier,' explains Miika Malinen, eCommerce Director. 'If people want a certain type of product, they tend to visit sites that specialise in that type of product because they expect a specialist to offer a wider range of better-quality products. We decided that the best strategy was to create a number of specialist sites for the main product categories we sell, and focus on building up communities of users who would help us to develop them.'

Sourcing help from enthusiasts

Finland has a number of very enthusiastic online fishing communities, and Hong Kong decided that its fishing equipment business would be an ideal candidate for the first of its new online stores.

'Fishermen are fantastic customers because they are very knowledgeable about the equipment they buy and use, and they are prepared to share their expertise with others,' says Miika Malinen. 'We decided to go to two of the largest online fishing communities in Finland and enlist 100 people from each. These 200 fishermen would be given user accounts for our new store a couple of months before it was launched. We would ask them to explore the store and the product catalogue, and use the social networking features of the site to help us improve it.'

Creating a technology platform

To make this strategy viable, Hong Kong needed a technology platform that could provide sophisticated social networking features as well as the more standard e-commerce functionality. Miika Malinen's team selected IBM WebSphere Commerce as the core of the solution, and chose software from Heiler and Bazaarvoice to provide rich product information and manage customer reviews and ratings. In addition, the solution would use IBM Coremetrics to provide analytics, Adobe Scene7 for imaging, and eCircle for e-mail marketing.

'We were one of the first companies in Finland to bring all these products together into a single solution,' says Miika Malinen. 'We wanted to ensure that the technology would live up to the vision that we and our customers had for the new store, so we needed a really expert partner to help us develop and implement the site.'

'We chose Descom because our team had previous experience of working with them, and we were impressed with their expertise in e-commerce solutions. They did an excellent job of translating our concept into a technical solution, including all the integration with our back-end systems, and they will continue to provide application management and development services as we go forward.'

A successful launch

With the technology in place, Hong Kong went ahead with its recruitment of its fishing community, and introduced them to the new kalastus.hongkong.fi fishing site a couple of months before it launched.

'The response was incredible – they wrote over 3,000 product reviews in one month and gave us lots of valuable feedback on how they wanted the site to look and behave,' says Miika Malinen. 'They even corrected spelling mistakes in the product descriptions! As a result, when we launched the site we were able to provide a rich user experience from day one.'

Enhanced sales analytics

Following the launch, IBM Coremetrics Web Analytics has helped the company to gain a deeper understanding of customer activity on the site. This solution is provided on a software-as-a-service (SaaS) basis, and provides new Insight into shopping behaviours.

'For example, we have discovered that the conversion rate for customers who read reviews is 250 percent higher than that of customer who don't,' comments Miika Malinen. 'This really shows the value of the 3,000 reviews that our fishermen wrote for us before we launched – it seems that a favourable review is one of the key factors in turning a browser into a buyer.' Going forward, Hong Kong will expand its use of IBM Coremetrics to enhance its cross-selling and up-selling capabilities.

'We are very keen to introduce the Intelligent Offer feature, which uses the "wisdom of the crowd" combined with personal order history to suggest other products that a shopper might be interested in,' says Miika Malinen. 'We just need to wait a few months until we have enough sales data to create an accurate statistical model, and then the solution will start to create links between products automatically. This will save us considerable time, and also give us greater insight into the kinds of products that sell best together.' The company is also considering using IBM Coremetrics to analyse the customer-generated reviews and ratings in the Bazaarvoice system and gain more Insight into what customers are saying about Hong Kong and its products.

Smarter Commerce boosts sales across all channels

In the six months since the online store launched, it has continued to outsell the fishing departments in Hong Kong's physical stores – but that is not the whole story. Sales in the physical stores have not declined; in fact, they have increased.

'The whole concept of having highly focused online stores was that it would help us build a reputation as a specialist in specific product categories,' says Miika Malinen. 'The results show that this has been a complete success: raising awareness of our expertise in fishing equipment online has actually brought more people into the fishing departments of our stores. So instead of cannibalising trade from our existing outlets, we have actually helped their sales to grow.' A targeted e-commerce website is not only a sales channel; it is also a marketing tool. By establishing itself as a haven for some of the most active online fishing communities in Finland, the site serves as an advertisement for Hong Kong's expertise in this market sector. By integrating sales and marketing in this way, Hong Kong has adopted a strategy that aligns perfectly with IBM's Smarter Commerce philosophy.

Looking to the future

Buoyed by the success of this first project, Hong Kong is now in the process of developing a second online store – this time focusing on DIY products. Again, the company is seeking help from existing online communities to create a richer user experience.

'The great thing about the solution we've built is that it gives us a template that we can customise and redeploy many times over. Instead of building the DIY store from scratch, we can re-use many of the components we built for the fishing store. Moreover, although the look-and-feel of the sites will be quite different, the back-end systems are exactly the same – so we can manage customer orders and deliveries consistently, whatever site they come from.'

About Descom

Descom is a Finnish IBM Business Partner that specialises in e-commerce, electronic work environments, social networking, process management and integration solutions, built on software from the IBM WebSphere, Lotus and Smarter Commerce portfolios. Descom also works closely with other IBM Business Partners such as Heiler to harness best-of-breed technologies that add further value to the solutions it creates for its clients.

Other Considerations

Using GPS through mobile – when in outlet range – and making offers to shoppers.

The importance of research to provide the Insights required for all three opportunities to message shoppers on the way to the store must be emphasised. The subject of research and obtaining Insights is covered in Chapters 17, 18 and 19. For brand managers, although there is the need to justify their budget spend, obtaining Insights from data is key to planning the marketing campaigns.

Summary

In addition to the engram, ESOV, encouraging the use of social media and developing a relationship are communications the shopper expects to receive from a brand, retailer or supplier.

Chapter 10
In the Store, On the Website

This chapter considers the messages the shopper should be sent in-store or on the website (include mobile site – see Chapter 9). Chapter 11 covers promotions, including price promotions (discounts), in order to not overwhelm the reader about what can be done in-store. And who is doing it? The In-Store survey 'Shopping Forecast' (June 2013) finds that POP activity and what used to be called 'above the line' (a term used to describe straightforward advertising in the second half of the 1900s) are being combined; that the POP budget is set by marketing directors (40 per cent) sales directors (35 per cent) and others (30 per cent); that messages are going to be more about passion for categories at the expense of promotional messages.

A bricks and mortar outlet has many ways to transmit messages to the shopper; on the walls, floor, ceilings (suspended from the ceilings), entrances, on doors, on security gates, on stairs – even on the steps, on escalators and lifts in the toilets/restrooms. Messages can be static or dynamic; they can use anything from a live human voice (town crier or salesperson), through video, holograms, interactive screens (just as online) or they can be simply visual – a rotating sign, a moving model or a flashing message. Innovation and creativity play their part as the shopper moves round the store. The purpose is threefold: to attract the shoppers' attention to the message, then hope that it is assimilated (taken in) by the shopper and finally acted on.

Further messages will then be delivered and in the immediate vicinity of products – shelves, gondolas and shippers. POP material has the potential to impact on both virtual availability (marking the product out on the shelf) and actual availability. The product itself is a further message carrier. Indeed the product may be the engram. The product with its packaging needs to be properly merchandised (set display, front facing) and stock replenished as it moves off the shelf. When the product is on promotion and/or the packaging contains a promotion, then adding additional shelf space in the form of display units or shippers may be needed and stock replenishment becomes most important (this point is repeated in the next chapter).

The marketer, having read through the first nine chapters, will have realised that the subconscious of the shopper will be working overtime as they move through the store, drawing on their engram bank for things that are familiar, placing them alongside the messages from ESOV advertising as well as recalling the relationship messages, probably in their order of impact and recency, alongside the remarks and reviews garnered from social media.

The shopper, of course, can ignore the lot as described in Chapter 7.

Online, the brand, supplier or retailer has the opportunity to require the shopper to view certain messages before proceeding. This is fine to an extent. There is the risk, however, that the shopper may at some point feel exasperation or disagree with the route that they are being driven through the website and abandon the journey. Research indicates that three pages is about the limit – certainly for dealing with the checkout process. Eye-tracking software will record for different nationalities and cultures the way the brain moves the eye around a screen and the mind takes in the messages. As for what the shopper takes in, the engram and other inputs will affect their interest as before. The mood of the shopper may well not cause the viewer to linger on any site if the messages and impact are too dull or the site requires them to surmount too many hurdles such as the demand for information.

Is Signage Important to Marketers and Retailers?

Research by IPM, in conjunction with fast.MAP in 2010, certainly shows that both marketers and retailers are intending to spend more in this area. So signage is understood by some to be important.

The research with 200 key executives revealed that in the five years from 2011 to 2016 they expected to shift money into the Path to Purchase. This poll was taken in a period of real problems in both the UK and German economy. The forecast UK trend would be for an 8.7 per cent growth in 2016, while Germany expected a greater increase, by 9.3 per cent.

Those surveyed expected that this investment would be drawn from other areas within marketing.

Can We Treat Online and Offline the Same in Terms of Location and Type of Signage?

In a report in 2009, Keyway indicated the fundamental differences between online and offline shopping.

For food and household goods they reported that e-shopping is a fundamentally different experience from offline shopping. This affects shopper behaviours and purchase patterns. There is a different relationship between the shopper and the retailer in-store and online:

- online grocery shopping is more functional than offline shopping;
- loyalty varies significantly; one large grocery retailer only has 15 per cent of shoppers returning (in 2009), another has 65 per cent+;
- purchasing visitors spend on average between 20–30 minutes on a site and will visit between 25–50+ pages dependent on the number of unique items they buy;
- e-retail grocery shoppers tend to do more of their full shop online but continue to use offline shopping for other shopper missions. The online 'full shop' differs from the offline 'full shop';
- as there is little impulse purchase – this throws up challenges when wanting to increase basket-size both in terms of value and the number of unique products. For a manufacturer, this also throws obstacles in the way of new product launches;
- purchase decisions are significantly more likely to be predetermined, in part because 'favourites' are a key mechanism to help the online journey. There is less willingness to try new brands online or to switch, cross-trade or be up-sold;grocery e-retail favours market-leaders; it favours habitual purchases;
- e-retail shoppers are more loyal to a single retailer than they are in the bricks and mortar outlets;
- in the UK offline shoppers on average shop at 2.7 grocery retailers; e-shopping it is 1.3;

- loyalty is different: online loyalty is currently driven by absence of negatives and lack of retailer choice than offline where loyalty is a more considered choice.

The Role of In-Store Signage

Many sources quote some POPAI US research to the effect that 70 per cent of shopper decisions are taken in-store. They also report that this figure is hard to track back to the original report.

Looking at grocery transaction data from the UK, analysing customers by their deal seeking behaviour, a clear conclusion is that there are significant differences by category and brand/product, so a 'catch-all' '70 per cent' statistic is of limited value – in fact, for certain brands around 70 per cent of the decisions appear to be made before entering the store (this confirms the engram importance). For what it is worth, an average number indicates that 47 per cent of customers are brand loyalists; another 17 per cent are brand loyal but wait until the brand is on promotion and stock up; only 12 per cent are driven wholly by promotions only buying what is on a deal, and another 18 per cent are brand-switchers, driven by variety. However, across categories there is huge variation. So, for example, across five categories, loyalists can vary from 58 per cent down to 16 per cent. Within a category, the brands may have a loyalty that ranges from 10 per cent to 70 per cent. Moreover, further research by fast.MAP (2010, Marketing Gap) showed that 20 per cent of people reported they had very little discounted product in their basket, but they did have a more than average percentage of product with an on-pack offer or promotion of some kind.

Messaging on the route to purchase clearly has a substantial role to play, but this can be different by category and by product. Research has consistently shown that whether online or offline there are four key shopper needs that need to be fulfilled to ensure that a return visit is made.

Help Me Chose, Tell Me about What's New, What's on Offer, Inspire Me, Let Me Buy

'What Shoppers Want from Shopping' (a report written by Colin Harper for Egg Research 2005/Storecheck 2010). Whether it is online or offline, shopper needs are the same and have to be addressed:

- Help Me Chose by ensuring that the customer gets to the right aisle and shelf and can find the products s/he wants. Shoppers are focused; they are there for a purpose and, whilst browsing can take place, the overriding need is to be able to buy what is required. As a consequence, a retailer needs to ensure that as a fundamental that navigation is clear, simple and perfect.

- Tell me about new brands and products. Shoppers want to feel that they know what is available and when new brands appear. (Whether the shoppers then buy is another matter.)

- What's on offer and ensure this is clearly sign-posted so I do not miss out. This is highly motivating for all shoppers and emotionally underpins the sense of being a 'smart shopper'.

- Inspire me to make purchases outside of my everyday essentials. Grocery shopping is mundane and weekly menus are repetitive. Inspiration cues can inject enthusiasm into the shop.

- Make sure what I need is in stock.

Consistency of Messages

The messages here need to be consistent with the activity on the way to the store or website and highlight any 'on the way to the store' promotion that might have been carried out through relationship marketing, social media activity or ESOV achievement. Research shows lack of consistency can result in a 30 per cent reduction in sales.

In the Store/Online Activity Where No Additional Messages are Provided Other Than on the Product

There are three key activities to carry out in-store or on the website, where POS and packaging are combined:

- the POS (Point of Sale also known as the Point of Purchase (POP)) material and positioning of the product should be easy for the shopper to find;the packaging can also be used to enhance the purchase;the product availability should be sufficient to match the shopper expectation, with contingency plans for additional delivery.

Potential Message: Content and In-Store Opportunities

Shopping is a journey that begins before the shopper leaves home or turns on the desktop, laptop, tablet or mobile phone. Asda now issue an app that allows the shopper to read bar codes of items that need to be repurchased at home that then produces a shopping list for the shopper to use in-store as a reminding list.

We have already seen the impact that state of mind can have on the way a shopper interacts with the shopping environment. Keyway show the key emotional points in a journey in their white paper 'Online Shopping Behaviour' (2009).

The message is that the shopper has to be mildly aroused to be able to take in messages – too relaxed and they have little interest in what is going on, while too stressed on the other hand, and they miss out on the detail.

The Constant Shopping Challenges

For the in-store shopper:

- Price versus quality.
- Where to start shopping?
- Is my stuff available?
- Where has it gone, the store layout has changed?
- Am I being sensible and smart?
- Is that what I paid last week ?
- Do I really need that?
- Who slipped the extra item into the trolley?

A similar look at the online shopper also revealed mood swings, with different, but still important challenges.

- The computer can freeze or crash at any moment.
- I cannot find what I'm searching for.
- The site navigation is not instinctive.
- Will the transaction be completed?
- Will the order arrive when specified?
- Will the order be correct when it arrives?

How Does This Help in Deciding Where to Place Promotional Advertising, and What to Say?

Evolution Insight (see the Appendix) spend their time seeing through the eyes of the online shopper to see how their attention pays out when they are shopping online. Their conclusions in Table 10.1 below give some considerable pause for thought, challenging some assumptions you might have about the process. They reinforce the dedicated way that, for example, shoppers approach the login page; totally dedicated to getting on with the job.

Assisting the Decision to Purchase by the Shopper – Building Interactive Consumer Decision Aids (ICDAs)

ICDAs are broadly defined as technologies that are designed to interact with consumers to help them make better purchase decisions and/or to do so with less effort. Fortunately, recent advances in information technology have made the development and implementation of such tools a realistic ambition. In fact, examples of effective ICDAs are becoming a part of everyday life for many people. Take, for instance, internet search engines, in-car navigation systems, personal video recorders (for example, TiVo), and RSS feeds (for example, for news and coupons).

Table 10.1 Evolution Insight analysis of the online shopper

	Common Assumptions	Our Research Suggests
Front page and login	This is the best place for your top offer; shoppers expect to see them at this stage. Fmcgs must support with their strongest promotions of the year. WRONG!	Page footfall does not necessarily equate to interaction with marketing initiatives – shoppers are very focused on logging in, booking their delivery slot and starting their shop.
Favourites	This section is used by most shoppers to purchase regular items. It is a good place to position alternatives to influence decision making. NOT REALLY!	The most likely to engage with favourites are frequent weekly online shoppers who use it primarily as a shortcut to buy their regular staples. They often move away from the favourites after this and complain about the length and lack of personalisation. One in three do not use favourites at all.
Key word search	Very powerful position for Shopper Marketing as shoppers typically search for specific items they already intend to purchase. WRONG!	Shoppers often search for specific brands by keyword, or use keyword search as a quicker way just to find the right department. Those who recalled marketing and offers complained about low relevance. It is suggested there is a significant opportunity to improve here.
The checkout	Best area for impulse purchases and new products. WRONG!	Better used as a reminder 'have you forgotten…?' Shoppers are focused on reviewing their basket and financial details. Relevance is key. Impulse purchasing in fact is very low.

In fact 'showrooming' is an example where people take their telephone to a store to augment this with a touch of the real world. But see the opening of Chapter 9 for remarks about apps and mobiles.

It has been demonstrated that, with ICDA assistance, consumers are often able to increase the quality of the decisions that they make while simultaneously decreasing the effort required to make these decisions (Todd and Benbasat 1999, Diehl et al. 2003, Haubl and Trifts 2000 – the authors are happy to supply all the references for these research papers). The latter, for example, conducted a large-scale experiment in 2000 to examine the benefits to consumers of using an ICDA to shop for a backpacking tent and a mini stereo system in an online store.

These researchers used two measures of decision quality. First, the share of consumers who chose the product that had been designed to be objectively superior to five other products when an ICDA was available was 93 per cent – but only about 65 per cent without such assistance. The second measure of decision quality was based on a switching task. After completing their shopping trips, subjects were given an opportunity to switch from their original choice in each product category to one of several attractive alternatives, all of which had already been available on the preceding shopping trip. Switching was taken as an indication of the (poor) quality of a subject's initial purchase decision. While 60 per cent of the consumers who had shopped without ICDA assistance changed their choice of product, only 21 per cent of those who had received ICDA assistance switched.

In addition, research suggests that the presence of personalised product recommendations enables consumers to make purchase decisions with significantly less effort than would be required otherwise. The researchers measured consumers' search effort on a shopping trip as the number of products for which a detailed description was inspected. They found that, on average, consumers looked at the detailed descriptions of only 6.6 products when they were assisted by an ICDA, while those who shopped without such assistance inspected an average of 11.7 alternatives. This finding is consistent with the notion that reducing the effort required to make a decision is a primary motivation for using a recommendation agent, which has become widely accepted both in the field of consumer research and more generally in the literature on decision support systems.

There are increasing numbers of ICDA sources around – and of course, the original was a friend or neighbour. The effectiveness of a source is, of course, wholly dependent on the value that you attach to the opinion you receive!

BPS research in 2013 showed that the key factors in choice of a retailer were equally split between advice from friends and family, and past experience. Close to home, face to face, and hands on, even in 2013, is still vital. The ranked list of reported influence is not the full story, however, if your concern is ROI. On-pack promotions, while down at the base for reported influence might actually be an excellent choice if all you have to do is print 'NEW' on it.

- **Top three**
  - Advice from friends and family
  - Past experience of brand or retailer
  - In-store sales discounts

- **High influence – 40 per cent or more**
  - Offers or vouchers through the door
  - Price comparison websites
  - Seen on TV
  - E-mail offers vouchers

  - Online customer reviews
  - Magazine/newspaper reviews
  - Internet offers (for example, Groupon)
  - Salespersons advice

- **Low – influence 10 per cent or less**
  - On-pack promotions
  - Professional advisor
  - Newspaper offers or voucher
  - Offers by post
  - Leaflets while shopping
  - Recommendations on social networks
  - Competitions
  - Brands on Facebook, Twitter
  - Mobile phone offers while shopping
  - Celebrity endorsement
  - Prize draws

- **The conclusions**
  - Offers and discounts are far more important than endorsements, competitions and 'buzz'.
  - Leaflets through the door are far more influential than those handed out while shopping.
  - Mobile is still very much in its infancy and should move up the rankings dramatically.
  - Online and offline reviews both matter equally.
  - TV is still important.
  - 'Real World' friends and family carry a lot more weight than 'virtual' friends.

Whether it is a retailers or brand setting up an ICDA, a site offering help, perhaps linked in to the pack or a QR code near it, seems to offer real promise moving forward in adding value to the product and to the store.

The Effectiveness of Point of Purchase (POP Displays)

POPAI examined the effectiveness of POP displays using ClipCam (a camera clipped on to a shoppers head). The shopper is typically exposed to large numbers of POP displays (between 33 per cent and 49 per cent) in a store when a supermarket is visited (with a total POP quantity in-store of between 2,394 and 16,383 POP – albeit some POP duplicated). How did the shopper react? Between 37 per cent and 49 per cent of items purchased were from POP displays with 60 per cent promoting extra free product and 46 per cent multibuys.

The POPAI survey found unsurprisingly that POP messaging has a significant impact. The impact ratio of messages was highest for messages using the word 'new' or 'value/saving' (50 per cent) alongside a new product with price reduction (50 per cent) and competitions (50 per cent) followed by discount vouchers (41 per cent); pricing (36 per cent) and quantity discount multi buys (34 per cent) were lower. It is clear that the single word 'new' is all that is needed. Short words are easiest. A '£1' sticker achieves better results than 'double loyalty points for two packs'. Vertical signage such as fins score well for impact when only carrying an engram – this triggers autonomic responses. Over millions of years, research finds humans have noticed horizontally moving, but vertically blocking, shapes – associating them with danger. POP above head height do not do so well (only 4 per cent notice). Floor graphics do work well. Think impact, engagement conversion but also location, location, location, for POP placed with low traffic flow near the toilets/restrooms 'will only attract the elderly and incontinent' according to the IGD. Full, by product, category findings of the IGD research are found in the document 'The Grocery Display Effectiveness Study' carried out in 2012.

The Psychology of Pricing

SBXL (Shopper Behaviour Xplained) have spent some years identifying the key measures that cause shoppers to track through the major stages in an in-store purchase. Stages identified as:

- stop from moving down the aisle;
- visit the shelf, looking closer;
- evaluate, pick up and look at a product or products;
- buy.

They do this with the use of CCTV cameras covering the aisle, tracking the way that individual shoppers move, in a number of categories, on many occasions. Using identical measures they are then able to see the difference when the environment changes.

SBXL have used a very large number of shoppers (8,128) in 11 key categories, across the three major supermarkets in the UK. In doing this, they have been able to distinguish some real differences in the way that shoppers behave to certain types of offer prices.

Their first observation is how little behaviour actually changes in what drives the shopper to stop in the first place. Non-promoted products in the majority of spaces on the shelf drew shoppers only marginally less to stop (2 per cent difference) than promoted products. As you track further down the buying pathway the gap widens so that at the end where products are promoted there is an 8 per cent difference. The observation that SBXL draw from this is that promotions are not the key draw to a category, shoppers look to what they know first, and then consider promoted product.

The key question is, what type of price offer actually persuades more people to buy? Here SBXL come to a perhaps controversial conclusion.

Firstly they deliver exactly the same Insight as POPAI on the impact of using 'save' on a pack or on the shelf. Then to underscore the fact that shoppers actually do shop, just printing the word 'new' actually drove more purchases than multibuys, introductory offer or extra product. 'New' is not far off 'save' either.

There is a moral here, which is that if you are launching a new product, the first thing you need space for on the pack is the word, 'new'.

Moving on though, to the price point and type of promotion that actually builds sales, they give the following advice;

- Promoted products accounted for only 4 per cent points more of product sales than they had share of shelf.
- Special offers are shopped more after something else has been looked at. If sufficiently interesting then shoppers will switch to them: secondary choice, more than primary visibility.
- When 37 per cent of products on-shelf are promoted, shoppers are 10 per cent more likely to buy one of them.
- At a more detailed level, once they show an interest in a product, shoppers are five times more likely to buy it if it is on promotion.

- Asda and Sainsbury's shoppers are more likely to buy after evaluating if the product is on offer; Tesco shoppers on the other hand are less likely.

- The best way to stop shoppers in their tracks is to present them with a BOGOF: this type of promotional mechanic was more than twice as effective as any of the others measured.

- In terms of getting shoppers to actively browse a product, then the clear winner again is the BOGOF.

- When it comes to getting shoppers to evaluate a product, once again, BOGOF was the most effective.

- BOGOF was the best way to drive sales achieving a sales rating almost three times that of an unpromoted alternative.

- A 'save' offer that ends on some 'random pence' is much less effective at all levels compared with finishing it with either a round pound or a round '50p'.

- When it comes to multibuys, the round pound ending is actually the least effective pence treatment for the offer.

- When looking at all offer types, and in particular the pence of the price point, we see that the round 50p is the most effective tool, by some margin.

- Rounder price points are generally more effective on promotions, and overall round pound and round 50p perform very similarly.

However, what the surveys cannot pick up is the extent to which customers are faced by the offer on the shelf, but are unable to find the product.

Keeping the Product on Display

There has been a great deal of publicity about the fact that all of the major UK fmcg retailers ran out of Easter eggs before Easter – see Chapter 6. The position is an outcome of the current focus on discounted product, which makes holding excess product after an event extremely expensive. When you combine this with inadequate space in-store to keep discounted product in stock, you have a recipe for disloyalty that increasingly forces retailers to spend more to attract new customers than satisfy their existing ones.

What Can Be Done About This?

Increasingly, retailers need to turn to brands to help retailers managing the localised demand patterns for core customers. Seasonal demand adds significantly greater strain to standard shelf space in core areas. These areas already have increased demand per square foot of shelf than the average.

Why this is important is analysed in Chapter 6 in the text, but in summary shoppers go elsewhere and buy other manufacturer's products. Fortunately, the use of current analytics allow brands to work very closely with retailers building demand, and supply, in tandem.

Product Availability

It is axiomatic that shoppers cannot buy something that is not there – or is there, but they cannot see it. For the former, a retailer fallback is to check with other outlets and arrange delivery.

Byron Sharp in *How Brands Grow* identifies achieving high actual and virtual availability as the key marketing task – making a brand easy to buy. His comment is that anything else is secondary. You would think that this was intuitive, given that it is a part of everyday life that anyone reading this book must recall instances where they struggled to find something that they wanted.

Moreover, it is within the experience of sales and marketing directors as they came up through companies to be taken to task by managing directors over why they could not locate their product in the local store. This could of course be that it was never there, or that the supply chain has failed in this instance. It could even be that, despite the visual acuity of the average managing director, they failed to spot it, or it was placed somewhere else. All of these mishaps happen to the average shopper, but with nothing like the motivation of the managing director on sales and marketing's case to sort it out!

The Last 30 Yards

A vital role for marketing spend is the 'last 30 yards'. This is often referred to as the distance from the stock room to the shelf, however, it is not a coincidence that this is also the distance that the shopper walks to be in front of the facing. Somehow, however, this marketing imperative seems to get lost in the split between the sales and marketing initiatives.

What goes wrong, and why? In the case of the web, this applies per click. How can you improve the perceived presence of your own product best? In the Path to Purchase this last 30 yards is vital in getting the maximum from your listing. In this role the shopper, and the store, are equally important.

But Can You Really Change the Store?

Yes, suppliers, you can. In fact retailers expect you to, it is the reason you get sales and stock EPOS data in the first place. So you can do for them what they cannot do for themselves, manage their categories, and your products, to maximise sales.

What Makes a Difference?

Back to Byron Sharp again, Director of The Ehrenburg-Bass Institute (financially supported by many of the world's leading corporations including Coca Cola, Kelloggs, P&G, British Airways, Mars and many more). His conclusion as to the vital importance of real and virtual availability is supported by work carried out by Colin Harper, an author of this book, (and of Storecheck published by the IPM in 2010 – 'In Place of Price'). What can you learn from the Storecheck Vital Statistics?

Firstly You Can Understand Exactly Who Buys Your Product

dunnhumby may say that Tesco serve the national average – which indeed they might. But a Tesco store in Wigan serves a very different customer to the one in Knightsbridge, even though they may be exactly the same size store serving the same size catchment of shoppers by number. However, Tesco category management processes give the same basic space allocation for your product to both. Moreover, if you run a promotion on the shelf, they also do not get additional allocations either. Tough if you were hoping for more shelf space and you happen to sell treacle toffee in Wigan, or champagne in Knightsbridge.

The first thing, then, to understand, is where your core stores are. These are the stores struggling to cope with the same shelf space as their peers. They will always be the first to run out of stock at the weekend. They also serve the shoppers that your advertising really needs to engage with. These are a retailer's core stores. The supplier too needs to have this information to react in collaboration to deliver appropriate quantities of product.

So how do you find out where they are?

- by region (so your advertising can be targeted);
- by geo-demographic definitions, based on which shoppers shops where (also what kind of people buy your product);
- by store size (how important really are smaller stores to each of your products).

In these areas you need to maximise your space, stock and stores (How to quantify this is covered in Part III). With this Insight you will benefit both your loyal shoppers *and* the retailers that service them.

Range and Assortment

Products with the largest shelf sales should be in the deepest distribution – allocated more stock.

Products with the greatest potential should receive the most stock.

In core stores the space on the shelves empties faster and fills slower than their peers. Work with these stores to improve your total brand sales. These stores will need to have more stock and space, in particular if there is a promotion (see Chapter 11). They are by no means always the largest stores. In your core areas all sizes of store will suffer. But they will also offer the opportunity to grow faster.

Stores Are Not Perfect

They can be slow on the uptake, and they can also stop selling. Why this happens is currently being researched. However, to see the impact of a simple change, just remove a shelf edge label for your competitor from the shelf of your local store and see how long it takes to be replaced.

It is possible to tell you: the stores that have stock and are not selling – ideal for new product launches when you don't have a ranging yet; ranged stores that have stopped selling (perhaps the fault of a competitor?); how much you are losing, so the stock allocation that goes out gets sales up immediately to where it should be.

As a bonus, at the same time, you can discover how much you would gain if you infilled stores for your leading products.

Summary

With knowledge of the behaviours of individual stores as part of the whole you can:

- improve your ranging into core areas;
- improve your promotion performance with stock and POP allocation.

With in-store messaging you can:

- increase sales;
- increase the value of your retailer relationship;
- improve your overall shelf sales across your products;
- optimise your distribution.

This is all 'low hanging fruit'.

Chapter 11

In the Store – Managing and Selecting Promotion Techniques

Promotions are designed to speed the process of getting a product into the hands of a consumer. They are a very important element of turning a warm body in front of a product into a sale. They can also serve many functions for an organisation or brand. However, our key focus here is how best to convert a shopper to a purchaser. Promotions work by presenting an incentive of some kind to stimulate action.

This chapter reviews the options, and gives an Insight into what they can do. First and foremost it is important to understand that, for many people, an offer of a benefit can be nearly as strong as the benefit itself. *Which* magazine in the UK reported that only 8 per cent of people actually claimed an offer made to them in any form. Obviously, 92 per cent of people are quite happy with the product or service alone. Of course this is an average; Hoover were basically destroyed as a brand and company in the UK by their over-generous free flights promotions offer. The promotional offer was worth many times the cost of the goods themselves. Below the two extremes of price discounts (that by definition reward all) and over-generous offers there are whole swathes of opportunities that offer better 'value for money' sales growth for the retailer or supplier.

Why Use Promotions?

In the current market conditions you cannot rely on people beating a path to your door (website, shelf space …) just because you are there. You need to let them know, and it might also help to make your advertising more impactful by running incentives alongside – presenting a reason to the shopper for the six message opportunities. The IPA commented in 'Models of Marketing Effectiveness' (see Chapter 5) that 'Advertising coupled with a sales conversion channel such as direct marketing or sales promotion is the most effective combination to drive hard business success.'

What Are the Choices and How to Choose?

Caution. All sales promotions are hedged around with legislation covering what you can and cannot do. The following review outlines the many options available. Before finally selecting your chosen approach, we suggest you consult either an expert in your local legal landscape or in managing promotions (promotion, marketing or advertising agency).

The Promotion Alternatives

Promotional techniques fit into a number of broad categories, each of which is outlined opposite (Table 11.1), along with examples from the IPM archives to give a vision of how well-produced promotions are carried through to a successful conclusion.

The key elements for consideration when deciding on a promotional approach are, in order:

- tailoring the incentive to the objective;
- tapping into the customers psyche immediately with the creative concept of the incentive;
- the long-term *as well* as the short-term impact of the activity.

TAILORING THE INCENTIVE TO THE OBJECTIVE

It is possible, and very common, to over-incentivise people. This is particularly the case with 'cash' rewards. Cash incentives can be used right across the company from sales through to human resources, where changed behaviour or improved performance can attract sometimes vast rewards (as witnessed recently with bankers' bonuses). For the target market, however, a downloaded itune may have a much greater perceived value compared to an affordable retail discount. Travel incentives work well with sales staff.

'Slippage' (the difference between the number of people that buy a product to take advantage of an offer and the number that actually do so) has the potential to magnify the promotional budget even further – according to a recent *Which* report only 8 per cent of people who buy a product for an offer actually go on to claim it. And with an 'instant win' promotion, only a small

Table 11.1 Categories of sales promotion

Technique	Mechanics Include:	End-user Proposition
1. Price Promotion (any offer where the customer gets a reduced price but does not get any other goods or services as part of the deal)	Coupons Discounts – Temporary Price Reductions (TPR) Extra free Multibuys – buy one/two get one free/ three for £10/and so on, otherwise known as Retailer Price Discounts	Save
2. A premium or Self-Liquidating Promotion (SLP)	Where branded merchandise is offered for sale to the consumer. Both the retailer and shopper benefit. The former makes a profit albeit smaller and the latter pays less usually for a quality product	Save
3. 'Free' promotion	Delayed Application offer Collection scheme Collector scheme instant In/on-pack Banded pack With purchase Sample Digital reward Reward for task Giveaways	Free
4. Prize promotions	Competitions Free draws Instant wins	Win
5. Off the shelf	The promoter buys an off-the-shelf package from an agency such as a hotel room, a package holiday and so on	Benefit
6. Cause-related promotions	Donation Sponsorship	Give

percentage of the prizes available are claimed, so the potential prize fund can be enormous and protected by insurance. With a price promotion, every single purchase costs money.

Often, however, when evaluating such promotions the cost and the benefit are often not even discussed. In the case of the bankers it is 'a price you have to pay to recruit and retain' (we are told). In the case of price discounts at supermarkets a similar argument is also deployed – 'it's just the price of doing business'.

However, all incentives must have a purpose or an objective that can be questioned and evaluated. Every company ought to know what options exist for alternate means of achieving that objective. Clear objectives are listed in Table 11.2 below and options for reaching them are legion.

COMMUNICATING THE BENEFIT – TAPPING INTO THE CUSTOMER'S CURRENT PSYCHE

Recently, in the UK, £1 has taken up the role that 99p used to have as a key price point. Just advertising that you sell a product at £1 seems to guarantee that it is a good deal, as Asda demonstrated when they launched their '£1 range'. *The Grocer* reported that a good proportion of the products in the range had been *increased* in price to meet the price point.

Similarly a recent entry for the ISP Awards played on the 'Scrappage Scheme' to promote the window replacement market. Would customers have responded to the approach so fast if the Government had not just spent a fortune elevating it to the must have essential home improvement? See also the Anglian Windows replacement campaign case study later in this chapter.

Communication should be designed to reach a customer as rapidly and affectively as possible. A recent IPSOS Mori report drawn from many markets, and thousands of adverts, nominated the creative approach as the one key element in the success of a campaign. It is vital to recognise here that you have, at most, a few seconds to get someone's attention, so this area cannot be underestimated. It should be clear then that the most important part of any promotion is the communication – and not necessarily just the value, since value is in the eye of the beholder.

THE LONG-TERM AS WELL AS THE SHORT-TERM IMPACT OF THE ACTIVITY

Considering the longer term might lead, for example, to offering a free branded item which may be more expensive than a cash discount, but if it has 'play value' for children it could offer substantial additional advertising to the target market.

You will probably be drawn to the conclusion, as you review the examples in the following categories, that the creative presentation is inextricably linked to the perceived value of the offer, so that an improvement in the communication, without any improvement in the actual value of the incentive, can result in much better results in the long and short term, than a much more costly 'cash' alternative.

Looking after the Loyalty

It is a moot point whether loyalty – repeat purchase – gained after a stimulating trial is the same as that gained after becoming convinced to try by advertising. But in the current market if it quacks, you might well be excused for thinking that it is a duck.

So if you feel the price for keeping customers loyal is an extended series of price reductions, then it may be reassuring to know that there are techniques designed specifically to build customer loyalty. These may be a less expensive option than price reductions.

If you feel that you need to offer more than just the standard product/price combination, then exploring alternative ways of *adding* value, perhaps also persuading customers to recommend your product/service to others, may be worth considering.

Promotions as Exciting as Porn?

The IPM in the UK worked together with iMotions – a radical eye-tracking technique that indicates the interest people have in a visual, as well as simply where people look first. The IPM examined the credentials of a range of award-winning promotions for their impact on the shopper. People respond to sights of interest by changing their blink rate, as well as their pupils expanding, both of which are externally measurable. iMotions has validated its approach on a scale of one to ten. In August 2010, the IPM put standard packs and promotions in front of consumers and measured the impact. The results, from their first release in *The Grocer*, led to positive worldwide reporting. The incentive varied from the very strong, such as 'free', to the weak, such as competitions. The Kingsmill Bread promotion adds considerable 'eye-appeal' to the pack as can be seen from the iMotions analysis. More to the point, you can see the difference in engagement – up from 3.5 to 4.1. This demonstrates the eye-grabbing appeal of a 'free' on-pack offer. Key to the success, however, was likely to be the fact that it coincided with the Wallace and Gromit film release, 'A Matter of Loaf and Death', as to the relevance of the subject of the offer to the brand.

In the Marmite case, of course, the impact has everything to do with the 'love it or hate it' advertising theme. The above illustration and Marmite's campaign of course stress the simple need for relevance in the promotion message to the engram you have developed for your products, either reinforcing, or contrasting.

ANGLIAN WINDOWS SCRAPPAGE SCHEME

As a further indication of the importance of relevance, and moving away from fmcg, we have the Anglia Windows scrappage scheme. This paralleled a scheme for cars that received wide publicity and was Government funded.

There was nothing special about the benefit – basically another way of offering a discount. What was different about this approach is that it tapped into a very top of mind issue in another market. The result of this is that you do not have to work hard to get the reader's attention – but you do have to make sure that the reader sees that the similarity is justified. Which in this case was perfectly carried out. As a result of this tight link to customer top of mind, the campaign took the industry by storm, and has been replicated by all the major competitors.

Britain's 26 million homes leak heat through their windows, accounting for 27 per cent of the UK's manmade CO_2. Traditional offers would have related to savings, but expressed as 3 for 2's, free fitting, cash back and free gifts.

The Campaign

Homeowners received an allowance when they traded in their old windows. This was communicated through Direct Response TV (DRTV), national press, online, door drops and foot canvassing.

The Results

- Against a target of 2,150 leads – £1.7 million worth of business, the campaign delivered 9,867 leads over the target period.
- The campaign peaked with a cost per sale of 12 per cent versus the same period the previous year of 21 per cent.
- Sales rose 126 per cent year on year, and in December despite spend being 11 per cent down on the previous year sales kept coming and were 68 per cent up on the previous year.

If you intend your promotions to compete against simply dropping the price, they have to be relevant at the point at which the shopper sees them. Get it right, and on-pack promotions, rated at number 13 in the list developed by the British Consumer Index, can soar up to number one.

Plus, if you offer something that seems to be a price offer on-pack (such as 'Try me free') this can have a high impact on-shelf browser. Power without the price – since the redemptions are a fraction of the cost of making a similar offer through the medium of discounting. Moreover, on-pack offers tend to target people who can afford to carry on buying at full price afterwards, since, of course, they buy at full price to be able to claim!

www.yousay.org, are a company specialising in rewarding through, and capturing information from, on-pack offers. These can be either added to a pack at the time of purchase or in-store by field teams, with the approval of the store manager. Either way, the result can be tracked via EPOS data against a pre, and post period.

In general terms, they report that an on-pack 'Try me free' offer, run according to their guidelines, should deliver 15–30 per cent uplift, for a redemption cost of less than 8 per cent. This kind of mechanic clearly offers much better value for money than a straight discount.

Couponing for Uplift

Finally, one of the preferred choices shows the impact of coupons, as well as the importance of relevance to the user in a Cravendale Milk promotion. What can you learn from this approach?

Even the most heavily advertised brand can benefit from a promotion to kick start an immediate trial, which, as can be seen, generated very significant loyalty. Of course, having a high-profile media campaign helped in giving the creative treatment high standout on the mat. This was amply demonstrated by a follow-up campaign with a logo-only approach that was significantly less successful. The reason for this can be seen in the eye response from iMotions.

While this is, of course, a high budget activity, the very flexibility of the doorstep coupon means that it could be considered for even relatively small campaigns.

Reviewing Your Promotion Options

PRICE DROP PROMOTIONS

Price promotions are where making a product or service more attractive is achieved by means of a (temporary) reduction in the price. There are a number of mechanisms to do this other than just cutting the price by discounting. These call for the shopper to act.

CASE STUDY: CRAVENDALE MILK DOORSTEP COUPON

Market Background

Arla Foods UK produces some of the country's leading dairy brands, including Lurpak, Anchor and Cravendale, a milk brand that keeps for longer in the fridge than other fresh milk.

The challenge Arla faced in driving sales for Cravendale is that milk-buying behaviour is very entrenched. Consumer tests show that once people try Cravendale they are very likely to keep buying the brand, but that most shoppers never consider switching from their existing choices. Arla needed to encourage people to look for Cravendale on the shelf and then provide them with the incentive to try it.

The Campaign

Arla regularly uses door drops to target its buyers' shopping lists, and recognised that this was another opportunity for a piece of well-timed activity. A heavyweight TV campaign featuring the three colourful characters — the cow, pirate and cyclist — ensured that awareness of Cravendale was at its highest when the door drop landed three weeks later. The incentive came in the guise of three coupons inside the leaflet offering money off a two litre bottle of Cravendale Milk.

To achieve standout on the doormat, the creative was simple but very distinctive. A die-cut front cover opened up to reveal the cow, pirate and cyclist at the bar, along with some key benefits about Cravendale, and finally the money-off vouchers.

With a budget of £970,000, Arla sent a total of 2.6 million door drops to a carefully selected target audience of families who were heavy consumers of milk but were not buying Cravendale.

The Results

The campaign delivered a very strong consumer response, with a higher than expected redemption rate of 5.8 per cent. More importantly, the response came from 40 per cent greater than normal new customers rather than existing ones who were buying their usual brand at a discount. This translated into 270,000 new buyers trialling the Cravendale brand. And post-campaign analysis shows that the campaign had a long-lasting effect: households who received the leaflet bought 14 per cent more Cravendale for six months, than those that did not. These were sales at full price, to boot.

Whilst manufacturers and retailers invest a considerable amount of time and money in opportunities to differentiate their products, leverage brands, set strategic prices and reduce the effectiveness of consumer search, little attention has been devoted to the impact of price from the viewpoint of the consumer.

Research commissioned by the OFT suggests that pricing practices may be less effective in conditions where consumers are readily able to make memory-based price comparisons, or have quick and easy access to price information, such as in online environments or using a mobile or tablet while shopping. On the other hand, pricing cues put forward by sellers both online and offline may still influence consumer behaviour, indicating that learning and/or easy access to information does not eliminate the impact of these practices. Short-term sales are positively affected by offering promotions.

The OFT research finds shoppers do not act rationally when presented with pricing; scientific research shows this conclusively. The presumption that a person makes a rational decision on pricing is incorrect. As human beings in today's complex shopping environment we tend to be persuaded by pricing clues. The effect of bundling (multi-offers) decreases cognitive effort and the belief that bundles involve discounts whether there is any saving or not. If the bundle is out of stock, shoppers may still buy an alternative as a result of lowered search intentions. Research on 'buy one get one free' is mixed – it may or may not have any effect. (However, see Chapter 10's conclusions by SBXL which tend to contradict OFT.) Reference pricing can have a significant impact even when consumers are sceptical. Partition pricing (base price plus surcharge) can positively increase shoppers buying because shoppers fail to adjust from the base price.

Examples quoted in the OFT research find we use mental shortcuts or apply rule of thumb which leave us open to external influences. For instance, restaurants are able to systematically influence customers' choice of wine, simply by manipulating the background music; stores have been able to influence people to buy the more expensive of two microwaves by adding a third even more expensive option; and researchers have been able to influence whether people choose a Sprite (green can) or an Orangina (orange can), simply by manipulating the colour of the pen people are handed by the researcher to write with (green or orange) when completing a survey questionnaire.

In many countries price discounting is the most prevalent way of delivering increased sales. In the UK well in excess of 50 per cent of fmcg product is now sold below what the brands would like shoppers to view as the right price.

Meanwhile, there is very rapid growth in people visiting retailers of white and brown goods to feel the merchandise and then get a better price online (this is known as 'showrooming').

However, the sheer ease of delivering volume by simply cutting the cost is mesmerising to many sales departments. Unfortunately, the task of improving sales when individual discounts have less and less impact demands – it would appear – more and deeper cuts.

Many companies turn to cost control, reducing the product for the same price just so they can keep offering generous price discounts. In the 1960s, Ford reduced the metal thickness of components to save cost until a Cambridgeshire policeman fell through the floor.

Certainly 'calls to action at the facing are often more powerful than discounts' in an analysis published in an IPA report in 2010. Perhaps surprisingly, this is a quote from dunnhumby, the Insight arm of Tesco Stores, who also offer club card analyses to major retailers around the globe.

However, it seems that even dunnhumby cannot prevent the lemming-like slide into commodity pricing that many brands seem to be taking. The whole aspect of discounting is so important that we have added a section at the end of this chapter devoted to an approach designed to help you manage it better.

COUPONS

Coupons are used by consumers to secure a discount, generally at POP. Electronic couponing technology now exists that can deliver a unique coupon to individual computers or to mobile phones and also provide an Insight into consumer response and behaviour.

Coupons cost more, of course, than just their face value. There could be print, distribution and the process of getting the coupons back from the point of claim. If, of course, the retailer issues the coupons, many of these costs disappear. If the coupons are distributed via the web, then distribution costs are also significantly lower – one reason for the massive growth in this approach.

Printed coupons are redeemed by retailers, who then bundle them up and send them to a clearing house, such as Valassis (www.valassis.co.uk). They reimburse the retailer for the face value of the coupons, their postage and a trade handling allowance. The coupon clearing house then recovers this payment plus a service fee from the issuer of the coupon.

MIS AND MAL-REDEMPTION

Mis-redemption is when a consumer deliberately or by oversight uses a coupon to secure a discount on their bill without buying the product. This practice is hard to prevent as the retailer typically fails to check that the coupon is being used against the promoted product. *Mal-redemption* describes those situations where retailers deliberately and fraudulently redeem coupons themselves without them ever having reached the consumer and request reimbursement for the value of those coupons.

The IPM has well-developed guidelines for coupon design covering minimum and maximum size, size of lettering, consumer and retailer messages, and so on. All coupons that are to be redeemed through the grocery trade should carry an EAN-13 barcode which identifies the promoter, the brand, the coupon value and the campaign reference.

Coupons can be a very cost effective way of attracting business. However, as with all price promotions, what is absolutely vital is to target current non-users. And only use coupons in areas where your product is in high distribution. Very sophisticated systems of targeting are now available and these must be used to avoid wastage. Tesco, in particular, can arrange to send coupons out to lapsed or potential users based on their customer data.

EXTRA FILL (FOR EXAMPLE, 25 PER CENT EXTRA FREE)

This is where free extra product is included in the pack either in standard packaging or a larger pack.

The trade likes to give away free product and normally the free product costs less than the consumer's perceived value. Where possible a supplier should use existing packs or the next size up.

BUY ONE GET ONE FREE (BOGOF)

This can involve packs being banded together but is more usually operated through the retailer's EPOS system. This is one of the retailer's favourite mechanics and can be hugely expensive for the supplier (who always has to pay for it – because that is the industry's common practice).

It is worth printing off a copy of the Government's 'Code of Practice for Traders on Price Indications' and checking it whenever communicating price, discounts or price comparisons in marketing material. The Code can be found in pdf format at www.berr.gov.uk/files/file8127.pdf.

How Much is This All Going to Cost – How Many Will the Shopper Take Advantage of – and of Which?

Redemptions are variable. Just how variable you can see in Table 11.2 below. One thing that does stand out, though, is that typically, you are not rewarding every purchaser. The one exception is online couponing. Some of the elementary errors made here did not take into account the fact that any unguarded coupon you make freely available, can be freely used. So if you make 100 available to colleagues, do not be surprised if this gets a much wider circulation! Basically, do not offer more than you think you can afford. If you are not sure, there are companies that can help by insuring your risk (the figures opposite are from Mando).

Managing Discounts

This aspect of promotions is so all pervasive, and so important, that it needs a section all to itself.

Price is not always considered rationally; the assumption by sales personnel that it is better to sell more at a reduced price may be flawed, when item profitability, brand, stock delivery and impact on cash flow are calculated, especially when a term purchase is contemplated. This treatment of price in such a cavalier fashion by many retailers and brands is widely practised in the experience of the authors.

Sales managers and call centre staff may have been set a target to sell a quantity, or receive commission for the number of products or services they 'sell' within a discount leeway. This makes them dangerous to brand, supplier or retailer. 'Me too' reaction can see a whole street of shop managers offering 75 per cent discounts without recourse as to whether this makes brand or commercial sense.

Table 11.2 Redemption rates

Category	Range %	
	From	To
On/in-pack coupons free product	4.87	30.65
On/in-pack coupons MONP (Money off Next Purchase)	1.17	16.04
Newspaper coupons free product	0.16	5.88
Newspaper coupons MONP	0.01	2.46
Magazine coupons free product	0.13	8.5
Magazine coupons MONP	0.022	5.4
Direct mail coupons free product	3.28	31.87
Direct mail coupons MONP	0.55	12.71
Door drop coupons free product	1.2	16.49
Door drop coupons MONP	0.19	20.66
Sampling coupons MONP	0.52	12.22
Online MONP couponstar – print	0.01	9.67
Online MONP couponstar – red from print	2	106.6 (!)
Instore free product	4.07	–
Instore MONP	0	0.68 per cent
Collector single gift	0.08	31.79
Collector single gift with contribution	0.19	3.37
Single gift single POP	0	38.93
Single gift single POP with contribution	3.43	–
Multi-gift collector	0.01	61.66
Multi-gift collector with contribution	0.01	4.46
Multi-gift single POP	0.7	28.62
Guarantee	0.0006	4.55
Cash back traditional	0.01	13.64
Cash back event	0	0.97
Try Me Free (TMF)	0.02	13.82
Challenge	0.04	10.8
TMF with statement	1.05	6.29
Click 'n' win	0.02	29.39
Text click Interactive Voice Response (IVR) to win	0.0004	17.12
Text 'n'win	0	4.48
Instant wins	0	33.33
Flat Panel Display (FPD)	0	10.17

Source: Mando, as at 4 February 2010.

Shoppers of course welcome it – they are acutely aware of price and actively (through their mobiles and tablets) seek price comparisons. Whereas traditionally the market should set prices – you would expect to pay more in outlets in wealthier areas – the advent of such comparisons and with online outlets too has levelled the playing field on price. Unless, of course, the convenience of owning the product or service earlier by buying on the spot at a higher price rather than waiting for a delivery or the shopper preference for the name of a well-known retailer as a warranty on the goods is valued sufficiently to be worth paying more.

Price drops or promotions are both ways of delivering a differential to competitor products and using alternative types of incentive to get more of a product in the hands of the shopper while they are in front of it.

Managing Price Promotions (Courtesy of Simon-Kucher and Partners)

Managing price promotions (discounts) is one of the most important issues facing the consumer goods sector, with increasing discount levels exerting significant downward pressure on margins. Getting promotions under control can appear a daunting prospect, given the sheer number of events consumer goods companies are now running. However, companies with the right strategies and a strong management process can achieve significant profit improvements. Promotions are time based both on when the start is to occur and the time for which the promotion is to run – called a calendar.

Every senior executive of a consumer goods company will have promotions somewhere near the top of the to-do list each year. Simon-Kucher works with a wide range of consumer goods companies and there is no other subject more likely to provoke a furrowed brow. There is no denying it is a complex and time-consuming subject, but the rewards for getting the promotional monster under control are enormous.

It is no exaggeration to describe price promotion in the UK consumer goods industry as a monster. Over the last 15 years the frequency, depth and costs of such promotions have grown inexorably and that growth is accelerating. In many categories discounting has become a zero sum game or worse. The promotional calendar for an individual category is already jam packed and ever increasing discounting levels are required to stay competitive.

Added to this, relationships with retailers are often combative and promotions have become a key bone of contention. Promotions are central to retailers' and suppliers' competitive strategies, but these objectives are often not aligned. Retailers push suppliers to fund ever deeper promotions, with suppliers pushing back on both discount and funding levels. Retailers also want suppliers to fund 'market-leading' deals linked to corporate marketing activity. Suppliers who do not fund these activities find themselves losing promotional slots and market share in their categories.

There is also conflict within suppliers themselves, as different account teams compete to get the best deal for their customer. With mysupermarket.co.uk giving a real-time view of in-market price to your buyer, the pressure to match or beat deals in other retailers is unlikely to ease.

Simon-Kucher identify five key steps to realising that potential value:

1. Develop a promotional strategy that gives you the right framework to build your calendar.
2. Identify which packs and promotions work best for your brands.
3. Create a strong calendar planning process that allows you to maximise your profits.
4. Look at promotions not only from an internal perspective, but also from a retailer and category perspective.
5. Developing an optimal stock allocation policy.
6. Put in place the infrastructure to sustain promotional management.

Developing strong promotional management takes time, but each step should deliver profit upsides. The more expertise you develop the more value you can realise, even a pilot project can help you to start reaping the benefits. The hardest part is often making the first step.

1. SETTING THE PROMOTIONAL STRATEGY

In many cases promotional strategy is owned by a wide range of stakeholders: senior management, sales, marketing, supply chain and finance to name just the obvious candidates. It is not unusual to have multiple objectives (for example, drive trial, secure listings, hit sales targets and drive incremental profit) all influencing the same promotional calendar. In this situation the sales team has the near impossible task of trying to reconcile all these conflicting needs and still hit their targets.

Having a clear promotional strategy is the key foundation to building the 'right' calendar. In the real world this involves making trade-offs and prioritising some objectives over others. Simon-Kucher commonly works with clients at the start of projects to develop an aligned commercial strategy for promotions. The key stages are:

- understand the objectives of different stakeholders;
- score these objectives in a quantitative way;
- bring the stakeholders together to agree the priorities and make the trade-offs;
- stress-test the output against the broader corporate strategy.

Equally, it is important to understand how your brands react to promotions. For example, is your brand expandable (that is, if shoppers buy more on promotion do they consume more?) or do consumers simply load the pantry? How substitutable is your product (for example, do you steal from other categories when you promote)? What is the relative size and penetration of your brand? Answering these questions will help determine what type of promotions you should run. For example, if your category is not highly expandable single pack deals may be more attractive than multibuy promotions, as they are less likely to 'block the pantry'.

With a clear context and strategy you can determine the objectives and key performance indicators for your promotions.

2. IDENTIFYING THE RIGHT PROMOTIONAL MECHANICS

Different promotional mechanics have an enormous impact on the uplift and incremental profit a promotion generates. Consumers will react very differently to the same price discount depending on how it is presented. For a product with an everyday price of £1.49, a half-price promotion can perform far more strongly than a 74p price down on some products. Equally, on a different product, a 74p price point may appear a very attractive price point.

SIMON-KUCHER PROMOTION POST-AUDIT METHODOLOGY

1. Build detailed calendar

- deal start and end dates, mechanic (for example, two for £3) and shelf price;
- display type and other feature;
- actual in-store execution levels (display, space and so on).

2. Volume lift analysis

- gather sales-out data (for example, IRI, Nielsen, retailer EPOS);
- model base run rate before promotion and analyse incremental lift;
- identify any cannibalisation of other products.

3. Promotional economics

- calculate baseline and promotional revenues analysis;
- add cost of goods and identify incremental profit by promotion;
- estimate retailer margins and retailer incremental profit.

4. Key promotion drivers

- analyse the multiple factors that influence promotional lift;
- store-level analysis to determine the role of display, space and so on;
- statistical analyses to determine which are the key drivers of lift.

5. Category impact of margins

- analyse competitor dealing calendars and estimate trade promotions;
- analyse impact of promotion on shopper panel behaviour;
- determine impact on category sales and profit of different promotions.

In determining which type of mechanic works best for your brand there are no hard and fast rules. There are a number of factors that influence how a mechanic performs and they tend to differ by brand and retailer. To name just a few:

- consumption patterns for the brand;
- shopper buying patterns for the brand;
- consumer perception of the brand;
- pack size/weight;
- everyday price levels and price perception;
- shelf space and on-shelf execution;
- retailer promotional strategies and advertising.

Simply plotting per cent discount or absolute promoted price and expecting consumer demand to react in a strictly mathematical way will lead to suboptimal decision making. There is, therefore, no substitute for post-auditing different promotions over a one to two-year timeframe. Many companies have the raw data already, and this database of promotions enables you to identify which promotion types perform for you, as well as enabling you to predict how new untried promotional mechanics may perform. The box provides a more detailed description of how to approach promotional analysis.

In a recent project it was found that there was no consistency between the relative performance of half-price and BOGOF promotions across a category and between retailers. Despite the promotional price and per cent discount being identical, there was a clear difference in performance between different brands and pack size within individual retailers. However, on one pack there was a clear benefit to half-price promotions. In order to really understand your promotional performance you need to analyse promotions individually.

The promotional mechanic is only one of a number of factors that influence promotional performance. The level of in-store execution is a key driver. Our analysis of promotions in different categories has found that store-level execution is often very different from the planned or agreed execution (Table 11.3). In practice, store managers have considerable influence over what goes on display. In a recent project we found that many stores were putting the product on display outside of head office guidelines, driving higher uplifts than predicted.

As you can see above, stock levels on promotion can vary widely, which can also have a significant impact on uplifts. The amount of space allocated to a product both on and off-shelf is a critical driver of performance (Table 11.3). Tracking actual execution levels of promotions (display, space, stock) is an important element in accurately post-auditing performance.

Table 11.3 Knowing which execution levers to pull and where to pull them is critical to driving maximum promotional uplifts

What You Manage at Head Office:	What You Manage at Store Level:
1. Promotional pricing and mechanic	1. Promotional space and gondola end display
2. POS and in-store displays	2. Off-shelf displays (pallets, dump-bins and so on)
3. Gondola end allocation	3. Promotional stock levels

The importance of promotional stock levels is covered in the next section.

Once you have a good understanding of which mechanics perform, you can start to build a stronger promotional calendar. Knowing which promotions generate the best returns also allows you to start improving profitability quickly.

3. BUILDING THE RIGHT PROMOTIONAL CALENDAR

A good promotional calendar is not just a piece of paper with a list of promotions; it is the process to turn a strategy and a list of mechanics into an executable plan (Table 11.4). A promotional calendar should encompass all the commercial activity within a particular retailer and work across retailers and channels. Price discounting is not the only option, as you have seen above, and a good calendar should contain a variety of tactics.

Table 11.4 Developing a strategic promotional calendar

Key Inputs into the Calendar	Key Elements of the Calendar Build
1. Rigorous understanding of previous promotions and the key factors that influenced performance	1. Build individual account calendars, using promotions that have performed well previously and new mechanics based on previous performance
2. Overall commercial plan for the period, to allow promotions to be tied-in with marketing or other consumer activity	2. Bring account teams together to understand cross-read issues and supply-chain constraints, iterate plan to create channel calendars
3. Overall strategy and financial targets for the period	3. Roll-up total plan to assess financial impact. Gain alignment to the plan across senior management and commercial team

The role of the calendar (Table 11.4) is to determine the pattern of promotional activity (for example frequency, depth and number of brands). This depends on the nature of the brand and the strategy you have adopted. Calendar planning should also cover all the key retailers and channels. One of the most important objectives of the process is to ensure that promotions in one account or channel do not have a negative cross-read impact in others.

Determining the correct discount levels for a brand is often one of the most contentious questions. Retailers will always push for the most attractive possible promotion, and there is often a clear trade-off for suppliers between sales and profit. We would always advise clients to follow a balanced approach, only proposing deeper promotions where you can do so at a reasonable return. For example, in a recent project Simon-Kucher identified that a shallower, more frequent promotional strategy would deliver much greater returns for one key brand than the current, less frequent and deeper promotional pattern. The deeper promotions performed strongly on some of their other brands, and retaining these promotions was important in maintaining engagement with the retailer.

A calendar planning process should aim to get ahead of retailer, competitor and supply chain issues. Planning six to nine months ahead allows time to make trade-offs and also allows time to revise the plan. Things will inevitably change, but it's easier to make snap decisions when a framework and strategy already exists.

With a process in place to plan promotions you will begin to develop more informed promotional strategies. As your stock of promotional audits increases, so will your ability to build your calendar to maximise profit.

4. DEVELOPING A 'WIN–WIN' CALENDAR BETWEEN RETAILERS AND SUPPLIERS

Understanding promotional performance from your own perspective is vital to developing an effective promotional strategy. However, the ability to analyse promotions from the retailer and category perspective is the key to successfully implementing that strategy. We frequently hear from clients: 'We know what the right strategy is, but the big supermarkets won't listen.' You will not truly know what the right strategy is unless you know whether it works for your retail partners as well.

The first step is to fully understand the retailer strategy, both at a buyer level but also at a more senior management level. If your buyer is focused on margin you should ensure that the promotions you propose are margin accretive. Similarly, if the senior management is focused on share, your promotional strategy should support this objective.

The second and most simple step is to ensure that all the analysis and planning of promotions that you do includes retailer margin. A good test of your promotional calendar for a subsequent quarter is whether it is margin accretive at a per cent or absolute level versus the prior year. A buyer is much more likely to be receptive to a shallower deal if the margin upside is shared between the retailer and supplier.

The more advanced step is to develop an understanding of how your promotions impact the category. A promotion which has a low level of cannibalisation of your products may drive little true incrementality for the category, and be unattractive to a retailer. Shopper panel data and consumer surveys can often give a good idea of how much volume is stolen from within the category. Understanding how your promotions perform versus the competition can often be the most insightful data for a retailer, and proposing a calendar that balances retailers and suppliers profit is a powerful win–win.

The diagram below show how promotions that appear the most attractive to a supplier may not be the most attractive to a retailer. The most effective calendar from a category perspective may be the one with a mixture of promotions that drive different results.

Table 11.5 Developing an optimal calendar for the category

2. Use strategically	1. Protect and sell to retailer
4. Remove from calendar	3. Re-balance margin share

Source: SKP project anonymised.

Framework for developing a 'win–win' promotional calendar

- a good promotional calendar will focus on building promotions in box 1;
- promotions in boxes 2 and 3 can be used strategically;
- promotions in box 4 should be eliminated.

Getting the category perspective on promotions enables you to get on the front foot with retailers and use promotions to achieve joint ends. The results of your analysis should form the basis for your selling story to your retailer partner.

5. DEVELOPING AN OPTIMAL STOCK ALLOCATION POLICY

When the product is on promotion and/or the packaging contains a promotion, then adding additional shelf space in the form of display units or shippers may be needed and stock replenishment becomes most important. Core stores have increased promotion uplift, requiring more stock and space than the average on top of a normal need for faster replenishment or more space.

Category management initiatives need to include promotion space – even though the promotion might be handled notionally from existing shelf space. Category intelligence needs to be delivered by store, and as an ongoing initiative to manage the impact that promotions bring.

How much more promotional stock?

First look back at your uplifts from a promotion and the stock cover that you need to get excellent performance. There is a very close relationship between the amount of stock a store has in place just in advance of a promotion, and its ability to perform well (ask for a copy of the white paper from Colin Harper at Storecheck 'In Place of Price' to look deeper).

You may need five or six times the stock cover to get a 20 times uplift in core stores. Less than this and there is not enough to build displays and manage the demand the first week. As well as this the gap between what you might achieve and what you do (average uplifts) grows ever wider as the discount increases.

Get the top level of allocation out to your core stores and advise them that they will really benefit from additional space as the selected products are more important to the category in their stores.

The level of discount which actually gives you the best overall return can also be found from this chart if merged with margin. It should not also be a surprise that store prominence (such as with added sitings on gondola ends) builds sales. However, it may surprise many people the extent to which added stock builds sale both promotionally *and* post-promotion.

6. PUTTING IN THE INFRASTRUCTURE TO SUSTAIN PROMOTIONAL MANAGEMENT

Getting your promotional calendar right should not be viewed as a one-off project. The commercial environment is fluid and a promotional strategy that worked in one quarter may not be appropriate if external factors (for example, competitor activity, retailer strategy) change significantly. Managing promotions effectively requires buy-in across your organisation, good quality data and an ongoing process to manage calendars.

That does not mean you should go out and invest significant amounts immediately. Kick-starting the process with a study of previous promotions for a specific brand or retailer is a good place to start. The data you gather should give you the evidence you need to justify a larger investment. Executive teams always want to see the money before making a bet on something new and untried in the organisation. Even a limited study can identify optimisation opportunities and you will find the account manager or brand owner becomes your most effective advocate internally.

However, in order to realise the full upside potential having a dedicated resource is vital. The analysis required is often complex and requires experience. Managing multiple retailers and channels adds complexity and more stakeholders to manage. In addition, the individual or team needs to build links across multiple functions (sales, marketing, finance, supply chain).

The ROI for a promotions team is frequently very high, as even small changes to promotional calendars can generate significant profit impact. A planned approach to promotions can, over time, turn them from being a challenge and a drain on your Profit and Loss (P&L) to a strategic lever that enables you to hit your objectives.

Summary

The right promotions will outperform simple discounts.

Price drop promotions need to be closely supervised by top management (above store level) to see that they do not harm brand, profitability, cash flow or affect the supply chain.

However, the impact of promotions lies in the how and where of the presentation as much as in the amount that is given away.

The best promotion performers also have the best retained sales in general after the promotion!

Chapter 12
After Purchase

This chapter recommends what the supplier and retailer can do to extract further sales (accessories, refills, complementary items, service support) as well as obtaining customer feedback after purchase. The shopper should be made additional offers (promotions) as well as allowed to comment on the product and encouraged to share their experience. This is well understood in mobile sales where a 'bounce back' contains a second offer. Few retailers other than those online do so – but generally only offer accessories – or similar or related offerings, alongside the first purchase.

A plan for a follow-up should always be considered.

Why Should a Follow-Up Communication be Considered after a Purchase?

The brand supplier and retailer can achieve through 'after purchase' contact:

- customer relationship building extracting information;
- additional sales of items associated with the product (often through a promotion);
- wider communication – especially sharing the positive customer experience with others.

The brand, supplier and retailer can find valuable information from the shopper either in-store or online or both, in two ways:

- the experience of the product or service;
- service and shopping experience.

The shopper feedback and review, language, and product/service experience can be used in subsequent marketing communications to other shoppers. If there are shopper mal-experiences with a product or service then these can be corrected before the purchaser has time to spread too many adverse comments – particularly in these days of social media.

In some businesses feedback is critical: for a die-casting business the feedback is obtained through a series of phone calls at different levels in the organisation. This is set up as an established procedure. The reason for the procedure is that die-casters tend to supply castings on a JIT basis. That is, castings go straight to the point in the assembly process that they are required, just before they are needed. If a casting is incorrect, it can stop an assembly production line. And what happens if a duff casting arrives in a batch? The word spreads rapidly up the supervision and management line to the top – reporting a failed casting as a cause of a halt or slowdown in production. A few failures here and reporting of this up the line will mean a new castings supplier will be found. For feedback let us apply what could be described as the marigold glove theory – that is, if hands wearing marigold gloves mesh, they are difficult to separate; just as hopefully the feedback system operates as marigold gloves when meshed. So how does it work? The driver delivering the castings at the gates takes the trouble to check the castings in to the factory, rather than just dumping the pallet. The casting foreman then shortly afterwards calls the line foreman to check that the castings are all OK, ideally at about the time they are to go on the line. The castings production supervisor calls the line supervisor a little later. If all is well the die-cast production manager calls his opposite number to confirm what he knows already; that the castings that were delivered were fine. If at any point there are any problems the die-cast firm sends across further castings as fast as possible without question. This is how relationship building is meshed with feedback and the contract retained. Fulfilment businesses are wise to do the same.

Once the purchase has been made, either at the time of purchase, but also subsequently, additional items can be offered – possibly with either a promotion or price discount to incentivise the shopper. The items may be a repeat purchase or associated – examples are, for an online shirt supplier, additional shirts or other items of clothing that go with the shirt such as a tie. A shirt might be offered with a tie for free. A time-limited voucher might be sent for a further purchase. A sale selection might be a further offer. A wine shopper might be offered a tasting. The imagination holds few limits (but do not offer free flights from UK to US with the purchase of a Hoover – it has been done already!). From time to time an incentivised feedback survey might be sent to the shopper.

The IBM Finnish Hong Kong case study (see Chapter 9) is an example of how reviews helped raise sales by 250 per cent as a result of them being fed back to prospective shoppers.

Content of Messages

Over time, a series of messages should reinforce the engram, entice the shopper to buy something else, ask for feedback on purchases and the shopping experience, obtain product and service reviews and build the relationship.

Building from the Single Purchase to More

It is entirely possible to build further purchases after the first if the way that it is presented is engaging enough. The Marmite promotion (iMotions analysis of the label is described in Chapter 7) is an example of how Marmite achieved 'eye candy' and they offer premium promotions (see the Case Study box). The free Horrid Henry audiobook download offered by Marmite was an example. Just take a look at the 'Marmite lovers' shop at http://www.marmiteshop.co.uk. Marmite is on Facebook too. Marmite is an iconic British Brand with an honest take on how it is received by the public. You either love it or hate it. The critical audience is mums with growing families. Their children are the number one priority for Marmite mums, so giving them the best start in life is hugely important. Children fed on Marmite are likely to become the Marmite buyers of the future.

What Can You Learn from the Marmite Approach?

It has to be hard making a promotion benefit out of the fact that many people hate your product. And also communicating this in a way that will get children to try, and then to use more. So the seeming improbability of getting a match at all shows that good, creative searching is vital to generate a sound basis for a profitable mutual link. In fact, the major benefit is not necessarily the giveaway but the media opportunities that the existing graphics delivered to the target market.

This identifies, as in other cases, that researching the market and getting a creative best fit is of paramount importance. And, of course, being on-pack had a major impact in the store.

MARMITE CASE STUDY

Strategy

Working with the Department for Children, Schools and Families and their 'Reading for Life' initiative, which aimed to get children into reading, Horrid Henry was identified as the best fit for the brand and the children. Over 14 million Horrid Henry books and audiobooks have been sold, the series has been translated into 25 languages, and the cartoon based on the books has quickly become one of CITV's most successful ever.The campaign centred around linking the two main characters in the Horrid Henry series, Horrid Henry and Perfect Peter with Marmite's traditional 'you either love it or hate it' dichotomy and was supported via national press and radio. In press fake ads and articles were defaced in Marmite by Horrid Henry and Perfect Peter. The message to mums was that Marmite will help keep your kids out of trouble, as well as giving away free audiobooks that would help them to get into reading.

Radio ads aired during the school run told the story about how Scheming Suzy and Shrewd Shaun plotted to get through their jars more rapidly so they could get all of the downloads faster.

This creative approach may well have been represented in the much heavier than average rate of usage experienced. The consumers were directed to a scratch-off panel at the back of the pack, redeemed through a site where the audiobook could be downloaded. Five could be collected, one with each unique code.

The results

1 Driving sales and frequency of purchase:
   - 10 per cent redeemed between two and five jars in the first four months;
   - a considerable increase on the standard rate of purchase of a jar every four months.
2 17,269 audiobooks downloaded from two million packs:
   - website results showed a 0.86 per cent redemption rate. The majority of the budget was devoted to the media with no cost for the downloads in exchange for the publicity.

Summary

It is worth the effort and, in this day and age, if you are in it for the long term with your shoppers and dare to be different (see the next chapter) then you should certainly communicate with them after purchase.

Chapter 13
Dare to Be Different

As a result of the research studied for this book, it is apparent that the retailer/supplier needs to assist the shopper with their journey to purchase in the following distinct ways, some of which might be combined. But beware at the search stage if you are a brand manager, supplier or retailer of 'coming on too strong', any search activity should feel as if it is independent of the supplier/retailer.

Dare to Be Different

Big brands and their products appear everywhere. That is what being big is all about. If you want to be a big brand you need to appear to be like them before you become one and consider this a necessary step on the way. It is the ever presence of messaging that makes the difference as to whether you appear big or small to the shopper: send a range of the six types of messaging to a shopper – and to them you then appear big. Case studies and examples in Chapter 10 confirm this.

This book also tells you that, no matter how often you repeat a fact, it will never sink in unless you make the message appeal to the emotions, and then attach this to a strong and recognisable symbol – the engram. Once this is developed, every product, POP, advert, article or discussion, any mention of the product by friends, family or the web then helps to cement this engram in place more firmly.

Much work has been done over the years on Share of Voice as a key predictor of advertising success. This book shows that the Share of Voice you need is that on the shopper's Path to Purchase and needs to be proportionally larger than your market share, that is, excess – especially if you want to build a brand and sales at the same time. In this book you are shown in various chapters why ESOV is important (Chapter 1), how you get it (Chapter 9), where you place it (Chapter 5), and how you can measure it (Chapter 16). When you are proposing to launch a promotion then ESOV is key to winning against the competition – achieve this locally, or within your niche. Plus the vital importance of synergy between demand and supply side – common sense really – making sure sufficient of your product or service is available to meet demand – generating your maximum real and virtual availability as you go.

Encouraging social media is again important – clearly participation should only be responding to correct misunderstandings or mistakes, but noting the feedback. The Hong Kong case study (Chapter 9, page 160) confirms the need for reviews to a prospective shopper.

The approach the book recommends is designed to work for any brand anywhere, although many illustrations are drawn from fmcg, since data is more readily available in this market. Companies, wanting to move forward to real ongoing profit, need to see their sales and marketing budget as one resource building both short-term sales and long-term marketing. Most companies still have a vast divide between these budgets.

Do You Dare to Be Different?

It is relatively easy to think short term only. Many suppliers and retailers do so where sales have a bigger influence than marketing. However, all the evidence points to the shopper seeking long-term as well as short-term messaging, in part because the human being stores the engram and builds on it, so sales and marketing need to work together. A sales campaign can unwittingly destroy the long-term shopper's mind impression. This then affects future product and service purchases at a great detriment to the bottom line. The research indicates ten days as the maximum a promotion or price discount should run. Brand managers probably know all this anyway and realise how so-called but extended short-term activity can damage a brand.

It seems clear that the shopper's purchase decision is made in the main below the threshold of consciousness. The influences to this are both recent – on the way to the purchase on the day (hence the need for ESOV), and also long term, based on subconscious simple symbol recognition – the engram – that acts as the focus for thoughts and feelings to the brand. Much of the build of this engram, a collection of thoughts and feelings based around a recognition feature of the product, are carried at a subconscious level by the shopper. New methods of research have spawned a range of qualitative and quantitative techniques that enable these thoughts of the shopper to be accessed and to measure them. This shows an engram build can be triggered by sampling for some categories, but to remain and be useful it needs to be reinforced by attitudes linking it to the rest of the buying universe.

So What Communications Do the Authors Conclude are Necessary?

Planting an engram in the shopper's brain is something that can be achieved by both B2B suppliers or brands or retail outlets. Even if the shop is local or the B2B supplier is a highly niche product or service, it significantly improves the chance of a sale if the shopper holds the engram in the mind. Even if the product or service is outside the normal value assessment of the shopper, the unconscious part of the brain will hold the knowledge. Thus on visits to shopping malls, large department stores or online social media sites such as Pinterest – even where for the shopper the stores are 'too high value outlets' for them normally – the sight of any brands will reinforce the engram, as will magazine or newspaper articles or advertisements, and similarly with television, outdoor or cinema advertisements and conversations with friends, relatives and colleagues. Of course, the shopper, should their fortune change or they are overcome by a feeling of 'I'm worth it', may lead to an override of their value instinct. The high-value retailer or supplier can but wait for the day and hope the shopper's needs may then well be met on a future occasion by such subconscious implanting and refreshment. The corollary is that anyone who sells anything, whatever their turnover or size, should certainly have an engram recognised by shoppers locally or by their target niche, or as a brand – nationally or globally – which the retailer/supplier should in partnership with the brand take steps to promote and refresh regularly.

There is a need in this age for 'other shopper' peer input and advice, to reinforce trust and obtain user views and experience of the product or service. Discerning shoppers will conduct their own search. But websites, printed material and QR codes offered by the supplier/retailer/brand should therefore assist the search by linking shoppers to social media where such advice can be obtained. They may print, report or offer 'satisfied customer' blogs on their own material but these do not have the same credibility. The retailer/supplier has to have, therefore, an active presence on social media sites placing messages that respond, and consistently, to shopper viewers about their brand. There are a few established retailers where the sales staff do give such equivalent trusted advice, such as John Lewis, and feedback up the delivery chain to the manufacturer such as Zara, but most sales staff are seen as just transaction order fulfilment persons – operating the till or credit/debit card payment and supplying a bag. It is assumed that the new Mary Portas towns in the UK will advocate staff training to match the John Lewis/Zara experience, but in any case all bricks and mortar outlets should do the same. There is no reason why online responders or call centre staff should not also offer advice. The shoppers' need for advice must be fulfilled by active support from the retailer/supplier. Sir Martin Sorrell, despite his statement about social media being just PR, has concluded a global deal with Twitter on behalf of WPP (June 2013).

The existing repeat shopper needs a relationship with the supplier/retailer which can be provided by sending out catalogues, mailshots, e-mails, mobile alerts and the occasional really good offer to tempt a further purchase. This additionally enhances the engram, the trust and the advice search, if blog links are quoted (see above) alongside such messages. The potential shopper, rather than the repeat shopper, probably needs at this stage an experiential opportunity or demonstration to be presented to them, or a sample provided. Now, and more in the future, the supplier/retailer may well find the shopper is content to order items – even clothing (on a sale or return basis) at home rather than visiting a bricks and mortar outlet. However, the opportunity to offer a visit to an outlet should always be made – and special treatment needs to be given to the shopper if the visit takes place and further offers made to entice a second purchase. A number of retailers (even eBay!) recognise that a bricks and mortar outlet should be offered to those shoppers who still prefer to visit an outlet. For them the invitation and visit should be seen primarily as entertainment or retail therapy but it gives the retailer/supplier the opportunity to sell. Data capture should be a part of this stage and set as an objective. Never forget that the in-store shopper can achieve instant gratification whereas the online shopper has to suffer the delay imposed by whatever delivery system is operating. Equally, for some people, not having to carry the goods home is an advantage.

ESOV should be achieved. Local outdoor signage or advertising gently reminds the shopper approaching an outlet of what is potentially available in-store though their engram recollection. The confectionary trade have recognised this for years and CTNs often have door and window displays including shop awnings to remind the shopper of a particular brand as they approach the store. Newspapers do the same. Local to any store, therefore, advertising and signs should be used. Local bus shelters, sponsoring garden displays, getting the local council to sign an outlet, all can point to a shop. The use of leaflets, handouts, local support from other retail outlets and local newspapers are ways to remind shoppers of local outlets. Local advertising needs to be in place for events, road shows, demonstrations or promotions. The retailer needs to increase the store presence locally. This increases Share of Voice to the Excess level. This reinforces the engram.

In-store, the retailer assisted by the supplier can have a field day with both on-pack, on-shelf and surrounding POP displays. These too need to be publicised locally and fully supported operationally. Remember the recorded research shows 70 per cent of the purchase decisions are made 'in-store', taking account of the influence of the subconscious engram, but the barriers to purchase – for example a failure to stock and place on-shelf – offers the shopper a chance to pick alternative 'on promotion' products or the services of competitors. Of course the shopper will be pleased with the retailer or supplier if the product is in place and available for purchase. It sends the message that here is a retailer who 'understands my needs' and its presence reinforces the subconscious engram.

In-store the retailer can add or use supplier initiated sales promotions – discount or any of other non-price promotions. These of course can be used in any of the on the way to the store message opportunities. But such promotions should not last too long to avoid affecting the shoppers' long-term perspective.

The need for collaboration between brand, supplier and retailer has been described earlier – when promotions occur, the need to stock appropriately to match actual local demand rather than an arbitrarily centrally organised uplift, with shelf stackers available to resupply as stock moves on a promotion and with contingency plans for urgent resupply. The need for sales and marketing to be as one for all purposes is similarly important, working alongside retailer and brand/supplier.

The corollary in all this is for the retailer and supplier acknowledging the six message points; it is better to have local, at most regional, promotions, where the stock, marketing/sales and outlet can collaborate to fully operate a promotion and increase to ESOV. The research also shows subsequent months in the store will also see an upsurge in trading at the selected local store. National promotions, research indicates, will never work as profitably as local ones.

The military analogy might be that a concentration of force at a point wins the battle but the expanding torrent theory suggested by Liddell Hart wins the campaign. Of course it is now accepted that the hearts – and significantly the minds – have to be won to win the war (the long term). The war for the shoppers' minds has yet to properly start but research is demonstrating it has been realised. The supplier and retailer, the sales team and marketing team, need to take this on board and act together in the six ways prescribed above.

Part III describes how to set about achieving the conclusions of the first two Parts.

PART III
What the Brand Manager, Retailer and Supplier Should Now Do

Donald Rumsfeld's quote has become famous over the years after first being used as a defence of the lack of information about weapons of mass destruction in the Iraq war. How, it says to us, can we know what we do not know unless we go out to find what it is.

> *There are known knowns; there are things we know that we know. There are known unknowns; that is to say there are things that, we now know we don't know. But there are also unknown unknowns – there are things we do not know we don't know. (Donald Rumsfeld)*

It seems, on the surface, to encapsulate everything about the environment that surrounds us that might drive the search for a marketing plan. It is, though, deficient in one, very important regard.

That is 'The things we think that we know, that are, in fact wrong'.

This part, written in a series of conveniently short chapters, looks at what a brand manager, retailer or supplier can do to implement the findings of the first two Parts.

Chapter 14

How To Do It: Successful Approaches Dissected

Much of the marketing environment changes very rapidly. Certainly annually, in some cases hourly, as entirely new approaches are launched. In some cases, in the search for this new marketing landscape, people actually throw away older techniques simply because they are old.

So the prime requirement for any marketer is to be self-challenging.

The start position then, for any successful marketing plan is a *true audit of the whole company results from past spend.*

To revert for a second to the Rumsfeld speech, an invasion of Iraq was based on the thought that weapons of mass destruction (WMD) existed based on a succession of reports that were very successfully disproved after the spend of some $1.9 trillion (Congressional Budget Office) by the US alone.

Where are the WMDs in your organisation? These are the assumptions carried forward from year to year. The unexplored areas that can be examined and then disposed of. The move into unknown territory based on gut feel, or because it is there, that might be unmeasured entirely or in the belief that we 'need to be there'. 'But we have always had a sale then.'

Central to this could be research such as the UK survey, 'The Marketing Gap' carried out by fast.MAP in conjunction with the IPM. This looks at what marketers believe about shopper behaviour, as opposed to what they say they do. This survey, produced annually, covers all aspects B2B and B2C. One finding is shown in Table 14.1. Marketers 'gut feel' is shown often to be wrong.

Table 14.1 The gap between marketers' belief about consumers and what consumers actually think

Do You Object to Receiving E-mail Messages?	What 2011 Consumers Said %	2011 Marketers Who Got the Consumer Figure Right %
Yes	75	15
No	25	none

The full report is extensive and should be read by all marketers.

The Objective of a Marketing Plan

The original concept (à la Kotler) of the way that a marketing organisation worked was that the discipline guided all of the activities of a company. Increasingly, decisions taken by the sales discipline prompted by the increasing strength of retailers has warped this vision, in some cases out of all recognition.

The authors believe that it is entirely possible to move back to a marketing-driven view provided that companies acknowledge that retailers have to be brought into the mix. Not just as the end result of the marketing process, but as active participants, whose needs must also be addressed.

In the new age retailers are under considerable pressure from all sides, not the least from the internet. The rate of high street retailers disappearing from the landscape is increasing annually, estimated in total as 61,930 shops over the next five years by the Centre for Retail Research. Manufacturers and services wanting to get the best from 'the now', need to have a present view that supports current retail appropriately, while developing their presence for tomorrow.

A marketing plan failing to take account of and work with the retailer landscape will have failed before it starts.

There has never been a greater need for knowledge and understanding of the options available. There are salutary lessons of simple marketing succeeding, while complex change has failed. One example of simple succeeding is the blender company Blendtech in the US. Their long-running series of extremely inexpensive 'Will it Blend?' viral adverts featured a wide range of desirable items such as iPhones, being blended down to powder. Not only did this have a serious impact on product sales, but Blendtech now sells 'Will It Blend?' merchandise. Meanwhile, there are many thousands of videos of blenders being used for their recommended use that get a handful of views.

On the other hand, it is entirely possible to spend a great deal of money and end up worse than you were at the start.

In January 2009, Tropicana introduced a new look pack with a heavy duty advertising campaign. A month later The PepsiCo Americas Beverages division of PepsiCo announced they were 'bowing to public demand' and scrapping the changes made to their flagship product, Tropicana Pure Premium orange juice. The re-designed packaging that was introduced in early January was discontinued and the previous version brought back in the next month.

'We underestimated the deep emotional bond' customers had with the original packaging, they explained at the time. 'Those consumers are very important to us, so we responded.' The new pack lasted only seven weeks before PepsiCo pulled it, following complaints from disgruntled Tropicana consumers. Perhaps more to the point, according to an article in *The New York Times*, Tropicana's sales fell 20 per cent, down $33million (though there is no hard evidence that this is linked to the pack change – though engram research would seem to support it).

Among those who underestimated that bond was Neil Campbell, President at Tropicana North America in Chicago, part of PepsiCo Americas Beverages. In an interview to discuss the new packaging, he said: 'The straw and orange have been there for a long time, but people have not necessarily had a huge connection to them.'

Reminded of that, Mr Campbell had said he added: 'What we didn't get was the passion this very loyal small group of consumers have. That wasn't something that came out in the research.'

Seven Simple Rules for Marketing

Byron Sharp, author of *How Brands Grow* (Oxford University Press, 2010), following Ehrenburg measurement principles, has established seven rules for successful marketers (republished here with permission):

RULE 1: REACH

Reach all shoppers/consumers of the brands service or product category, both with physical distribution and marketing communication. All these people are potential buyers of the brand.

RULE 2: BE EASY TO BUY

Physical and mental availability drive market share (be there, and be seen to be there) as they make a brand easier to buy, in more situations, across time and space. Your brand needs to be where people would expect to see it. Just signing a contract with a retailer is not the end of the process – getting it onto the right shelves and keeping it there is an ongoing responsibility.

The penalty for disappointing people reasonably expecting to find a product where they shop can be severe. The IGD figures for this are given in Chapter 6.

In the US, Leo J. Shapiro and Associates reported that 20 per cent of shoppers disappointed by not being able to find a brand continued their search at another store while another 20 per cent delayed a purchase. Meanwhile those who bought substitutes spent 6 per cent less for the alternatives.

Non-availability represents a 'lose–lose' for brands and retailers alike. (Reported in 'PromoCast A new Forecasting Method for Promotion Planning' *Marketing Science* for University of California at Los Angeles.)

RULE 3: GET NOTICED

In an age of multimedia getting the message out has never been easier, but getting it across, never harder. Shoppers regularly avoid advertising et al. media. So embed an engram.

RULE 4: REFRESH AND BUILD APPROPRIATE MEMORY STRUCTURES

Re-invigorate and remind enhancing the engram.

RULE 5: CREATE AND USE DISTINCTIVE BRAND ASSETS

In-store, as the Tropicana example clearly indicates, shoppers navigate by what they instinctively recognise. The product had not changed in the case of

Tropicana, but the appearance of the product certainly had. Research shows that shoppers navigate stores using brand images they are familiar with (the engram). Shoppers expect these brands to be easy to see – even if they do not choose to buy (possibly substituting cheaper or own brand options).

Sharp isolates three reasons why a distinctive brand asset is so important. It is something a customer can be loyal to, as well as pick out in a crowd, it allows shoppers to tie this back to advertising, and, of course, as a result of the first two attributes, it gives stand out. However, standout can also be acquired temporarily by grafting on a well-known and sympathetic image. The Wallace and Grommit and Marmite examples both gave positive pack benefits, while the brand image for 'Britain's Got Talent' negative ones. It is, of course, possible to measure and predict the impact on the eye of pack or brand asset change. Companies such as P&G wisely insist on an 'eyeball' check before any pack is changed.

RULE 6: BE CONSISTENT, YET FRESH

Brands outlive people, and companies. They do this by delivering a consistent message across generations. However, this consistent message needs to be constantly re-imagined to get cut through to new generations of potential users/consumers.

RULE 7: STAY COMPETITIVE – DON'T GIVE A REASON NOT TO BUY

In the UK in the current climate, key fmcg brands are on discount at retail over 90 per cent of the time. However, many companies have found that merely dropping the price does not bring the same level of sales as a discount does. Nor, paradoxically, does it actually lessen the need for discounts – even own brands are discounted.

This is in part because discounts, while run on brands, are not necessarily run for a brand's benefit. Supermarket chains vie with each other to prove that they offer the best value for their shoppers. Much of this comes down to retailer perception that shoppers like offers as a substitute for value. As a result, marketing strategy needs to encompass the thought that, for the moment, discount offers, like death and taxes are always with us.

Under these circumstances, brands need to focus on getting the best value for money from their discount events, while making sure that their core users – the loyalists who would buy at full price – are not disappointed in discount availability.

Key Features of a Successful Marketing Plan

MEASURE EVERYTHING

A marketing plan needs to be measured, in an increasingly data heavy world. You will want to look at appeals to the shopper that maintain and build your image and brand values, alongside those that bring them to prominence at the POP. The latter approaches can all be measured for their varying effectiveness, and should be. (Check out the *Value for Money Marketing* – new edition about to be written – by Roddy Mullin.)

The ability to measure is coming on in leaps and bounds. However, few companies actually audit the resources they do have available.

SET APPROPRIATE TARGETS

Nowadays it is easier than ever to identify where your core customers are, and lay out a strategy to reach them. Whether you are B2B or B2C, database management should be core to where you are and a base for where you are going.

However, it is important to distinguish yet again, the Rumsfeld factor.

KNOW WHO YOUR SHOPPER REALLY IS

Often a product finds another market from that intended at the time the product was imagined. Examples of this would be Organix products – primarily bought by young, organic caring mothers for their children. However, analysis of purchasing patterns shows a heavy loading in stores frequented by a high proportion of grandparent-age upmarket shoppers. While this may not change the focus of the advertising, it does leave open the chance for sampling gift packs at gifting times.

KNOW WHERE YOUR CORE CUSTOMERS ARE AND WHERE THEY SHOP

Identify the stores. Market to people in and around core stores. See Chapter 10.

KNOW HOW YOUR PRODUCT IS PURCHASED

Times are changing. For high ticket items increasingly the shopper browses in a high street store but purchases online. However an item bought in a convenience store has a fraction of a second to make an impact. (Remember research shows this to be 0.9 of a second!)

How much of the process is considered and discussed with other people, and how much is purchased after viewing comparison sites, or special interest sites such as mumsnet?

If you know the touch points of your brand it can be very easy to get a positive outcome from your spend.

KNOW WHAT YOUR SHOPPER IS LIKE WHEN THEY PURCHASE

The shopper modes have been described in Chapter 7. The way that they take in messages depends on stress levels (Chapter 18 describes this).

KNOW WHAT THE SHOPPERS FEEL ABOUT YOUR PRODUCT WHEN THEY HAVE USED IT

Many promotions as well as online activities have the potential to give real feedback on the reaction to tastings and the usage experience. Advocates for your product can crop up all over the place.

On the other hand, people not liking what they find can also find a voice they could not use in the past – complaining through social media.

KNOW THE TRUE DISCOUNT PERFORMANCE OF YOUR PRODUCT AND THE TRUE COST OF THE ADDITIONAL SALES YOU MAKE

Research carried out by author Colin Harper with the IPM in the UK revealed the vast gulf between discount events with proper stock support – and that without it. This was reported in 'In Place of Price' (IPM 2011). The downside to the non-availability that also caused the poor performance is covered elsewhere in this book (see Chapter 10). However, if brands need to run discount events (which they do) then maximising the performance could offer the chance of getting both better predictability, as well as less cost (given the key money that often accompanies such events). A clear case where less is more; *less* events, giving *more* sales.

Proper discount event performance is an important task for the marketing department wanting to reach effectively more people, and reduce attrition.

Pull the Organisation Together

It is often surprising that one part of an organisation can have information that would help another to succeed. An example of that is in the UK where under half of all fmcg marketing managers make use of the store by store EPOS data that is freely available to their companies to measure marketing impact. This information, however, shows how poor actual distribution can be in core retailers, as well as how poor availability is. This is covered in Chapter 10.

A Recap

The key lessons from Parts I and II to remind you (Do You Dare to Be Different? – see Chapter 13) are:

It seems clear that the shopper's purchase decision is made in the main below the threshold of consciousness.

1. Planting an engram in the shopper's brain is something that can be achieved by both B2B suppliers or brands or retail outlets. The engram acts as the focus for thoughts and feelings to the brand. An engram build can be triggered by sampling, but to remain and be useful it needs to be reinforced by attitudes linking it to the rest of the buying universe.

2. There is a need in this age for 'other shopper' peer input and advice, to reinforce trust and obtain user views and experience of the product or service. The retailer/supplier has to have, therefore, an active presence on social media sites placing messages that respond, and consistently, to shopper viewers about their brand.

3. The existing repeat shopper needs a relationship with the supplier/retailer which can be provided by sending out catalogues, mailshots, e-mails, mobile alerts and the occasional really good offer to tempt a further purchase. Building trust and data capture on the shopper are this stage's objectives.

4. Local outdoor signage or advertising gently reminds the shopper approaching an outlet of what is potentially available in-store though their engram recollection. Local to any store, therefore, advertising and signs should be used. The use of leaflets, handouts, local support from other retail outlets and local newspapers are ways to remind shoppers of local outlets. Local advertising needs to be in place for events, road shows, demonstrations or promotions. The retailer needs to increase the store presence locally to ESOV level.

5. In-store the retailer, with the supplier, can have a field day with on-pack, on-shelf and surrounding POP displays and retailer or supplier-initiated sales promotions. Remember the recorded research shows 70 per cent of the purchase decisions are made 'in-store', taking account of the influence of the subconscious engram, but the barriers to purchase – for example a failure to stock and place on-shelf – offers the shopper a chance to pick alternative 'on promotion' products or the services of competitors.

6. Add a sales promotion.

The need for collaboration between supplier and retailer has been described earlier.

The Next Chapters in Part III

Part III, here, comes up with answers. This Part is about how *you* can do it, and what the industry thinks about the next five years. So having looked in Part I at the players and drivers – the customer and their preferred communication means and message format, the facilitators with their channels and media available and the barriers to purchase – then in Part II examining the shopper journey starting from outside 'the store' and continuing all the way to purchase, what is the solution to placing the appropriate messages to the customer through what media and at what points in the shopper journey to ultimately persuade the shopper to buy your product or service rather than competitor offerings?

Targeting Better is Best

As an overview – you need to optimise the effort. This is achieved by limiting the number of stores or outlets you consider each time. Too large a number of stores or too large an area – the effort does not work and the target shopper is unidentifiable. Only a small focused team can deliver the result.

Tracking the Shopper Journey

The shopper makes two journeys. One is the actual journey from the home to the store. The second is a virtual journey from 'wholly unaware' to 'satisfied purchaser on a regular basis'.

That the two can complement each other is shown by IPA research that shows the content of successful campaigns.

Discover if, in the company, 'we have anyone who has tracked a shopper' that we can use.

In Chapter 17 the power of three is described, where advertising viewed in a relaxed environment is three times more likely to be noticed by the shopper.

Where are Your Core Stores to Focus On?

Core stores are surrounded by more people likely to buy than non-core stores. For some companies, the difference might be slight. For others the difference can be vast. See Chapter 10.

Pick your core stores. Research and profile the customers that use that store. You need then to stock the brands, products and services those profiled customers prefer. (Part III shows you how to research shoppers and persuade suppliers to support you.) Then, the authors believe, you should concentrate on six (not three, as recommended by the IPA) communications with the shopper. After building the engram and ensuring social media is on-side, you need an advertising awareness initiative – locally to the store applied (outdoor, local TV or radio, or newspapers), with local to the store 'direct marketing' to the local individual shoppers. You need to use any personal databases to communicate with the local shopper as individuals (mobile, e-mail) ideally as part of relationship building and you need to ensure that stocking levels are correct and shelf facings are in place with some in-store promotion display. Finally, if you are a brand supplier, an on-pack message or sales promotion (not necessarily a price discount) is required.

In other words, by segmenting people and the stores they use, limiting your communications to the local area with some direct and general promotion, and in-store preparedness and communicating the product promotion in-store and on-pack, you become a focused Shopper Marketing Organisation. Find your core stores, access that from data you already have and find the media you could use – and remember to measure the impact.

Chapter 15
The Shopper Marketing Organisation

Supposedly, the organisational structure of businesses at the millennium (2000) was evolving from the hierarchical and silo structures that had worked for previous generations, into the flatter, holistic, increasingly agile, shape of businesses being made ready for the twenty-first century. To supply this business need – whereas they had previously used existing trades and skills to establish a workforce organisation competent to perform all the operations a business required – new multi-skilled persons were sought to undertake tasks that change flexibly in scope and constantly require the learning of new skills. The rate of change of technology, especially in communication, and the rise of the supremacy of the customer and the customer expectation of service, have meant that no longer can any part of the business hide from customer involvement, so staff have to have a customer-facing capability too. This has increased the need to keep all staff up to date with internal changes and awareness of the customers of the firm.

But has the structure of businesses changed?

Sadly the reality is, just like the 61 per cent of firms which, according to research findings that are not measuring marketing effectiveness, many firms still operate their businesses as hierarchies and with silos. Staff are not trained to deal with modern customers, nor are they kept up to date with a firm or organisation's brand or marketing. All organisations need to deal with these problems and focus on the customer.

The story of Virgin One Account in Chapter 6 is not unique. Virgin Media also have silos that operate online and at different call centres that do not communicate internally. The operator rules are inflexible (they can take no initiative such as overriding IT automated responses) and clearly the training is poor from the different stories that emerge each time when dealing with staff in customer services, accounts, collections and a silo that 'looks for sums paid in to Virgin Media' to name a few. The Virgin Media marketing silo, of course, at the same time sends out door-to-door letters seeking new customers – but these are intensely frustrating to existing customers who see fantastic offers that, as loyal customers, they are unable to take up. Then there is the clear impression that there is innate distrust of the customer when talking to staff even when they are supposedly 'valued'.

There should be no silos.

And what about central control? The Waitrose example and others quoted show central control is not the answer. Because of the need to match the customer, either local or niche, the decisions on what to stock and how to operate must be delegated to the local manager. She or he must be a trained collaborator, capable of working with all suppliers and the organisation's internal support services, from delivery through merchandising and marketing – able to handle the myriad of promotions that run throughout the year as well as conduct local or niche research into customers and understand and act on the findings. There needs to be a two-way dialogue with the centre. Zara does this well in the world of fashion. Others such as dressipi.com are similarly heading to a full meshing with the customer – really understanding them as shoppers, then supplying their needs.

And where should a firm be to be ready to take on the market in 2013? IBM envisages the Chief Marketing Officer (CMO) as the person that marries the culture of the organisation, the brand and customer data. Interestingly, as part of restoring focus, Unilever, under Keith Weed, CMO, completely removed the corporate social responsibility department, declaring the task as universal – the responsibility of all.

As to the size and shape of an organisation, an examination of the databases of professional organisations finds that there is an optimum ratio for maximising profit between the number of fee earners, technical support and administration staff. The ratio changes over time and needs to be regularly updated. This ratio can be applied to engineering consultancies and then to other professions. The ratio has changed over the years as technology has reduced the need for the latter categories using software as a replacement. The ratios can be applied to the medical professions, engineers, solicitors and accountants. One very large professional engineering consultancy firm with a surprisingly out of skew ratio and consequent poor profitability was forecast to go into administration, and it did a few years later as the problem was not addressed.

Managing people – leadership – and determining an appropriate people specification is often not considered as a strategic necessity, particularly for customer or client-facing posts. People often tend to be employed to meet a workload shortfall and then stay on or carry out an extra task (often essential) which is handed to an existing staff member without the management being aware that this has occurred. Experience of working with solicitors' offices found that many legal professionals in effect work alone. They have scant knowledge or experience of managing people. The people employed as solicitors' receptionists are not trained to handle potential clients in what is nearly always a stress-related purchase. Here sympathy is replaced by the receptionist's perception that the task requires them to keep the public away from the legal professionals at all costs. In another profession, one receptionist with a remit to be welcoming and friendly, who was excellent at the task in a large IT office, was handed the key to the stationery cupboard by the accounts manager – as it was close by – and of course the very welcoming and friendly receptionist allowed office staff to help themselves. Only after the cupboard was bare and thousands of pounds of stationery had vanished, did management realise that 'control of stationery' was not part of the receptionist's job description, nor appropriate to her lovely welcoming and friendly demeanour for which she had been recruited as a customer-facing person.

Local or Niche Empowerment and Action

This book concludes that local or niche-focused organisation is the best place to increase profitability. As an outlet manager, wherever you work and face customers/shoppers (even in a bank, even online) you need to persuade the centre, the boss, the area management, that you need to have delegated powers. Next make sure that your shopper has an engram in their subconscious that your outlet is their prime choice for whatever it is you sell. In order to serve the shopper, decisions on what to stock or the service to offer and what to put out on promotion, requires data about your shoppers. You probably need a data controller who works directly for you and keeps you (and the staff) updated on what the shoppers purchase. If you can afford it from your budget you may commission local research. Your data controller may be able to extract data from a central database to find out how your exclusive shoppers shop and/or buy your services. Your staff needs to have a culture ingrained in them that they are the key interface with the shopper. They need to report back on shopper behaviour – what they say and ask for, what they hover over, what they have on their wish list. The till will report what they actually buy. To shape and control the culture should remain the focus of your bailiwick. Lead by example – also talk and listen to your shopper/customers.

Implementation

1. Remove silos – the top level of management should just oversee and consider strategy (see Chapter 20) – and to do this they need to be informed about shopper/customers in great detail. The company focus should be on the buyer/shopper – for only they provide income. The annual report should include marketing information. It is a little acted on statistic, but shopper 'bonding with the brand' is a better forecaster of future company performance than financial data. (Investors please note!)

2. Go for local – the organisation should empower those who control the outlets that interface with the buyer/shopper. They need to be trained (as above) and trained to understand research findings and how to listen to customers. If they are unable to take on the workload they would need a team member to coordinate sales promotions and employ a customer (research/customer and sales data) analyst. Within the team a change manager capable of leading change (whether it is re-labelling for a new VAT rate or physically moving categories) is required as is a stock/replenishment manager, an HR person and an administrator/finance person who also oversees contract services. The outlet team all need to learn how to lead. (See *Learn How to Lead* by Roddy Mullin.)

3. Train all staff to be customer facing and keep them updated.

4. When the strategy concludes that a change is required in the operation, as it will, then the change manager should prepare for and oversee the change.

5. The above would suggest that at the level above the outlets (online or offline), as the outlets are customer facing, they would report to the CMO who also has the marketing support team within his/her bailiwick. There is an operations support team led by an Operations Support Officer (OSO) which covers the remainder. A business development person is concerned with the future, considering change and procurement. The Board level should only be concerned with strategy consideration and decision taking.

As an aside, where a start up is contemplated, the person in charge too should learn how to lead from day one – research by the IITT in conjunction with Go Lead Ltd (www.helmsmanship.co.uk) shows that an entrepreneur who knows how to lead will succeed earlier with a greater chance of success. Clearly, as their organisation grows, the entrepreneur should empower operations managers and concentrate on strategy. An understanding of marketing is essential, understanding the findings of this book is important too.

Chapter 16

Measuring Effectiveness

The in-store POP survey (June 2013) finds that 86 per cent of brands use sales uplift as the measure of POP success though they recognise this is probably inaccurate. Only about 25 per cent of POP projects are measured in depth and of these only 44 per cent go on to establish ROI. Many would still rather invest in more POP than do any measuring.

Measurement was for many years scorned – particularly by advertisers who felt it was better to spend what might have been spent measuring on more advertising. There is the famous quote about 50 per cent of advertising being wasted but not knowing which 50 per cent. But now as a result of EPOS and data collection it is possible to measure the effectiveness of marketing. This is particularly important to record for future campaigns. A log of each marketing element has to be recorded: at minimum details of what it was, its spend, its duration, its target and the result. The key to measurement is to keep it simple. Do not use jargon or academic mathematical formulae, except for those who are specifically tasked to provide the management with Insights – which itself should be couched in simple terms – into marketing activity effectiveness.

Dealing with Accountability

The importance of being able to demonstrate that the marketing communications budget is not being wasted is covered here, suggesting ways to measure effectiveness – ensuring marketing spend is contributing to the bottom line. One author, Roddy Mullin, has spent time with clients devising ways to measure the effectiveness of marketing communications because of the difficulty of relating it to ROI in the short term. The problem is that there is a time lapse, particularly with B2B campaigns, because of the human psyche. No buyer is going to switch 100 per cent to a new supplier until they are certain that delivery, price, product reliability and quality are assured. That takes time. The buyer's job depends on the reassurance from successful trading. A small test order is placed and if all is well then the following order sizes are increased. But there are ways of measuring – matching a new customer's profile to existing good customers – which a finance director can undertake. So effectiveness can be measured in indirect ways.

First, the need and belief in measuring marketing effectiveness must come from the top – the Board, the chairman and the managing firector. This is an early strategy decision to make – if not already made – all marketing activity will be measured for effectiveness and the result recorded in a log for future access. Second, for each element of marketing (or sales) expenditure, someone must be made responsible for it and that responsibility must include a statement of the expected outcome and, most importantly, the measure to be applied to determine whether the outcome has been achieved or not. The actual measurement is carried out by someone else – preferably in finance and the log held by finance too. To incentivise the success of the responsible individual, just as a promotion incentivises a shopper, the outcome is taken as part of the individual's annual assessment appraisal – in other words achievement of marketing effectiveness is a work objective.

If the authors' proposal to adopt core stores in local areas is adopted, then most of the effectiveness is relatively easy to measure. The spend on the ESOV advertising, the cost of any promotion, can be assessed fairly rapidly against the data on increased shopper spending as a result – and all this is readily measured by finance.

It would be easy to load a marketing activity with indirect costs – extra staff to fill shelves for example, but this would be wrong. Marketing costs should be seen as different from operating costs and treated as revenue expenditure, in the way that it costs the same to run a store when it is open, as a generality, whatever marketing (or sales) activity occurs.

B2B is different. Marketing effectiveness is not so readily measured because of the very human sensitivity of buyers to avoid making mistakes on purchases. If tasked to obtain new clients, a B2B marketer (or salesperson) should still forecast the outcome of marketing activity and expect finance to measure the effectiveness. ROI is not measurable in B2B because no buyer working for an employer is going to switch in toto to a new supplier on a whim, but will first place a small test order. Subsequent orders will increase if all is well with product, service and delivery acceptability confirmed. So what to measure? The marketer must supply finance with a profile of existing 'good' clients. When test purchases arrive then finance should check the profile of any new client against the preferred client profile. If it matches, then the marketing activity has been effective – the marketer can be rewarded. In the long term – say two years – there will be an impact on the bottom line, assuming that the new client is properly pursued by the sales team in the interim.

Measuring Improvement

Many companies use second-remove measures to divine success in activity. The problem with associated change that is not financial is well illustrated in The Rosser Reeves Fallacy.

'Follow your audience' is the fundamental mantra of media planning. Today, that audience is spread increasingly wide and thin, and the fact that an audience is present on a media platform does not necessarily mean that advertising there is effective. The evaluation of media's effectiveness is the single biggest issue for planners today (or at least advertisers hope it is) and there are a variety of effects that contribute to the confusion surrounding it. One common mistake is confusing cause and effect which is a specific example of the Questionable Cause Fallacy (QCF). See Chapter 6.

The question posed in Chapter 6 was 'Is there a direct lesson for media here?' Yes. All media suffers the same plight: namely that more often than not, proxy measures such as brand and advertising awareness are used to measure effectiveness. 'Yes I saw the advert and noticed the brand' is not the answer that a brand manager, supplier or retailer needs. They are not true measures of effectiveness of a brand and its advertising, unless the shopper actually then buys the brand. The key measure for success, over any other, might be, 'I saw the ad for A and so I bought brand A.' This book clearly shows that retailers should measure real sales as a result of any combination of the six communications advocated here and then compare that with all six communications being applied together – if the authors are correct – only all six applied will produce the optimum return. This should be relatively easy to test if a core store is selected and the shopper Insights obtained so the brand sales can be measured with relationships built, with social media on side and the store stocked and displaying the brand offering some form of sales promotion.

Stock Measurement

The management concern is to figure out what to order by way of stock for an upcoming promotion event. The scale of the problem can be daunting with typically 20 million promotions over two and a half years against a 150,000 UPC. The length of the promotion is important (sales will vary from day to day and week by week) as is the promotional mix. Is the promotion to be advertised, direct marketing used, is there a discount and a POP display? Is the store one which often has promotions, has the product been promoted before, what about the time of year and the seasonality of the promotion? Certain categories move slower than others when promoted. Combinations of major, minor or no ad, with a major, minor or no display have quite different sales profiles over each week. Cooper, Baron, Levy, Swisher and Gogos consider 69 variables in their promotion planning forecast model.

You can stack promotions on top of discount events to bring people into the stores.

Summary

SPECIFIC MEASUREMENTS

Just for completeness, measuring the six recommended opportunity message points:

- The engram is best measured through analysis of social media under the eight category headings (as used to measure the response to the 2013 Easter egg fiasco). A specialist firm such as Spectrum Insight (see the Appendix) can assist.

- The ESOV (as described above), if applied to a core store as recommended in this book and plotting (increased sales) against the days when the advertising applied, particularly if it was used with a promotion.

- Relationship marketing should be measured against coded shopper responses; that is supplying a shopper with a code to enter at the time of purchase.

- Social media effectiveness – same as for the engram.

- POS effectiveness again will be seen as increased purchase of product.

- Any promotion – an increased purchase of the promoted product should be recorded.

As an aside, should the stock run out, it will be possible to record the drop in sales of product – compared to times when product availability for the shopper was 100 per cent. Social media and eye tracking will record adverse shopper reaction (Easter eggs!) to a failure to stock (be prepared for a shock!).

DON'T FORGET THE LOGGING JOB

Remember that any marketing activity and the result should be logged and retained for future use when planning further promotions.

Chapter 17

Researching the Consumer/ Customer 'in Their Community'

I notice increasing reluctance on the part of marketing executives to use judgment; they are coming to rely too much on research, and they use it as a drunkard uses a lamp post for support, rather than for illumination.

David Ogilvy

Preamble to Chapters 17, 18 and 19

Any marketer realises that to produce products and services that sell and to communicate meaningfully with their customers, they need to carry out research. Research, however, is only beneficial if it provides customer Insight into – what, how, where, when (The Offer – Chapter 3) – they might purchase and what communications persuade them (Part II of this book).

But there is further dimension to research. The power of the retailers in the UK with their retailer-based research, which has spread widely around the world, has meant that brands and suppliers not only need research for self-enlightenment but also for presenting to retailers, to gain retailer support and to place their products in-store or online. Few companies have the budget for pure research, so any research by those undertaking it, culminating in Insight, needs to be marketable far and wide. The question for marketers then is: 'What research can you actually commission or use that will deliver broadly valuable insights?'

The subject of research that provides Insight is complex and marketers, as they delve into what they should do about it, tend to shy away from undertaking any, or rely on agencies (how often are they fully briefed by the marketer?), or just repeat the formula used for previous years ('but we always have a sale then', 'we always advertise there'). Marketers need to 'bite the bullet' and think about what they need to know. Research providing Insights is further complicated by the fact that the consumer as a shopper can be influenced by the retailer, so pure research into the customer can be invalidated because the shopper/customer changes their mind in-store or online at the POS as the result of some retailer activity. The authors have discussed at length how to present their findings to the reader on the subject of gaining Insights and decided, for ease of understanding, to write three separate chapters even though they know the decision is flawed, because research and Insight of these three parameters are interlinked in every way.

Gaining Insight

Research is, or should be, designed to bring *communicable Insight*. Insight gives you a new view of your problem that allows you to move forward. Insight is a function of the interpreter and of the user, and not inherent in the research. Judgement brings you Insight, research delivers facts. Insight is not the same thing as research.

There are basically three types of research (hence the three chapters) that companies could involve themselves in: consumer/customer research per se (who is your customer?), in the shop – shopper research (the consumer/customer in the shopping/purchasing environment – both in-store and online) and retailer research (information gleaned by the retailer from their own data about shopper preferences and purchases).

The first research type is to do with the individual shopper/buyer, and revolves around their view of the product, the usage experience, the advertising messages they have seen and their future intentions. This is something only a business can investigate from its knowledge of who its customers are (that can be researched too!) and such – usually commissioned – research will provide valuable Insights into how to communicate with their customers, what their customers want by way of products and services and the delivery, and how to best to establish a relationship with their customers (The Offer – Chapter 3). Researching the shopper as customer/buyer, to gain Insights, needs to cover: 'before entering the store' or going online and the way the shopper goes about their search; their experience of the purchase, in-store or online; and then their experience of the service or product itself post-purchase (social media/feedback). It is all part of the view from the customer. The customer/buyer as shopper research is covered in this chapter.

The second area to look at is the in-store behaviour or the way the shopper reacts to their shopping environment in-store/on the website – through observing how they react to the layout, the positioning of product and so on. The retailer can influence this. The research here looks at shopper behaviour in the store and at the facing (see Chapter 10). This can be very powerful, and deliver important uplifts from change. Mostly these are camera-based, either fixed in the store or eye tracking. Eye-tracking research is covered in Chapter 18.

A third area is to look at the retail side: the store EPOS data. This information is generated as a result of the sale and is not, per se, research into the shopper. This is, therefore, covered in Chapter 18. On top of this you have information from shopper actions, such as social media reporting or on-pack promotion take-up. This comes from the research into availability issues and work with yousay, also given in Chapter 19. More singular research such as neurophysiological and accompanied shopping is also available to the retailer.

Customer Research

First, looking at research of the shopper customer, this book has already provided Insights into what other businesses have achieved. The specific case study that follows provides an example of the results that Intersperience Research provided for Virgin Atlantic. For further information and contact details for Intersperience Research see the Appendix.

So How Can the Marketer Obtain Insights on Their Shopper Customer?

One of the downfalls of conventional research is that the questions are provided by the researcher. Often the shopper has problems that may not be properly understood simply because the right question is not being asked.

The current plethora of opinions on the web in Twitter, Facebook and others are, of course, well known, but how can they be used to produce a reliable and consistent picture of what real consumers and shoppers actually feel?

What is needed is to turn the mass opinions you can find into something more tangible and measured that you can really work with. There are a number of search engines and companies offering feedback on these opinions. However, what is needed is some academic rigour in showing that these can actually be measured and to deliver correlated Insights into shopper behaviour.

CASE STUDY – VIRGIN ATLANTIC: RESEARCH CARRIED OUT BY INTERSPERIENCE

Sector: Aviation

Country: UK-based+ offices worldwide

Employees: 9,000

Website: www.virgin-atlantic.com

Insight provided for Head of Product and Service, Virgin Atlantic.

Intersperience services utilised

- International research;
- Customised research;
- Board presentation.

'Intersperience has a very different model – an international skill base, multi-language team and strong cultural insight and knowledge. It gives them a critical ability to explain the "why" behind the "what".'

Business need

Virgin needed to determine how cultural differences impacted on passengers' perceptions of their journeys on flights to Nigeria, China, Japan and India, where customer satisfaction scores lagged other routes. The airline wanted to ensure that all passengers, regardless of cultural background, enjoyed a world-class experience with Virgin.

Solution

Intersperience conducted in-depth research into passengers' experiences from check-in to arrival, using mixed methodology including face-to-face interviews, diaries, in-flight observations and an online survey. A multicultural and multilingual team accompanied passengers and crew on each route, accurately identifying every cultural nuance affecting customer satisfaction.

Benefits

- produced independent authoritative Insight on passenger experience;
- helped secure Board support for resources and service enhancements;
- resulted in new cultural awareness training for staff;
- identified requirement for changes in in-flight entertainment and menus;
- paved way for upturn in passenger satisfaction on targeted routes.

Delivering superior customer service is in the DNA of the Virgin brand, underpinning Virgin Atlantic's status as one of the world's most popular airlines. The airline has a simple mission statement:

'To grow a profitable airline where people love to fly and where people love to work.'

The Virgin Customer Experience Team has particular responsibility for ensuring that every passenger, regardless of their cultural background, has a great experience. The team decided to engage a consultancy to ascertain the extent to which cultural issues affect passengers' experiences and decided to focus on routes where cultural differences were greatest. Virgin needed a consultancy capable of tackling a complex multinational project with a team of native language researchers. It also required a consultancy with broad research capabilities and techniques, a deep understanding of multicultural issues, and the ability to deliver actionable Insight within a challenging timeframe. Virgin decided that Intersperience fitted the bill.

Intersperience then worked with Virgin to devise a wide-ranging study which included detailed research into the experiences of passengers and ground and cabin crew on flights to Lagos, Shanghai, Tokyo and Delhi. The mixed methodology project was designed to cover the entire customer experience from check-in to boarding procedures, safety briefings, in-flight entertainment, meals, and arrival at the destination. Research techniques included face-to-face interviews with 160 passengers and also 40 crew, as well as diaries, observations and an online survey.

Intersperience matched native speakers to routes, which meant that passengers and researchers had a shared cultural heritage, allowing them to pick on cultural nuances. The brief was to ascertain whether the current customer offering was sufficiently relevant and enjoyable and, if not, where it fell short.

Intersperience identified several cultural issues which had a significant impact on satisfaction, including meal choices, in-flight entertainment and the presence of native language crew aboard planes, as well as subtle differences affecting staff–passenger communication – including tone and volume of speech and body language.

Virgin said: 'We found that apparently little differences matter and we gained a new appreciation of how different cultures rate different things ... The research absolutely helped us secure resources to address the issues because it was based on objective third party data which was respected enough to be taken seriously at board level by Virgin.'

The research led to a number of changes being introduced by Virgin, including new cultural awareness training to enable crews to deliver a more positive passenger experience as well as new in-flight menus and entertainment offerings. Virgin also decided to recruit more native language crew on certain routes where this was important. The airline saw a marked increase in customer satisfaction scores following the implementation of these changes.

Virgin said: 'Our directors were all very supportive because it addressed a performance issue for passengers and enabled us to make things better for them.'

At this point they would become really useful tools as they can potentially replace two stages of research – the focus group looking for pressure points and the right questions to answer, and the actual quantitative research itself.

Cranfield University in the UK are leaders in marketing thinking, and they have looked at an approach called Qualimetrics from Spectrum Insight.

This looks at Twitter data and the prevalence of certain words as indicative of the state of mind. This has a real resonance with the way that words are used in looking at the mindset of shoppers via semiotics (definition in Chapter 2, also see Chapter 18 on shopper research in the shop).

MEASURING EMOTIONS USING TWITTER DATA

Twitter data is captured by web crawlers. These develop real-time feedback on a brand and a related emotion.

Emotions can be identified in Twitter data using a computerised content-analysis tool called the Regressive-Imagery Dictionary (RID). The RID tool was developed and verified by academics several decades ago (Martindale 1975). This dictionary contains 3,200 words and seven emotional categories (Table 17.1). (Note: Other companies use eight categories.)

Table 17.1 Seven emotional categories

Emotion	Example Words
Positive affect	Cheerful, enjoy, fun
Anxiety	Afraid, fear, phobic
Sadness	Depression, dissatisfied, lonely
Affection	Affectionate, marriage, sweetheart
Aggression	Angry, harsh, sarcasm
Expressive behaviour	Art, dance, sing
Glory	Admirable, hero, royal

Source: Martindale 1975.

Furthermore, as each Twitter comment is date-stamped it is feasible to match aggregated Twitter data with aggregate behavioural measures at specific points in time. Plotting these measures over time allows us to draw conclusions about the impact of consumer feelings and perceptions on brand performance.

All the Tweets on a particular theme, such as excitement, bad service, high prices or executive pay, are then divided into time periods, such as weeks or days (or even hours of the day). Increasing or decreasing volumes of Tweets can help spot critical trends such as the failure of a newly created marketing campaign or a potential PR crisis boiling up. (It was possible to foresee the departure of the Barclays Chief executive.)

This Qualimetric data quantifying volumes of Tweets on important qualitative themes can then be matched statistically with measures of brand performance, such as brand consideration and sales to see how much these trends matter.

Cranfield took as their basis Aaker's (1997) five dimensions of branding:

Table 17.2 Five dimensions of branding

Brand Personality Dimension	Traits
Competence	Reliable, responsible, dependable, efficient
Sincerity	Domestic, honest, genuine, cheerful
Excitement	Daring, spirited, imaginative, up to date
Sophistication	Glamorous, pretentious, charming, romantic
Ruggedness	Tough, strong, outdoorsy, rugged

Source: Aakers 1997.

Developing a Time-Based Tracking System

Taking these five measures, they produced a high quantity of feedback over time (see Table 17.2), which they were able to place into the bins in the Aaker's dimensions.

One aspect typically missing from qualitative feedback is a linkage to eventual result, and Cranfield cast around to find a published source of sales data they could link the 'over time' data they were having fed back.

Using two independent measures of Waitrose success – sales and Twitter contemporary feedback – they first built a picture of what was driving the average Waitrose shopper. They found that the lead emotion was excitement, followed by competence. Interestingly, competence was not closely associated with the Tesco profile.

Given that Twitter feeds have the main objective of bringing friends and followers up to date, and not to be the grist for the researchers mill, it may be expected that high quantities of praise relates to a shared good experience. Meanwhile, bad experiences also travel well.

Cranfield found that excitement such as with finding something new or a special treat was highly correlated with positive sales uplift. Meanwhile experience and self-esteem were negatively correlated to sales.

So, poor service, making you feel small, and not finding what you wanted would reduce sales.

Tracking both together explained 53 per cent of the variance over 12 months, while just the good experiences (excitement) on their own, 42 per cent. These correlations are at a very high level indeed (over 99.9999 per cent).

Cranfield commented that this strong correlation between the Waitrose value-in-use categories and sales performance demonstrates the usefulness of Electronic Word of Mouth (eWOM).

This may be the first time that you can actually get qualitative data behaving like quantitative data.

It is early days yet, but this might be used to track the impact of advertising in a way that could be related directly (although possible with a time lag) to sales.

It could also track the impact of the message – with the caution that, of course, advertising with no discernable message has proven to be very successful.

Lastly, close inspection of change in the volume of tweets and their nature could be used to track the impact of marketing techniques designed to stimulate people-to-people talking (providing that the right kind of tweets can be benchmarked in advance quality *and* quantity).

This interpersonal communication remains a vital element in marketing. The impact of local communities getting behind messages has been very well demonstrated by an award-winning piece of research by the BPS.

The BPS carries out monthly face-to-face omnibus surveys in very carefully matched rolling areas that match the UK population. They build over time, as well as showing local and national trends.

They show the real importance of actual experience and personal recommendation in choosing to shop in one retailer or another.

Shoppers as Part of a Community

THE IMPLICATIONS OF 'STRONG 'NEIGHBOURHOOD INTERACTIONS

Some areas respond much better to certain types of local media than others. BPS also analyse promotion and advertising to spot underlying trends. In working with Red Nose Day (a biennial fundraising, media-supported exercise based on the UK's comedy talent), they analysed the way that different areas responded to the same basic marketing techniques. They then recommended a change in techniques based on individual communities response, and gained a large improvement in the ROI from the activity.

CHARITY: COMIC RELIEF/SPORT RELIEF

Partner: DataTalk, Streetwise Analytics, the BPS

Entry: Sport Relief 2012 registrations – leveraging an 'infectious brand'

Challenge

Comic Relief had a target of over one million participants in the Sport Relief Mile 2012, requiring an increase in registrations of over 33 per cent. Though recruitment budgets were frozen, it was hoped increased attention on sport as a result of the Olympic Games would help.

Solution

Initial focus was on doing what had worked previously as effectively as possible, so Streetwise Analytics worked with DataTalk and the British Marketing Survey (BMS) to refresh the existing household level segmentation and add depth to the understanding of segment communication preferences.

Results

Data exploration driven by Insight derived from BMS consumer engagement tracking enabled exploration of views, opinions and preferences of consumers that live nearby. People who anticipated 'engaging in charity communications' alongside 'health activities' formed localised hot spots, with an index of over 145 compared to conventional intention distributions. This identified the segments most open to engagement with Sport Relief participation.

Historically the database split into two groups: fundraisers who originate events, actively participate and generate sponsorship; and donors who provide revenue mainly via payment on the night of TV events. Fundraisers generated a high proportion of the income and were the traditional focus of all outbound communication activity.

Localised analysis of historic transaction data around participation in and donation to Red Nose Day and Sport Relief showed that, not only are fundraisers much more valuable individually than donors, their presence generated nearly six times the value of revenue from donors. Density of donors is nearly three times higher in the vicinity of a fundraiser, with almost double the value of donations. This fact had never been identified before. Composition of teams involved in Sport Relief events was also explored. Over 60 per cent lived within 400m and intriguingly formed linear-like shapes, indicating local street geography was having an impact.

Fundraisers and donors were matched to Channel Spectrum, a communication preference directory derived by DataTalk from the BMS and other data. Differing preferences for the two groups showed the influential groups were more engaged with direct channels, whereas the passive groups opted out of these but were open to localised communications such as newspapers and leaflets.

Comic Relief explored how supporter engagement could change. A new strategy saw the construction of a marketing directory, used with household demographic segmentation to coordinate communication with active fundraisers and stimulate behaviour of donors/team participants. As a result Comic Relief began to invest in acquisition communications for the first time.

Conclusion

This Insight into the cross-over effect of 'real' neighbourhood relationships completely re-focused CRM activity, and shows how data analysis can fundamentally change the perspective of an organisation. It demonstrates that word-of-mouth communication between supporters, particularly with an 'infectious brand' such as those built by Comic Relief, can cross internal organisation boundaries and generate an unforeseen but significant uplift.

Comic Relief were able to identify completely new communication methods during the subsequent highly successful Sport Relief 2012 campaign. Dramatic effects have been seen, such as an uplift index of nearly 600 for a localised campaign in Belfast, and Comic Relief is now able to extend the reach of their TV exposure.

What the judges said

This project shows a holistic understanding of the relationship between Insight, marketing, human behaviour and brand. The genuine discovery of something new challenged conventional thinking and led to a significant change in the way Comic Relief conducted its communications strategy.

Source: BPS.

Both the last illustration, Twitter feeds and the case study relating to unspecified local interaction, show that interaction tracking is vital.

Identifying the Hidden Persuaders

Typically, in marketing measurement, a model will be devised that assumes that each individual in an analysis set has a series of different attributes – be they demographic, transactional or attitudinal – that can be used to predict propensity to make different purchases or other behaviours. Implicit in these models is that the inevitable variations around the model predictions are random and independent of all other elements of model. This independence assumption is a crucial element of the model that is taken for granted.

In analysing the tail of activity that is normally removed as outliers, they found real significance in communities that clearly talked to each other.

They recommended to the Red Nose Day Organisers a switch to doorstep leaflets. These can be shown to other people and discussed – in which sense they are, like Twitter, social communication. In identifying those locations that were more sensitive to such interpersonal impacts they also reduce the number of household impacts necessary.

A New Grassroots Directory

The findings led to the new strategy beginning with the construction of a grassroots marketing directory, to sit alongside the previous household demographic segmentation. This directory is now able to coordinate the ongoing communication with active fundraisers and stimulates the behaviour of both donors and passive team participants. As a result, for the first time,

Comic Relief began to invest in acquisition communications during the Sport Relief 2012 campaign. This new activity is based on the potential to utilise word of mouth within neighbourhoods – particularly when referring to infectious brands such as Comic Relief.

The effects of these new communications and methods have already been dramatic. For example, a localised campaign in Belfast this year has generated an index of uplift of nearly 600 and allowed Comic Relief to extend the reach of their exposure on the TV.

Summary

It is now possible to track people by their attitudes and actions as well as just their simple demographics. Such targeting can have real impact on both the marketing budget *and* the sales targets.

Chapter 18

Researching the Shoppers' In-Store Behaviour

Even if you're on the right track, you'll get run over if you just sit there.
Will Rodgers

In-Store/on Website Shopper Research

If you are not large enough to do it yourself as a brand, supplier or retailer then you need professional help. As a result, one of the first ports of call for research has to be dunnhumby or Nectar-based research which links the shopping basket to the purchaser. The information they have to offer is drawn from shopping baskets linked in to a geo-demographic view of the person owning the basket derived from their address.

Online/website research is covered in Chapter 17 and in Chapter 7 and from data – following the shopper as they move through the web pages. The impact of the environment is mainly introduced by the individual. This chapter deals with the store.

Obviously, as well, retailers can get a great deal more from looking at the contents of a basket. As an example of this, an area heavily populated with young couples would gain additional meaning if they were buying quantities of nappies and baby food.

There are other sources for information on what the household is like – for example, Nielsen Homescan (National Consumer Panel in the US). Nielsen Homescan has the advantage of covering all the retailers and is basically a diary of purchases, which has the advantage of more Insight into the household, but the disadvantage of less scale, meaning that, if you are a real minority brand, you may not show up in a representative manner, purely because the numbers are too small.

Store information is, of course, freely available as well to the store buyer. There are, however, real advantages in delivering additional Insight to the standard, for the retailer as well as the brand. There are also significantly less expensive ways of getting the same Insight as from the above approaches that might be considered. These can work for any type of retailer.

The Insight here is gained from research that relates to the way that the shopper goes about the process of purchasing. This covers their relationship to the store, the environment the store is in, the pack as they see it in context (and how they themselves go about seeking information before they go out to purchase – covered in Chapter 17). There is much available research here that can be purchased. A large part of this book reflects the acquisition of research published by other sources and developing Insights based on the extensive experience of author Colin Harper.

Of course the shopper may not be the consumer, so one of the influences on the shopper may be the actual consumer. That is, the shopper is buying for the family or for another relative. The difference is important. If there is one thing this book should have shown you it is that many decision processes actually depend on, or are triggered by, the shopping process, whether this is online or offline. What advertising and other forms of conditioning provided in-store by the retailer do is to smooth the way and make the product that is purchased stand out from the rest in the eye of the beholder.

But what research specifically targets the shopper and sheds light on changes that can be made on the Path to Purchase?

Can this research show the way to directly impact more purchases, and can the effect be proven? In Chapter 1 you can see that stacking messaging is additive, but what messages should you stack, what should they be and where? This is the information that shopper research provides.

The Market for Research

Unlike consumer research, shopper research also needs to bear in mind that the owner of the outlet determines the real or virtual availability of a product. The power of retailers in the UK and abroad, and the fact that they also deliver their own shopper research (that has spread widely around the world) shows the importance they place on the shopper. As a result they are a prime target to demonstrate why they should devote more of their space, and prominence to any one, over any other. As well, the brand owner needs to be convinced that investment behind their product is more important than any other.

The best product in the world will die if shelved at the darkest corner of the stores, or six clicks down online.

Shopper research should bring reality to bear on the position a brand finds itself in. The case studies and findings earlier on in the book should lead you to exactly this point.

Out of Sight – Out of Mind

You can start your planning for research with semiotics (see Chapter 2) – a view of the importance of the environment interaction with your message – then move on to look at the interaction with your display. This display interaction is research that looks at shopper behaviour in the store and at the facing. This can be very powerful and deliver important uplifts from change. Mostly these are camera-based, either fixed in the store or eye tracking (see later in this chapter for examples of eye tracking).

You can pull back from the purchase information of your own by adding a promotion to the pack asking people to contact you and to give you more information as a requirement to getting the reward.

A store manager can also get information back from the sales and stock data that is made available by the key retailers.

Interaction with the Environment

Ruth Lawes of Lawes Consulting Ltd and a partner in Lawes Gadsby Semiotics LLP believes that semiotics offers a unique approach to developing products in their sales environment. Typically this would benefit a retailer, however there are serious messages for the advertiser on the way to, or indeed at, the POP.

Semiotics (or semiology) is the study of signs and symbols. It is descended from linguistics, which makes it useful for crafting messages, and also from anthropology, which makes it useful for understanding physical environments. Semiotics takes an interest in verbal and visual communications and built environments because it regards these things as points of access to consumer culture. The point of commercial semiotics, then, is not to decode signs and symbols out of mere academic interest, but because those signs are culturally specific. They reveal something about the cultures and subcultures within which consumers operate and are, therefore, a very valuable source of information about why consumers behave as they do.

Examples of Shoppers in Physical Environments

People's propensity to buy things, to become engaged with retail displays and environments and their ability to absorb messages are all strongly influenced by two things: environmental triggers and their cultural expectations (in the mind – engrams).

Is your retail environment bent or straight!? – grids versus curves. It is a noticeable feature of supermarkets and malls around the world that supermarkets are square while malls are round. That is, supermarkets usually conform to a grid-like aesthetic with precisely measured aisles, angular strip-lighting and industrial-looking shelving in which everything is at a right angle to everything else. In contrast, malls are full of curves; the more luxurious the mall, the curvier the architecture and interior design. The malls of Kuala Lumpur are fine examples. There are slopes, spirals, domed ceilings and portholes. They make the Guggenheim Museum in New York look spartan. A simple recommendation, then, if you want to make your supermarket display more sexy is 'break up those straight lines'. Introduce 'mall' curves into the supermarket environment.

Author Colin Harper has also seen supermarkets introduce 'nightclub' cues in their interior design, producing a novel and exciting effect. This can be done with certain types of spotlighting, floor coverings and signage. Another option is to introduce 'circus' cues in the form of aisle decorations, which are appropriate for children's products and confectionery.

SIMPLE VERSUS COMPLEX MESSAGES

If you want to display advertising or POS messages, tailor your message to the environment. People who are highly aroused, in either a positive or a negative way – that is, people who find their surroundings either exciting or stressful – are not good at absorbing complex messages. They need signs and advertising which are light on text and do not include puzzles, in-jokes or anything too clever that requires a lot of mental capacity to interpret. However, people who are highly aroused are sensitive to emotional content, more so than if they were calmer. A particularly emotionally compelling ad or a strict warning will elicit a stronger response in people in this situation. In contrast, people who are more moderately aroused, hopefully in a pleasant way, which consumers call feeling 'relaxed', are much better at absorbing complex messages. They can absorb and retain ads with more text and they can process more unusual and complicated messages. Environments vary in how pleasantly arousing they are. At the airport, most people find check-in stressful, security somewhere between stressful and boring, and then they are released into the International Departures Lounge (IDL), an oasis of coffee, iPhone accessories and luxury cosmetics. Their interpretation of their situation immediately becomes more positive, that is, they cheer up, and at this point the IDL, much like the mall, has the potential to be both 'exciting' and 'relaxing' depending on what is going on in different areas, which is something you can deliberately tailor through things like interior design, as discussed above.

CHOOSE COLOURS APPROPRIATELY

Think carefully before allocating a particular colour to a certain area of your store, mall or airport. Colours are powerful semiotic signs. If you have a lot of signage around your store, or around certain departments of your store, and certain colours dominate, you are giving off a very strong message that may or may not support your brand values and the kind of experience that you want customers to have. For example, be careful with red. We all know that red is attention-getting. However, red-and-white signs and red-and-yellow signs have been heavily used in Western consumer culture at the extreme 'economy' and 'value' end of the market in most categories. This is also true to a lesser extent of orange. These may be good colours to use if your store is a mass-market grocery store, a petrol station or a pound shop because consumers will be able to recognise and process the 'low prices' message with no effort and from a distance away but if you are selling luxury goods or women's fashions in what you hope is an upmarket environment, then we would urge you to use more muted, tertiary colours (these are six combinations of primary and secondary colours) to mark out the territory, and indeed the semiotics of taste and design trends can tell you which colours will be best for your category and your local market.

Semiology practitioners like Ruth Lawes would say that, in order to produce the best possible results in terms of shopper engagement, absorption of advertising and propensity to purchase, the following pairs of things need to work together:

Firstly, brands and retailers need to work together. A lively and cheerful brand can be suppressed if it is housed in overly severe, grid-like surroundings.

Secondly, environmental triggers and cultural expectations need to work together. You need to know what your consumer expects from the situation, whether it is a department store, an airport, a coffee shop or whatever, and what they expect from similar retail situations, and you need to build an environment that appropriately responds to those needs. Semiotics will help you find architectural devices, lighting, flooring, signage, colour schemes, aisle decorations and promotional displays that support the experience you want the customer to have, whether that is 'great value', 'premium', 'innovative' or whatever you choose.

Semiotics/semiology is an ideal approach when working very closely together to understand how, and where, to present a more effective front to the shopper. The principles should be borne in mind whenever deciding on the quality and nature of communication.

Lawes Consulting worked closely with JCDecaux, evaluating the impact of a poster for a non-existent brand in various locations, and with two types of messages – high and low detail. In conjunction with measuring the amount of stress, positive and negative, that the shopper was experiencing, they also picked up the amount of detail the shopper retained from the poster campaign.

When the research was finally released it was published under the title of the 'Power of Three' (see Chapter 17), since the shoppers retained nearly three times more of the message from a non-stressed environment. It is of interest that the stressed environment was a high street: the relaxed environment was a mall.

In Front of the Product – Through the Eyes of the Shopper

Much in-store and online research is literally done using cameras to track exactly what the shopper looks at before they actually reach out their hand (or their mouse finger) and buy.

Here you can research in the store, or through a screen, holding the product. iMotions have benchmarked the impact of a message on the eye of the beholder and, having a benchmark, are able, as with SBXL and Spectrum Insight to validate their results against performance in the store. This means that, even for reasonably small samples, they are able to see a difference appearing between, say, a standard pack, and a new design.

CASE STUDY FOR THE LAUNCH OF A NEW FLAVOUR OF STIMOROL GUM, WHICH DEVELOPED A RADICALLY NEW DESIGN APPROACH. A DESIGN WHICH MIGHT HAVE BEEN SEEN TO BE TOO EXTREME

Background/Objectives

The client wanted to evaluate a new packaging proposal for their 'Senses' brand in comparison with their existing packaging. Both packages will carry the same product, but different flavours. The intention was to launch the new one (watermelon) without pulling out the old one (tropical), having them both in the market at the same time.

The results were significant:

- The watermelon package produces a higher emotional activation, thus stronger stopping power.
- The watermelon package has less communication elements which allows more attention to the remaining elements, enhancing the understanding of its message and capitalising on the branding of 'Senses'.
- The branding of the watermelon package is organised delivering a clear message and proper brand communication hierarchy reading.
- The 'Stimorol' brand receives the same amount of attention (5 per cent) in both forms of packaging, even though the size of the logo in the watermelon package is much smaller than in the tropical one.
- According to the respondents, the watermelon package 'looks like condoms' which could be a subconscious advantage as it implies sex and potentially explains the higher emotional activation.
- The elements that attract the most attention in the tropical package are 'Senses' (21 per cent) and 'the Piece of Gum' (12 per cent).
- The elements that attract the most attention in the watermelon package are: 'Senses' (28 per cent), 'Flavor (watermelon)' (9 per cent) and '14 gums + sugar free' (8 per cent).
- The view order of the elements in the Tropical package is: 1. 'Senses'; 2. 'Enjoy the Experience'; 3. 'Piece of Gum'; 4. 'New'; 5. '14 gums'; 6. 'Flavor' (US spelling on packet) (tropical twist); 7. 'Stimorol'; 8. 'Sugar free gum'.
- The view order of the elements in the watermelon package is: 1. 'Senses'; 2. 'Stimorol'; 3. 'Flavor' (watermelon sunrise); 4. 'New'; 5. '14 gums + sugar free'.

The watermelon package is better than the tropical one in the following aspects:

- better branding;
- better hierarchy of brand communication elements;
- better distribution/order of brand communication elements;
- higher emotional activation/stopping power.

Price, Price, Price

Many people will have you believe that it is all about price nowadays. As a rider to this chapter, The Marketing Gap, as study published by fast.MAP in 2010, contained reports from 1,000 people matched to the UK population exploring the typical contents of a shopping basket.

This found that while 80 per cent of the population had a variably extensive discount element in their grocery shop, 20 per cent had very little. Just the amount you would get if you went out to shop only to find that your regular purchase is on offer at the time.

Summary

In-store research of the shopper concentrates on the impact of the environment and the stress on the shopper. Eye tracking is a most useful technique to see what catches the eye of the shopper. Is it your engram? Is it your POS material? Eye tracking will find out what attracts the shopper.

Chapter 19
Research from the Retail Side

Any business arrangement that is not profitable to the other person will in the end prove unprofitable for you. The bargain that yields mutual satisfaction is the only one that is apt to be repeated.

B.C. Forbes, Forbes Magazine Founder

After the purchase you can get a great deal from retailer data. You can turn to dunnhumby or Nectar-based research which links the shopping basket to the purchaser. They hold sales data by postcode with personal details, so they deliver basket research. A second area is to look at store EPOS data.

The Retail Trade Magazines Both Online and Offline

These magazines report on general statistics and movements by retailers. They also collate and publish or point to surveys carried out by their sponsors.

For example, the British Retail Consortium (BRC) stated (May 2013) that online, especially through mobile, purchases (one in five) are growing, with high street sales falling, adding that consistent cross-channel pricing is what retailers are starting to apply.

The following useful links to trade magazines listed below are given in the Appendix:

Mobile Marketing
Internet Retailing
In-Store Insights – POPAI and the MARI results
Promotional Marketing
The Grocer
British Retail Consortium

Then we need to go online. A number of firms publish reports that are free – see the Appendix:

Booz
Deloittes
Bronto
Juniper Research
ABC and the results from the Co-op

As you move further from the purchase, you can turn to the unadulterated views of the shopper on what they have found from social media reporting or from on-pack feedback reporting.

Going for New or Old Customers?

In 2005 only around a third (36 per cent) of retailers were spending more on gaining new customers than retaining existing ones. In a report in 2010 from research carried out by *Retail Week*, the UK's high street retailers were spending an increasingly large proportion of time, money and effort on acquiring new customers. In 2011, 55 per cent of retailers were expected to invest more on acquisition than retention. In 2015 almost two-thirds (63 per cent) will be spending more on acquiring customers than retaining current ones.

These findings were based on research from 280 senior-level decision makers and C-level management from household names in the UK retail sector. The research shows that 63 per cent of UK retailers achieve a higher profit margin from an existing customer against a new one (19 per cent say it is significantly higher). Knowing loyal customers are more profitable, why are UK retailers prepared to increase their new customer acquisition spend? Later research in this chapter shows this strategy of targeting new shoppers to be flawed. Research consistently shows a few high-value existing customers spend the most in almost all sectors including B2B and B2C. More research supporting this is given below. Like Myer in Australia, you need to find out who they are and cosset them. They are the real spenders. If you do not look after your real spenders of course they will drift away.

Losing Loyalty: The Consumer Defection Dilemma

At almost the same time (2009), a report by dunnhumby, for the IPA – 'Price Promotion during the Downturn, Shrewd or Crude' – looked at the position of loyalty to brands. They reported:

> *Economic pressures and the growing presence of price promotion have resulted in a general drift away from brand loyalty towards a promiscuous 'deal seeker' mentality. There has been explosive growth in the use of price promotions in UK retail over the last 12 months (2008 to 2009).In some categories where this is particularly prevalent there has been considerable erosion of loyalty and substantial growth in the proportion of sales made 'on deal'. This will adversely affect profitability and is likely to take some time to rectify after the downturn has ended. There have also been considerable reductions in advertising and marketing communications support for brands over the last 12 months. This may already be exacerbating the drift away from under-supported brands. The data show that brands that broadly maintain their media presence appear to be more resilient.*

What do these authoritative reports have in common, and what impact should this have on where marketing monies are actually spent? The clue lies in the measures that were identified as being key loyalty drivers for retailers. Heading the list was product or service availability. The IGD says (Shoppertrack, October 2010) that 17 per cent of shoppers are 'not satisfied' with the frequency that promoted products are not in stock when they want to buy them. This repeats the 2003 finding (see Chapter 6 for more on this).

What Loyalty Means to the Bottom Line

The truth about brand loyalty, and its frequently transient nature, may surprise many seasoned brand marketers and retailers. Research was conducted using Catalina Marketing's vast database of household-level purchase data, conducted by Catalina partnerships through shopper purchasing dynamics, with more than 200 major retail grocery, mass merchant and pharmacy chains across the US. Pointer Media Network and Catalina Marketing continually track the purchases of more than 150 million individual shopper identities, with a multi-year history of brand purchasing for an estimated 76 per cent of American households. The study authors claim the study is 'unique' in the breadth and depth of consumer data used in developing Insights.

For the purposes of the study, loyalty was measured as the percentage of category sales using standard CPG categories defined by Information Resources Incorporated (IRI). The study measured loyalty only for individual product brands, not for master brands as a whole. High-loyal consumers were defined as those consumers who made 70 per cent or more of their category purchases with a single brand during a 12-month period. Switchers were previously loyal, but moved to buying less than 70 per cent of their goods from a brand. Defectors are those formerly defined as High-loyal shoppers who have stopped buying the brand altogether, but still shop the category. The findings are based on an analysis of the individual buying patterns of more than 32 million consumers in 2007 and 2008. Their core findings are;

- Loyalty erosion and consumer defection are pervasive and costly problems. Their impact is increasing dramatically in the current economy.

- For the average brand in this study, 52 per cent of High-loyal consumers in 2007 either reduced loyalty or completely defected from the brand in 2008.

- Only four out of ten brands retained 50 per cent or more of their High-loyal consumers from year to year.

- For the average brand, approximately one-third of all High-loyal consumers in 2007 completely defected to another brand in the same category in 2008.

- The current economic downturn is having a significant impact on brand loyalty. Many leading brands experienced a drop in the total number of highly loyal consumers between 2007 and 2008.

- Loyalty and consumer churn have a huge impact on brand revenue and value. Some major brands could have increased overall revenues by more than 20 per cent in 2008 if they had eliminated churn among High-loyal shoppers – who have stopped buying the brand altogether, but are still purchasing in the category – to the benefit of competitors.

All Loyalists Are Not Created Equal

Loyalty, of course, is not the only critical determinant of a consumer's present value to a brand. Some consumers are highly loyal, but not major category buyers. It is the high-volume brand buyer that really drives revenue. In December of 2008, Catalina Marketing and Pointer Media Network, in conjunction with the CMO Council, released a major report entitled, 'Discovering the Pivotal Point Consumer'. The study introduced into marketing lexicon the 'Pivotal Point Consumer' – the high-volume brand buyer who, along with her or his peers, accounts for 80 per cent of your brand's sales. This breakthrough research showed that a surprisingly small number of consumers – just 2.5 per cent of shoppers for the average brand – make up 80 per cent of brand sales.

These High-loyal, High-consuming people are the people you really need to keep onside. They are the most likely to be advocates and to be annoyed by being unable to find you where they expect the products to be.

And they are only 2.5 per cent of your shoppers. These comprise the core you need to keep happy. Measures then need to be considered by the Board that recognise and reward these shoppers. Such rewards should then incentivise more of the 95 per cent to seek favoured and recognised status.

Data

Data exists from loyalty cards, purchase history, segmentation, customer polling, attitude and demographic research, behavioural analysis and now social networking sites.

Sir Terry Leahy stated in his *In-Store* interview (June 2013):

> *In so many companies there's no shortage of data but it's in the wrong place, at the perimeter of the business. The key decisions are taken at the heart of the business. Often the most powerful in the organisation are the least informed. That's the reality. So we [at Tesco] had to push that data right into the parts of the organisation where it needed to be. Now is the time to invest in data which, unlike other retail business costs, is falling in price. The key is to use data to get a better management of supply chain and operating systems, also to understand their customers better. In that way they can create more relevant benefit for the customers and in that way create loyalty; from that comes more spend and more*

profitable spend. That's basically the economics of data. The challenge is that the theory is known but not being practically applied. There are relatively few examples of genuinely multi-channel engagement with the customer. There are practical problems of getting old systems to work on new platforms. That's a lot of the work that companies have to get through. If you keep focused on how that will benefit customers and therefore benefit the retailer; at least that provides a lot of motivation and momentum of getting through difficult systems development. But data on its own is not enough; values, culture, purpose – these actually matter as much to success as the technology and data. Even today when there is limitless data, limitless potential, actually the values matter even more. They speak to the heart in the way that data and technology speak to the head.

Data and analytics are a key source of targeting and conversion advantage, Booz reports (May 2013), charting a new frontier for collaboration between brands and retailers. If a retailer can deliver tailored messages and product personalisation better than its competitors, consumers will choose to return there again and again (the retailer will 'win the trip'). And those same messages and recommendations will lead consumers to buy more each time (they will 'grow their basket'). For example, Amazon's highly effective product recommendation engine is powered by transaction data and Insights across its entire customer base. This keeps consumers returning to Amazon for each incremental purchase, and purchasing more at each visit as complementary products are showcased along the way. The access to shared data across partners is expanding this value even further.

Driving more effective digital promotions, developing compelling original content, and using 'big data' and analytics in more sophisticated ways is the way ahead. But for most retailers and brands, determining which ROI metrics are the most reliable (for example, click-through versus page visits versus time spent), or which ad formats will persist into the future (for example, display, banner, rich media and 'shoppable') remains a struggle. High rates of innovation and experimentation across both fronts are creating a wide variety of options, but little informed Insight on what is really working – and few, if any, standards.

Google have introduced Google Shopping which is providing (three times) better returns than Google Product Search but retailers have to optimise data to achieve this. Google advises of the need for the use of words such as 'free' or '% off'.

Summary

Only businesses know the data they hold. This chapter can only emphasise the importance of analysis to draw out Insights about the shoppers using any store. The authors, in trying to simplify the understanding of research, split the topic into three chapters – but in reality all Insights are interlinked. The chapter has also tried to indicate that there is a lot of information available from the trade journals both in print and online – much of it 'free'.

Chapter 20
Strategic Scenarios

Knowledge dispels fear.
Motto of Royal Air Force Parachute Training School

From a Basis of Knowledge Take Risks

Businesses seem too cautious when thinking of the future, other than the large chains, though they can make mistakes sometimes too.

Decisions regarding change are often delayed. There is often no process applied, with strategy consideration just a reaction to something happening in the retail environment. Copycat activity within categories occurs – car advertising is a prime example. Lack of process may cause a failure to make any decision. Lack of process may be a result of the fear of what is observed in others. Government sets a poor example, hampered by the many processes put in place to protect taxpayers in that civil servants will only act after parliament has cleared policy sanctioning actions or purchases. Fear of making the wrong decision may postpone a decision. Often that fear is based on a lack of knowledge. However, indecision is often much more costly – postponing decisions sometimes even results in total failure. A process is required to consider strategy. That process should not be the prerogative of those involved day to day in the operation of the business (though they should examine the final outcome of the option selected for a reality check) but is the responsibility of the director level – the Board. They must, however, have all the facts to hand.

For brands, suppliers and retailers, in dealing with the shopper, strategic analysis should start from the premise that the search is for the future market position of the company or organisation – to be best placed to serve the customer in the future while making a reasonable return. To establish that future market position the directors should call for a broad range of scenarios to be considered, even scenarios that seem 'off the wall'. The scenarios should be researched and a number selected that are possible within an estimate of the future commercial environment and the likely future shopper needs. For each scenario chosen, options for implementation can be described and examined for their practicality in terms of the resources that are available. A rigorous examination of the options should determine which is most likely to be profitable and realistic to implement. The future position of the company or organisation can then be defined. The task of implementing the change from the present position to the future position is a matter of change leadership – persuading all the interested parties of the need for change and why the selected future position has been selected. (Future Kindle books on change and strategic leadership are scheduled for 2014 in the *Learn How to Lead* Kindle series by Roddy Mullin.)

Key components of the future market position of any brand supplier or retailer are the shopper or buyer and the business environment. How they shop or buy is covered by the 6Cs constantly reviewed in the light of technical advances, economic, social and cultural pressures and what they buy by product and or by service development. Desk research should establish the environmental factors – legislation, future business rates and tax liabilities, the eco environment and the likely political, social and cultural backdrop. What the shoppers are likely to buy in the future requires both research and data collection of the customer/shopper and research into potential product development in the areas or categories in which the business is engaged.

Insights into how the shopper is likely to lead their life in the future is important. For household item categories, an observer might foretell the demise of the separate dining room. Cooking however is re-emerging as a home activity as a result of TV viewing, after a generation that used ready meals and the microwave. Wet rooms seem the fashion over shower cubicles and showers replaced baths as the cleansing fashion. It will be interesting to discover whether the simple bath will again find favour – rather than just modified as an upmarket Jacuzzi which provides the soothing jets for aching muscles – as a bath is seen to have no beneficial effect other than for frowned upon luxuriating. Decoration itself might move into the theming of rooms. What today is a Moroccan lounge may become a Caribbean sitting room with extensive *tromp l'oeil* views tomorrow. Indeed it might be possible, with wall-by-wall screening, to be able to create any habitat with the flick of a switch – Swiss meadow, New York apartment, Parisian chic or English country garden at a moment's notice. Mirror TVs hide the screen when not switched on – but they could also show works by artists – Picassos today, Modiglianis tomorrow – or just family photographs instead of being mirror facings. Moving walls and turntables, like theatre stage sets, change the living space from large to intimate.

Creativity and innovation will play its part alongside material science development. Heatherwick is a leading design consultancy who have in recent years moved the boundaries of material capabilities forward. The rate of development itself is likely to be faster with the introduction of rapid prototyping – now even available with a specialist printer using colour printed paper to replicate intricate design in hours rather than weeks, months or years. Jewelry designers have been using rapid prototyping for years – it is only a question of time before the technique becomes universal – available to all.

From the marketing communications perspective, the engram research indicates that it is most unwise to change the engram once established. Examples of much publicised potential changes to the brand identities of Shell and BP with the final result – despite spending millions – looking very similar to the original are to be applauded for effectively retaining their engram. The engram, however, can be alongside new products to introduce and to endorse them, but only if the 'parent' has an engram implanted already. Confectionery and detergents apply this concept. The distinctive colour for Cadbury should be retained. There are some colours or combinations that are very persuasive of purchase. A client of Helmsmen Business Consultants (owner – author Roddy Mullin) has discovered one such colour combination. It is in effect their engram and is distinctive in turn on their client's shelves. If a firm is without an engram (research will decide this) for its customers (shoppers or buyers) then this should be given strategic consideration. It is dangerous to produce too much variation from the original engram. It will be interesting to see how 'PO Cruises' is valued by the shopper now that the '&' has been removed.

Strategic consideration should be applied to the marketing communications plan. Resource should be applied to shopper research as inputs to other strategic considerations. Resource should also be set aside to confirm the effectiveness of marketing subsequently. Once the shopper or buyer is defined then from the Insight, analysis can determine initially whether there are sufficient shoppers or buyers to provide turnover and profit to sustain the business. The research should also determine The Offer (the 6Cs) to be made to shoppers or buyers and the channels and media to communicate with them. If the need is for more shoppers or buyers then there may be a need to implant the engram to a larger audience. The next task is to determine the core stores or business to sell to and plan both relationship building and ESOV alongside encouraging social media as appropriate for reviews and feedback for the local or niche shoppers targeted. Whether a promotion is to be run or discount offered may provide a reason for the activity. Delivery to store and the quantities to stock may require strategic production decisions.

The reality check should be taken most seriously once the change has been determined – but before the change is implemented, as the operational team will have to make the change and then run with it. The process, once established, can be made to run fairly smoothly. Feedback on the strategy consideration process should be welcomed too by the Board.

Summary

Strategy consideration should be a serious and ongoing process. Investors should applaud and be happy to remunerate a Board that get the future right and implement the changes so the shopper remains with them – not with a competitor.

Chapter 21

The Future Prognosis of Shopping

Predictions about the future are possible and with time are found to be correct. New products and services can be assessed rationally as to their success, through a process that considers their deployment in a range of scenarios, which are then examined, with selected scenarios developed as options to be exploited. The options are reviewed against a background of technical, commercial, market, government, legal, social and cultural trends within the geographic scope, capabilities and resources of a business or organisation. The selected option can then be more widely tested in the marketplace.

Roddy Mullin has produced successful strategic predictions in print – in 2002, for example the third edition of *Sales Promotion* (now in its fifth edition) with a replacement entitled *Promotional Marketing* published in September 2014, forecast the rise of the mobile phone and the need for measurement and marketing accountability – and a section of the book was headed 'It's all in the mind of the customer'. How prophetic that has turned out to be in the light of the discovery of the part an engram plays in a shopper's decision to buy.

So the authors feel we should make some predictions as to the future. Clearly the future of shopping depends on the shopper. The 6Cs view of the shopper will continue to dominate and firms CVPs must be related to The Offer. Insights from research, data and feedback (a two-way conversation?) will be the core backdrop of successful retailers as they segment through RFM scores. Loyalty linked to status and rewards may retain shoppers for a time but shoppers will apply RFM in reverse to retailers: shoppers will question: 'Is the retailer offering value and, over time, do the retailers communicate with me, the shopper, through the channels and with the frequency I prefer? Do they value my custom and treat me well always and are they easy to shop with and convenient?' Someone will invent an acronym for this; like the 4Ps became the 6Cs. It will be RFM in reverse (MFR?) My Favourite Retailer is … because … who knows?

The power of social media will increase and settle down to industry standards but only for a time – when some new system will take over (instant scoring of retailers just as in some TV shows?). Just as cassette tapes, videos (VHS winning), CDs, DVDs all had their day, so too will one or two social media will dominate for a time. WPP global support for Twitter (May 2013), however, cannot just be on a whim. Understanding and taking in shopper power will be even more widespread. The power of the tweet will grow further. One early result: Unilever (June 2013) has reformulated Flora back to its 2010 taste as a result of tweets.

What of shopping itself? Unless retailers in town centres pull together, the shopper will increase their online and mall shopping activity. *Sold out,* a book by Bill Grimsey, foresees the end of the road for the high street. In his view it is no longer a retail place but a community place and that is what the future holds for it – it is past saving in terms of retail (unless it is a tourist attraction). Retailers on the high street claim business rates place them at a disadvantage to online stores and are seeking an online retail tax. Shoppers want a worry-free (traffic-less) environment for shopping. Convenience will be the shopper catchphrase – combining 'location' with ease of value purchase. Repeating the shopping experience will occur where it is a pleasure to shop (and the shoppers are recognised, appreciated and welcomed) and declining shopper visits will occur with a decrease in visits where barriers have to be overcome. No longer will retailers survive if they fail to deliver and, most importantly, fail to communicate in a shopper-preferred way.

Reduced (inconvenient) opening times of any outlets will drive shoppers to alternatives such as service station/garages with their co-located 24/7-open shops. Perhaps there will be a return to automats in shop walls where out-of-hours purchases can be made. Do not underestimate the volunteer manning of post office cum shops in rural communities which seem here to stay (rightly because of the 'community spirit' they embrace). The love of car boot sales in the UK may see short time migration to towns for a time with multi-stall shops located in presently empty premises. But the same difficulties of all towns – parking, traffic, limited opening hours – will probably kill them off.

Fortunately for the UK, the increase in the UK as a cruise ship destination will see coastal towns benefit from tourism and its associated shopping – and coach-guided tours to the UK's many sights, often cruise liner-based, will be taken up by European and other global travellers. London is establishing cruise terminals at Greenwich and Tilbury, and Dover now takes cruise ships along with established ports such as Southampton, Liverpool, Harwich, Belfast,

Newcastle and Greenock. Entrepreneurial coastal towns should be reviving their piers to take cruise ships. Unsurprisingly, more Bicester shopping villages are planned (some even in foreign parts) – for top-end retailers. However, the fashionistas are likely to demand more home visits for high-end items or multi-online delivery of items to try on, returning those that don't suit. See more on this below. For the middle section shoppers, time is at a premium with many demands on their precious 'free time' – the online assistance with purchasing given by firms such as dressipi.com will be a blessing; firms that match what a shopper likes with what is available on the high street or online.

Where is Technology Taking the Shopper?

Technology will enhance the shopper journey further. The new material that is to replace silicon – graphene – will make it possible to make items smaller yet more efficient electronically, and stronger. Graphene can be made in sheets an atom thick. It is a superb conductor of electricity. It is at least three times stronger than carbon fibre. Samsung, among others, is researching how graphene can be used in commercial production and for use in many electronic situations. Other materials are also being reduced to atom thickness. Building up layers of alternate materials, each an atom thick will allow, for example, painting a layer on anything, that will then light up, transmit sound or show photographs. Wristwatch-sized devices will do anything that PCs used to do. So technology has a long way to travel – some of it will appear shortly. (Even a model railway can be controlled by a mobile phone – ask Hornby! Talk to the train.)

An astounding increase in use of mobile and tablet by the shopper for search, compare and purchase is forecast. Carphone Warehouse 'It's a conversation' mobile software, if it works, will transform the communication between sales staff and the shopper (see Chapter 4). Unless Microsoft comes up with a cheap version of its Windows software for mobiles its demise is forecast too, going the same way as Nokia (though purchase by Microsoft may save it if mobile Windows works) and Blackberry. The shopper can expect the retailer/brand/supplier to be using the shopper's location, through GPS, to make relevant offers when in the vicinity of stores, restaurants and bars. Proximity-commerce WiFi will be everywhere. Even through bus stops, shoppers now can use their mobiles to communicate, reading QR codes with their apps or connecting through Near Field Communication (NFC). Mobiles will be the same as money, acting as a wallet. More shoppers will purchase big ticket items using their mobiles. Even those without bank accounts will top up their 'wallets' and adopt electronic shopping. NFC (as used on Oyster cards but fitted in mobiles) will speed up transaction times and make better use of staff time. Asda now offers an app that can be used to zap barcodes of items at home that need replacing, stored as a list for their next shop or online venture.

The Future of Bricks and Mortar

The future seems to be bleak for retailing; for the shopper in-store view, read the earlier paragraphs in this chapter above (unless the outlets re-locate to malls or coastal towns or towns inland on the cruise ship itinerary, and unless the in-store shopper has a preferred in-store layout as described in Chapter 18). The Centre for Retail Research (in May 2013) forecast that one in five shops will close by 2018. That is, in their estimate, a total of 61,930 shops. The rising cost of conducting business and the falling of consumer spending are blamed. This will lead to a loss of over 300,000 jobs. Pharmacy and health and beauty shops would account for some 5,100 stores closed. DIY outlets will also decline. Sixteen major store chains are expected to close with some 2,000 outlets going into administration. On the bright side, the number of supermarkets is expected to rise – and they will increase their non-food offerings. As this goes to print, clearly Sainsbury's have got it right and are benefitting from a rise in sales and profits.

Professor Joshua Bamfield, a Director of the Centre for Retail Research, is reported in the *Daily Telegraph* (26 May 2013) as saying: 'Customers now shop in multiple ways, checking a store's website, visiting stores, reading reviews, and making online price comparisons with smartphones while shopping. Retailers have to make clear and find strategic responses to the changing pattern of how consumers shop, which includes tactical decisions about store numbers and locations. They also need to fully integrate these physical stores with their websites, smartphone offering and social media community coherently.' The authors can but agree with the Professor.

Chris Grigg, the Chief Executive of British Land, is optimistic about the future of British shops. British Land is a publically listed company that invests in shopping centres (malls). He wrote, at the time of the opening of a new centre (May 2013) between Portsmouth and Southampton – that saw 47,000 shoppers on its first day – that shops will be different in the future. Many shops now are too pokey, in the wrong place, boring and staid. British Land classify shops under three headings: 'convenience' – places where you regularly shop in flagship stores; 'functional' – the superstores and DIY (mainly out of town where there is free parking); and 'experiential' – where you go for the experience (for example, pubs, restaurants, cafes, cinemas and bowling) to meet and chat with friends. British Land are negotiating with BT to provide free WiFi at their centres in recognition of the digital age, they are also trialling with Google indoor maps and are proposing Treehouse pop-up events and shopping spaces, a location for community uses or where new shopping concepts can be tested. If the malls do offer community centres this will further deplete the high street's ability to survive!

There is also the Mary Portas effect on town centres to consider – Margate town (Isle of Thanet, Kent) may convert its high street to a fun-filled land-based pier (but a decision to locate a Tesco supermarket not too far away has caused Mary Portas to think the Government is only paying lip-service to her campaign); the Cornish town of Liskeard might become a source of local quality food. But the bickering and non-decision taking, or scant support she receives for her great ideas, set out in her December 2011 report 'The Portas Review', does not bode well for the retailers in either town, despite earlier Government support for her thinking and recommendations. Hopefully in the long term her recommendations will be adopted or bricks and mortar outlets in town centres will cease – just as Liskeard and Margate have nearly succumbed.

Unless retailers work together along the lines advocated by Mary Portas, the shopping mall and out-of-town sheds will take over from town centres. Town centres will see less actual shopping (other than niche one-off outlets), and be used more for retail therapy and joint entertainment/community purposes – so a town centre might be successful should it offer cinema, theatre, restaurants/fast-food outlets (often combined, for example, as at Berkhamstead, Colchester), activity centres (ice rinks, pools, gyms), market stalls for local produce (farmers markets) as well as shops, but also offering fashion shows, personal demonstrations (hairdressing, manicure, pedicure, health and beauty) and providing experiential marketing and road show sites (test driving cars, bikes, gardening items). But there has to be a will from amongst themselves to take the town and its traders forward. Clearly though, local independent shops care for their future in town centres, large chain retailers, brands and suppliers probably care less – after all, it doesn't matter to them where they sell, only that sales occur.

Interestingly, Mary Portas (The Queen of Shops) has chosen not to write much about the need to undertake marketing communications, though in her programmes she talks, instructs and implements marketing communications plans. In one author's experience of running 'surgeries' (free consultancy sessions) at trade shows, a lamentable majority of (in fact most) retailers have scant knowledge of marketing or of how to discover what their customers think of their products, service or delivery. They fail as a consequence. Because of pressure from a local paper, several have usually, and disastrously, spent money on local advertising that saw scant return in terms of any resulting shoppers who spent money. They had not analysed the readership and matched it to their target shoppers. With their fingers burnt they stopped any further marketing communication relying solely on word of mouth – hopeless. An absolute classic example of this 'once bitten twice shy' attitude is the Silver Vaults in London off Chancery Lane. They offer a wonderful shopping experience if you are looking for something special – in silver. But they have never ever really marketed their wonderful arcade of shops, because on the one occasion they used a PR firm for marketing, that firm spent all the money on one binge party; they have never promoted themselves since and paid the penalty for it in a much reduced footfall. Every visitor to London should be enthused with the same appeal for the Silver Vaults – if only to look at the wonderful silver craftsmanship – as the Bicester Shopping village has for the Chinese.

Sir Terry Leahy in an *In-Store* interview (June 2013):

> *The high street will need to be attractive because people will only spend time on things that are engaging and attractive. Human beings are social and will want to gather together in nice places, there'll probably be more residential, a good thing anyway. There will be care homes, GP practices, health and beauty services, opticians, nail bars, physios, etc. There'll be a lot of stores of different types. There'll be virtual display stores [such as those Tesco launched in South Korea] that you can transact with, click and collect for online, eating places. There'll be a different mix of things. Food will be there – it's hard to see all of food moving online.*

What of the US experience – supposedly often ahead of UK? On Big Island Hawaii, where the locals shop in out-of-town or resort malls until late, you find the best restaurants are now co-located alongside Walmart and other superstores. The downtown areas are increasingly only occupied because of the recent introduction of daytime farmers markets with niche craft stalls alongside, but they and the downtown shops close early and town centres are silent at night and the future looks sad … unless perhaps they become places of historic interest or encourage more cruise ship stopovers (two per week currently) – both unlikely to happen!

In future there will probably be a substantial increase in demonstrations, sampling and experiential marketing – all offered in-store and online and, where appropriate, at road shows and exhibitions. Gaming at store entrances, which has started in the US (Body Shop uses the technique) means shoppers draw a card on entering and a variety of alternative promotions are offered – each card being different; typically discounts on category items are the reward. Pop-up shops will offer very small local retailers the opportunity to combine for a stand each, for a fortnight or so, in taking an empty high street retail outlet (the equivalent of bricks and mortar car boot sales?). Is it likely to last? Charity shops will continue as before.

The future then is more ordering direct from the supplier online and trial, rather than sampling, will increase – especially for high-value items such as fashion, watches and jewellery. More sale-or-return home ordering, for example for clothing and shoes, will occur as firms such as dressipi.com and Mywardrobe become known, where they store data on shoppers' personal statistics and preferences with their consent and then match that data to clothes and shoes being offered at retail outlets or websites that they research, constantly updating. Home delivery for commodity groceries is expanding and forecast by BT 'as the future' although for many this is happening now – and with secure delivery stations (nationwide) introduced as an alternative to home or in-store collection after ordering online, it has a strong proposition to the worker. Amazon is developing delivery/return points, eBay has teamed up with Argos. Test 'delivery lockers' are already being trialled, for example in the City of London. Sainsbury's is trialling mobile scan and go, and its online business is increasing at a rate of 20 per cent a year (approaching £1 billion), with more than half of shoppers using click and collect for non-food online orders. Virtual stores, where shoppers scan barcodes for delivery later, have been trialled (used at Japanese railway stations). These will probably appear in the UK soon.

Mobile payments are set to grow according to *Internet Retailing* (May 2013) with 20 per cent of mobile owners already doing so and another 30 per cent keen to do so.

A study (June 2013) by the Local Data Company and the Oxford Institute of Retail Management reports that an average of 14 per cent of shops on the high street are empty across the UK and foresees the reduction of stores owned by chains continuing by a further 8 per cent (5,000 shops). This supports the Centre for Retail Research finding. This is offset by the increase in value (Poundsavers type) shops, pawnbrokers, pay-day lenders, betting shops, health and beauty shops, food stores and multiples. The study forecasts successful high streets as being increasingly diverse, incredibly adaptable while accommodating online business.

Deloittes Consumer Review reports that, in the UK, mobile smartphones are owned by 72 per cent of the population with 57 per cent using them as a shop assistant and 50 per cent using them to buy products. 48 per cent of 16–24 year olds use apps to shop. A third of shoppers had used an online wallet and 12 per cent used contactless pay systems. Ben Perkins, Head of Consumer Research at Deloittes, commented (*The Daily Telegraph* 24 June 2013): 'There is no doubt that mobile is rapidly redefining the way consumers and brands interact even more than the internet did. Consumers are expecting convenience, simplicity and security in exchange for their loyalty. It is only by embracing mobile's full potential with the right strategy that a consumer facing business can compete in mobile-centric world.'

Digital coupons and vouchers will be used more by the shopper to give as birthday or other presents.

The authors give their opinions in this chapter. Retail will not die. It will just be quite different. The realisation of the need for long and short-term marketing communication will dawn on suppliers, retailers and brands – hopefully as a result of this book. The authors advocate the focus on core stores and their shoppers alongside the empowerment of the store manager – providing all the data at the outlet, currently held centrally – to achieve the six message points of communication effectively. Shop-floor staff should have the same access to information about products online as the shopper – so they will have to carry smartphones/iPads or the new generation of all-in-one mobile/tablets.

The future could be rosy, the future will be local! As this was written (June 2013) Ernst and Young were forecasting a 1.2 per cent growth in consumer spending so that should cheer up retailers, suppliers and brands. Alex in *The Daily Telegraph* sees the future of equities as fantastic (though the FTSE was falling then) alongside more quantitative easing and a continuation of almost zero interest rates. Amazon is entering the online groceries business and Tesco is to fight Amazon by increasing its online music and film download side by adding books. The authors still worry that the Tesco engram is falling out of favour with shoppers and needs serious treatment. But we probably won't lose too much sleep over that. (Authors note: Since this paragraph was written the retail environment has continued to be difficult for the large supermarkets. Small businesses and convenience outlets and those that do not discount are doing well. Tesco at last recognise the 'need to be loved' but they and Morrisons are both instituting a price war, which is applying the wrong solution. What is required is work on their brandgrams to change the shopper perception to a more favourable one. See *Promotional Marketing* by Roddy Mullin which details the answer.)

The future will be mobile and a personal relationship with each shopper is expected – and brands, suppliers and retailers need to take the six message points seriously to help them shop. Remember, as far as the shopper is concerned, they see no difference between in-store or online, they just want to enjoy the shopping experience – so help them!

Chapter 22

Implementing the Changes Pragmatically

The aim of this chapter is to start you thinking about how to apply the contents of this book in your job in the B2B or retail sector – whether brand manager, supplier, store manager or in a future career as a marketer, or if you are just setting up in business and want to know how to start marketing communications.

Think too of the future of shopping, with successful outlets as locally tuned to the shoppers they serve or a niche market on the website or in a niche outlet. Dare to think both long and short term. If you just needed sales, anyone can do that by selling at a ridiculously low price. Clearly the future is also definitely going to be one where change has to be accommodated and the pace of change would seem likely to accelerate – so allow for change. Change means a business has to be flexible – but for the shopper you need to keep one item constant – that is the core element of the engram that is in the mind of your shopper.

For the shopper, the reverse of change is true with the position an engram holds in the mind; the shopper seeks something stable in the subconscious mind on which to hang everything related to the product or service – the core of an engram. As additional knowledge or experience is acquired relating to the product or service, it is attached in the mind to build the engram. This does not mean that the engram cannot in itself accommodate change but the engram has to be developed with one core element of its features as constant with the building elements – consistent, certain and stable. The value of the engram to the individual is not necessarily related to any cost of the service or product or its delivery. It may relate to location or the proximity or availability of products or services. It may be the association that the product or service has with its core element. Typically the core element of the engram is stored in the mind as a sense. It may be visual, a sound, have a smell or have a feel, or be a combination of some or any of these; it will affect a sense and it will be distinctive. It may be a logo, either pictorial or in writing, it may also be related to colour. Examples of the core elements of engrams are the easyJet logo (a particular font, one word, lower case – except for the capital J and a distinctive orange colour), Shell and its symbol, the white Nike flash or McDonalds yellow arched 'M'; the series of notes for a jingle, for example 'Go compare', or 'Just one Cornetto'; or a phrase such as 'Because you're worth it' for L'Oreal or Audi's 'Vorsprung durch technik'. The subconscious mind of the shopper will hang everything that features the core element and build the engram in the mind.

So, deal with the engram first. If you are already in business or a supplier or retailer, survey your customers to find out how they describe your products and services, what they think of your outlet(s) and or website. A quick sample test survey should give you a steer. Does it match what you think you are selling? (If it has a large mismatch or if you think it is wrong or has a bias with which you are unhappy, you may need to commission a full statistically significant survey.) If what the survey is telling you produces a consistent response and they all refer to your logo or business name – you have the core of an engram; if it is praised, then you have something to really build on.

If you do not have an engram then you need to find and establish one. This requires much thought and creativity. It has to be distinctive – unique. If your early customers come up with a catchy, new, innovative way to describe your products and or services – test it, then adopt it. The shopper – the customer – is usually right. Use the core element of your engram everywhere. To give it credibility you may be able to use a joint promotion with a well-known brand and piggy back on their reputation to establish yours. Otherwise, establish locally, or in your niche, the marketing communications activities recommended here and, only once that is confirmed through Insights, expand the business.

Of course, if you are a brand manager all this should have happened already. However, it is wise to check from time to time whether what you think is your engram is actually in the minds of your customers and that their description of your engram matches the image of your product and services you want them to hold. Remember an analysis of social media can assist here.

The second most important part of the marketing communications process is measurement. You cannot hope to develop your marketing communications unless you understand what works and what does not – see Chapter 15. You need shopper or buyer Insights to keep your products or services on the long and winding road to sales.

Be flexible and react to what shoppers feed back to you. There is a range of options now available to analyse social media, but you should also encourage feedback through relationship building and through marketing communication.

The third point is to apply synergy and consistency. It is becoming ever clearer that you need to reinforce your engram on the way to a purchase, whether this is online or in the store. Moreover, in-store, understanding that price discounts are a way of life means they should be properly integrated into a communication strategy at all message points. If you can get stock managed properly you will avoid damaging your engram – there is nothing then stopping you stacking promotions and advertising on top of each other.

Checklist

Chapter 19 looked at strategy. Here is a checklist of how the authors envisage you proceeding.

- Is each shop (and every aisle) or every outlet or web page, innovative, creative, fun and not boring? Check this with Insights from your shoppers.
- Think of your Offer (the 6Cs) under the same innovative, creative and not boring dimensions and then examine – this book's particular purpose – the marketing communication you propose and apply the same criteria. Ensure that stock support matches the communication in terms of delivery.
- If you are a brand manager or supplier concentrate on confirming (and implanting or re-implanting if required) the engram then building and refreshing it. Next set up a team to encourage social media and respond to feedback about your brand. You need to work with each retail outlet (key account management!) to support their communications plan – of course as brand manager you can offer promotions to inspire the retailer (a core store) and their shoppers but they should know best what works best for each brand with their unique group of local shoppers.
- As a retailer your organisation should place the manager at the outlet or shop or website as overall responsible for anything that is customer facing. If the outlet is not the centre, ask why not? What is the barrier

to doing so? The store/outlet manager will need an appropriate team and suggestions are given in Chapter 14. The manager (who will be carefully selected and be trained as a leader) has to have delegated powers to research then use the Insights to optimise the outlet to the shopper/customers/buyers that are local or in the niche you are in. They must also control stock, promotions and communications in conjunction with the brand manager and supplier.

- First and foremost the store manager must discover who their buyers/shoppers are. Obtain Insights. The store manager will need to spend money here, but so be it. Budget for it. If you are a niche retailer/supplier and your market is precise and well known to you, make contact with every buyer/customer shopper – it is called relationship building. Over time build a full picture of each one. If you are area-based then you need to know who is in the area round your outlet. Fourteen miles is a typical average for a UK shopper to be prepared to travel (figure from Forrester research). Obviously less distance in towns; further in the country. Count the number of shoppers regularly – from EPOS data you can check their average spend. Now as an incentive how do you increase that? Who are your top shoppers (VIPs/RFMs)? Build up a calendar of promotions with your suppliers. For each promotion you need a plan – for POP, for stock, for shelf filling and so on.

- If you are a supplier, you need to work with retailers. Check the store has the right profile and its shoppers have the right profile – similar people cluster together and chose the same local stores – and buy the same brands. Check the store has the capability to manage extra demand. Unfortunately, typically, centrally located planograms dictate how much stock is kept in front of the shopper, regardless of the profile of the shopper and the area demand – fight to change that, dare to be different.

- It is important to communicate with existing customers to maintain their loyalty. Modern shoppers are not as loyal as they used to be because of fierce price competition and the experience of recession, but if you serve them with what they want they will remain loyal.

- Have a look at the website or store – is it conducive to shoppers and easy for them to buy while being sufficiently interesting to inspire purchases? Mall curves are preferred rather than the rectangular designs of supermarkets, remember!

- Now set the communications strategy and devise the communications plan. It may be a good idea to involve local events or charities – even be a sponsor – or speak to suppliers to find suitable promotions. Does the retail outlet have an engram? Essential! How is the signage on the way to the outlet? Liskeard has a number of shops post-Mary Portas combining offers. This increases coverage. Any similar possibilities with your outlets?

Awareness

Decide on a local outdoor or TV campaign or radio or press. Local cinema? Local transport? Remember you need ESOV. Tailor the messages to the promotion and involve others.

INDIVIDUALS IN THE AREA OR NICHE – THE RELATIONSHIP DIMENSION – COUPONING

Local press, agencies or Royal Mail will deliver. Or hand out a voucher with each sale – advertising an event or promotion, but also offering a promotion itself. Supermarkets offer vouchers at the till; typically £3 off, if you spend £20 on your next visit within the next week. Time limiting works on such offers.

WHAT VALUE COUPON TO USE

Chapter 11 covered this – it does not have to be large, in any case redemption will be small – but it will attract shoppers.

CHECK – WHO TO TARGET?

This is where data comes in. Who bought what? New car to launch? Why not invite previous purchasers to a launch party. Dare to be different – attract back existing shoppers – you spent money on the engram, now call in the shots.

WHERE TO TARGET? (WHICH STORES IN WHICH AREA)

Central headquarters should examine the data to discover which their core stores are. Storecheck can help here (see the Appendix).

WHEN TO FOCUS DEMAND (BETWEEN PRICE DISCOUNTS)

Data will show you when your shoppers buy and what they buy – encourage them at the same time next year, or do something totally different which Insight finds your shoppers will support.

OVER WHAT PERIOD TO INCREASE DEMAND?

The research indicates that a ten-day promotion is about right. Those shoppers that miss it and hear about it will be keener next time.

WHAT TO SEND OUT WHEN?

The strategic communication calendar plan should decide what products and services are promoted to which customers and when, tied into any promotions. The messages then fall into place in the six message points.

WHAT MESSAGES YOU WANT TO CONVEY

On the way to the store – there is an event, a promotion, that is innovative and creative (we know this from our shopper Insights) which as a store (you know our engram) we are holding for ten days starting from (this date). (This should be repeated on advertising, relationship marketing – here's a coupon, and we have created a buzz on social media.)

In-store – well signed, plenty of product, wonderful POS and the sales team have access to the internet so you can double check on the value.

And on-pack – there is the promotion! Thank you brand! Or supplier.

May Your Sales Be as Sweet as Your Promotional Messages

A final message from the authors – who believe you make your own luck – we wish you the best of luck!

Appendix

Further Information

Useful assistance for readers (mentioned in the text) is in this part which includes brief description and contact points (text provided *in toto* in some cases by case study providers). See also the Index which, in addition to a general index, lists brands and organisations and persons mentioned in the text.

Admap website: http://www.warc.com/

Andrew Ehrenburg (1 May 1926–25 August 2010) was a statistician and marketing scientist. For over half a century, he made contributions to the methodology of data collection, analysis and presentation, and to understanding buyer behaviour and how advertising works.

Atom

Blendtec website: http://www.blendtec.com/

Booz and Company website: http://www.booz.com/

British Airways website: http://www.britishairways.com/

British Consumer Index (BCI) website: http://www.bcindex.co.uk/

British Council for Shopping Centres (BCSC) website: http://www.bcsc.org.uk/

British Land website: http://www.britishland.com/

British Market Research Bureau website: http://www.mybmrbsurvey.co.uk/

British Population Survey (BPS) website: www.thebps.co.uk

British Retail Consortium (BRC) website: http://www.brc.org.uk/

CapGemini website: http://www.uk.capgemini.com/

Catalina Marketing website: http://www.catalinamarketing.co.uk/

Charities Aid Foundation website: https://www.cafonline.org/

CIPR website: http://www.cipr.co.uk/

CMO Council website: http://www.cmocouncil.org/

Cranfield website: http://www.cranfield.ac.uk/

Deloittes website: http://www.deloitte.com/

Dressipi is an excellent example of being at the forefront of online shopping. It provides the answer to women shopper's questions: Got a wardrobe of clothes and nothing to wear? Never have time to shop or check out new brands? Dressipi is a *free* fashion advice and recommendation service for the shopper. After creating an accurate profile for a shopper, called a Fashion Fingerprint®, which is based on the shopper's own body shape, style and preferences, the online service then finds the most inspiring and flattering and best types of clothes and brands for the shopper. The clever bit is Dressipi's top styling team alongside Dressipi's search technology which identifies all brands online from high street to high end that suit the shopper›s profile. The team gives a free personal Style Guide to the shopper that includes a list of the shopper's wardrobe Must Haves and the styles the shopper should avoid. To see the website, go to www.dressipi.com.

dunnhumby website: http://www.dunnhumby.com/

Econsultancy online magazine: https://econsultancy.com/

Engram – The engram discovery and how it works (contact the authors for a copy of the paper by Grimes Barker Elliott and the presentation by Elliott) which highlights the need to be aware of both the short-term and long-term impact of messages on the shopper to generate brand growth over time, as well as real sales now.

EPIServer website: http://www.episerver.com/

Facebook website: https://en-gb.facebook.com/

fast.map website: http://www.fastmap.com/

Global Loyalty Pty Ltd. Sarah Richardson General Manager © 2012 Global Loyalty Pty Ltd, Level 2, 710 Collins Street, Docklands VIC 3008, +61 438 923 300 I Tel: +61 3 9097 1764, E-mail: sarahrichardson@globalloyalty.com.au

Go lead Ltd website: www.helmsmanship.co.uk, *also* Helmsmen Business Consultants

Harvard Business Review website: http://hbr.org/

IBM website: http://www.ibm.com/uk/en/

IGD Institute of Grocery Distributionwebsite: http://www.igd.com/

IMRG website: http://www.imrg.org/

In-Store Insights (POPAI magazine) website: http://www.popai.co.uk/Instoreinsights/

Information Resources Incorporated (IRI) website: http://www.iriworldwide.com/

Instagram website: http://instagram.com/

Internet Retailing (magazine) website: http://internetretailing.net/

Intersperience Research offers business advice and market research across industry and for small and large brands. We have 25 years of research in customer and user experience giving us a clear understanding of how consumers interact with services. Intersperience operates worldwide with headquarters in the UK. Our team is a blend of psychologists, statisticians, business consultants, sociologists and marketing experts. A versatile team, we translate results into business-led consultancy, advising our clients on their future direction. We use a full spectrum of qualitative, quantitative and blended techniques. We employ researchers from 62 countries, creating a multi-national team of native language researchers. Customer-centred Insight is available through bespoke research (as commissioned by Virgin Atlantic) and through the application of our knowledge in workshops, tailored reports or through a knowledge subscription. We work with you to improve your understanding of your market and your customers.

We synthesise data into knowledge and recommend appropriate research to fill the gaps in understanding. We ensure our client's products and services meet their customer's needs and deliver the best return on investment. Through our consultancy we ensure they are best placed to meet their customer's needs for the future. Our four key areas of strength are:

> *Futures and Foresight* We explain digital trends and technology's impact on consumer behaviour and apply that to your business, with a key emphasis on current multi-channel behaviours.
>
> *Customer and Market Analysis* We provide you with market comprehensive intelligence and forecast demand for your products, to create a clear business plan helping you stay ahead of the market.
>
> *Testing and Validation* We work with you to ensure your new products, concepts, ideas and services meet your customers' needs.
>
> *Performance and Experience* We measure customer experience to ensure your customer service, web and shopper experience are continuously at their best.

website: http://www.intersperience.co.uk/

IPA Institute of Practitioners in Advertising website: http://www.ipa.co.uk/

IPM Institute of Promotional Marketing website: http://www.theipm.org.uk/

JC Decaux website: http://www.jcdecaux.co.uk

KeyWay Worldwide Tel: + 44 (0) 7791 876914 +44 (0) 20 8742 2256. Website: www.keywayworldwide.com, contact: gthomas@keywayworldwide.com

Kogan Page website: http://www.koganpage.com/

Lawes Gadsby website: www.lawesgadsbysemiotics.com

Mando website: http://www.mandogroup.com/

Marketing Attribution 2013, A Buyers Guide – Econsultancy. Website: http://econsultancy.com/uk

MIT Sloan School of Management website: http://mitsloan.mit.edu/

Mobile Marketer website: http://www.mobilemarketer.com/

Mobile Marketing (magazine) website: http://www.mobilemarketingmagazine.co.uk/

Moneysupermarket.com website: http://www.moneysupermarket.com/

Nectar website: http://www.nectar.com/NectarHome.nectar

Neilsen Homescan website: http://www.paidsurveysuk.com/blog/nielsen-homescan-uk/

Office of Fair Trading (OFT) website: http://www.oft.gov.uk/

Outdoor Media Centre website: http://www.outdoormediacentre.org.uk/

Pinterest website: https://www.pinterest.com/

ResourceNation website: http://www.resourcenation.com/

Responsys website: http://www.responsys.com/

Retail Week website: http://info.retail-week.com/

Royal Mail website: http://www.royalmail.com/

Saatchi and Saatchi website: http://www.saatchi.co.uk/

SCALA Consulting website: www.scalagroup.co.uk

Shopper Behaviour Xplained (SBXL) website: http://www.sbxl.co.uk/

Shoppertrak website: http://www.shoppertrak.com/

Spectrum Insight website: www.spectrum-consulting.net

StoreCheck website: Storecheck use retail and consumer data to identify core area communication policies designed to build faster, and stronger brands working across sales and marketing disciplines. The data analysis is offered through their website: http://retailvitalstatistics.com/; www.storecheck.co.uk

The Centre for Retail Research website: www.retailresearch.org

The Grocer (magazine) http://www.the.grocer.magazine.co.uk

Twitter website: https://twitter.com/

UKCSI website: http://ukcsi.com

Valassis website: www.valassis.co.uk

Velti website: http://www.velti.com/

WPP website: http://www.wpp.com

Code of Practice for traders on Price Indications: www.berr.gov.uk/files/file8127.pdf

A Number of Firms Publish Free Reports

Auros – the internet consultancy and technology company Tel: +44 (0)117 946 6800, website: http://www.auros.co.uk/media/114799/are_you_serious_about_mobile.pdf

BARB website: http://www.barb.co.uk

Bloomberg website: www.bloomberg.com

Bronto – Marketing Platform for Commerce Bronto offer trigger based e-mail messaging, website: http://bronto.com/

BRAD website: http://www1.bradinsight.com/

Campaign (magazine) website: http://www.magazine.co.uk/magazines/campaign

Egg

Empathica website: http://www.empathica.com/

Evolution Insight website: http://www.evolution-insights.com/

iMotions website: http://imotionsglobal.com/

Lawes Gadsby Semiotics LLP website: www.lawesgadsbysemiotics.com

Local Data Company website: http://www.localdatacompany.com/

Museum of Brands Packaging and Advertising website: http://www.museumofbrands.com/

Oxford Institute of Retail Management website: http://www.sbs.ox.ac.uk/centres/oxirm

POPAI website: http://www.popai.co.uk/

POPAI and the MARI results website: http://www.sheridanglobal.com

Simon-Kucher and Partners (SKP) specialise in consumer goods and promotional management. SKP is the world's leading pricing consultancy and advises leading companies on a range of projects to deliver smart profit growth. The Chapter 11 section is extracted from the paper 'Developing 'win–win' Promotional Calendars with Retail Partners', website: http://www.simon-kucher.com.

Sitecore's leading Content Management System software is the first to cohesively integrate with marketing automation, intranet portal, e-commerce, web optimization, social media and campaign management technologies. This broad choice of capabilities enable marketing professionals, business stakeholders and information technology teams to rapidly implement, measure and manage a successful website and digital business strategy. Businesses can now easily identify, serve and convert new customers with Sitecore's Digital Marketing System, part of its encompassing Customer Engagement Platform. For more information about Sitecore CMS, visit www.sitecore.net.

SLI Systems website: www.sli-systems.co.uk and learn more at http://sitesearch.sli-systems.com

Further Free Resources

FREE additional charts and an elevator pitch. For Dropbox access please send an e-mail to shoppernomics@storecheck.co.uk.

References

The authors decided that as this is not an academic text but written for practitioners they would not produce meticulous entries for every reference but sufficient to find them through Google. Should a reader have any difficulty please contact the authors. The Chapter 2 references are included for interest (in the Cranfield thesis approved format) as most marketers seem to have scant understanding of learning and how communication works – essential when plying their profession.

Grimes Barker Elliott

Andy Tarshis, AC Nielson Co quoted in Mayer (1999, 179–180)

Jonah Berger and Grainne Fitzsimons (2008) at Halloween

Villarejo-Ramos and Sánchez-Franco (2005)

Palazon and Delgado (2005)

Sponge 2013

Phillip Adcock

Professor Greenfield, Oxford University, *The Private Life of the Brain*

Rosser Reeves

Bath University Robert Heath

Aakers (1997)

Martin at Cranfield

BOOK REFERENCES (LESS CHAPTER 2) ARE LISTED BELOW

Ailawadi, Kusum L., Karen Gedenk, Christian Lutzky and Scott A. Neslin (2007). 'Decomposition of the Sales Impact of Promotion-Induced Stockpiling.' *Journal of Marketing Research*, 44(August), pp.450–467.

Ainslie, Andrew and Peter E. Rossi (1998). 'Similarities in Choice Behaviour across Multiple Categories.' *Marketing Science*, 17(2), pp.91–106.

Bawa, Kapil and Avijit Ghosh (1999). 'A Model of Household Grocery Shopping Behaviour.' *Marketing Letters*, 10(2), pp.149–160.

Bell, David R., Jeongwen Chiang and V. Padmanabhan (1999). 'The Decomposition Of Promotional Response: An Empirical Generalization.' *Marketing Science*, 18(4), p.504.

Bemmaor, Albert C. and Dominique Mouchoux. (1991). 'Measuring the Short-Term Effect of In-store Promotion and Retail Advertising on Brand Sales: A Factorial Experiment.' *Journal of Marketing Research*, 28(May), pp.202–214.

Blattberg, Robert C. and Kenneth. J. Wisniewski (1987). 'How Retail Price Promotions Work: Empirical Results.' *Working Paper* (43), University of Chicago, Chicago IL.

Botti and Iyengar (AMA) (2006).

Ehrenburg, Andrew Professor. Strongly persuasive or nudging see www. http://marketingscience.info/professor-andrew-ehrenbergs-publications.

Huck and Wallace. Details of price framing experiments.

Inman, Jeffrey J. and Robert S. Winer (1998). 'Where Rubber Meets the Road: A Model of In-Store Consumer Decision Making.' *Working Paper*, Marketing Science Institute (October), Report No. 98–122.

Iyengar, Jiang and Kamenica (2006).

Iyengar and Lepper (2000).

Kalwani and Yim (1992).

Kotler, Phillip (1988). *Marketing Management: Analysis, Planning, Implementation and Control*. 6th editon, Englewood Cliffs, NJ: Prentice-Hall International.

Krishnamurthi, Lakshman and S.P. Raj (1991). 'An Empirical Analysis of the Relationship between Brand Loyalty and Consumer Price Elasticity.' *Marketing Science*, 10(2), pp.172–183.

Kumar, V. and Robert P. Leone (1988). 'Measuring the Effect of Retail Store Promotions on Brand and Store Substitution.' *Journal of Marketing Research*, 25(May), pp.178–185.

Mace, Sandrine and Scott A. Neslin (2004). 'The Determinants of Pre- and Post-Promotion Dips in Sales of Frequently Purchased Goods.' *Journal of Marketing Research*, 41(Aug), pp.339–350.

Manning, Kenneth C. and David E. Sprott (2007). 'Multiple Unit Price Promotions and Their Effects on Quantity Purchase Intentions.' *Journal of Retailing*, 83(4), pp.411–421.

Martínez-Ruiz, Maria P., A. Mollá-Descals, Miguel A. Gómez-Borja and J.L. Rojo-Álvarez (2006a). 'Assessing the Impact of Temporary Retail Price Discounts Intervals Using SVM Semi-parametric Regression.' *International Review of Retail, Distribution and Consumer Research*,16(2), pp.181–197.

Mayhew, Glenn E. and Russell Winer (1992). 'An Empirical Analysis of Internal and External Reference Prices Using Scanner Data.' *Journal of Marketing Research*, 19(June), pp.62–70.

Meat and Livestock Commission (2002). 'The Shopping Decision Tree: Understanding the Consumer.'

Molenarr, Cor. *Shopping 3.0.*

Mulhern, Francis J. and Robert P. Leone (1991). 'Implicit Price Bundling of Retail Products: A Multi-product Approach to Maximizing Store Profitability.' *Journal of Marketing*, 55(Oct), pp.63–79.

Mullin, Roddy and Alison Williams. *The Handbook of Field Marketing.*

Murray and Haubl.

Raju, Jagmohen S. (1992). 'The Effect of Price Promotions of Variability in Product Category Sales.' *Marketing Science*, 11(3), pp.207–220.

Rao and Thomas (1973).

Rust and Thompson.

Schacter, Danial, Professor. *Searching for Memory*.

Underhill, Paco. *Why We Buy the Science of Shopping*.

Urbany, Joel E., Peter R. Dickson and Rosemary Kalapurakal (1996). 'Price Search in the Retail Grocery Market.' *Journal of Marketing*, 60(2), pp.91–104.

Wansink, Brian and Rohit Deshpandé (1994). '"Out of Sight, Out of Mind": Pantry Stockpiling and Brand-Usage Frequency.' *Marketing Letters*, 5(1), pp.91–100.

Wansink, Brian, Robert J. Kent and Stephen J. Hoch (1998). 'An Anchoring and Adjustment Model of Purchase Quantity Decisions.' *Journal of Marketing Research*, 35(February), pp.71–81.

CHAPTER 2 – THE COMMUNICATION CANVAS

Based on a literature review carried out by Roddy Mullin for a PhD thesis at Cranfield University

Ace (2001). *Successful Marketing*. CIM/Butterworth.

Akin (1987). 'Varieties of Managerial Learning.' *Organisational Dynamics*, 14(3), pp.19–32.

Allan (2005). interview 24 October 2005

Allen-Mills (2006). *The Sunday Times*, 22 January, p.23.

Ambler (2000). *Marketing and the Bottom Line*. Harlow: Pearson Education Limited.

Argyris (1976). *Increasing Leadership Effectiveness*. London: Wiley.

Argyris, C. (1993). *Knowledge for Action: A Guide to Overcoming Barriers to Organizational Change*. San Francisco, CA: Jossey Bass.

Argyris and Schon (1996). *Organisational Learning*. Reading, MA: Addison Wesley.

Atwater, L.E., Dionne, S.H., Avolio, B., Camobreco, J.F., Lau, A.W. (1999). 'A Longitudinal Study of the Leadership Development Process: Individual Differences Predicting Leader Effectiveness.' *Human Relations*, 52(12), pp.1543–1562.

Avolio, B.J. and Gibbons, T.C. (1988). *'Developing Transformational Leaders: A Life Span Approach,'*in Conger, J.A., Kanungo, R.N., *Charismatic Leadership: The Elusive Factor in Organizational Effectiveness*. San Francisco, CA: Jossey-Bass, pp.276–308.

Bartram and Green (1998). *Initial Assessment to Identify Learning Needs*. Further Education Development Agency.

Batley, Tom. (1998). 'Management Training of Professional Engineers in New Zealand.' *Journal of European Industrial Training*, 22(7), p.3.

Batra and Stayman (1990). 'The Role of Mood in Advertising Effectiveness.' *Journal of Consumer Research*, 17(September), pp.225–233.

Beane and Ennis (1987). 'Market Segmentation.' *European Journal of Marketing*, 21(5).

Bee and Bee (1994). *Training Needs Analysis*. Institute of Personnel Development, p.8.

Bee and Bee (2003). *Learning Needs Analysis and Evaluation*. CIPD. The Learning Wheel diagram, p.xiii, p.51, p.131.

Bennis (1985). *Leaders*. New York: Harper and Row, pp.2–4.

Bennis (1985). *On Becoming a Leader*. Reading, MA: Addison-Wesley, pp.114–141.

Bennis (2000). 'Foreword' in Gibber, David J. II. Louis L. Carter and Goldsmith, Marshall. T. *Best Practices in Leadership Development Handbook*. Linkage Press, p xiii.

Bishton and Allan (2005). 'Businesses, Universities and Engineering Management,' University of Bath School of Management, Paper, September.

Bloch, S. (1995). 'Coaching tomorrow's top managers.' *Executive Development*, 8(5), pp.20–2. p.21.

Blythe (2003). *Essentials of Marketing Communications*, 2nd edition. Pearson Education Limited, pp.2–30, pp.37–38 and p.40.

Bond (1977). *Liddell Hart: A Study of his Military Thought*. London: Cassell.

Boydell (1976). *A Guide to the Identification of Training Needs*. British Association for Commercial and Industrial Education.

Brown and Posner (2001). 'Exploring the relationship between learning and leadership.' *Leading and Organisational Development Journal*, 22(6), pp.274–280.

Bruce (2001). *The Psychology of Executive Coaching: Theory and Application*. Ann Arbor, MI: Sheridan Books.

Burgoyne (2004). 'How Certain are We That Management and Leadership Development is Effective?' Second Seminar on Management, Learning and Leadership, Lancaster University.

Burns (1978). *Leadership*. New York: Harper and Row, pp.201–240.

Caciopp, R. and Abbrech, S. (2000). 'Using 360 Feedback and the Integral Model to Develop Leadership and Management Skills.' *Leadership and Organization Development Journal*, 21(8), p.390.

Cambridge Programme for Industry (CPI) (2002). *How Do People Learn?* CIPD.

Chan, K.Y. and Drasgow, F. (2001). 'Toward a theory of individual differences and leadership: understanding the motivation to lead.' *Journal of Applied Psychology*, 86(3), pp.481–498.

Charlesworth, K., Cook, P. and Crozier (2005). Survey: 'Leading Change in the Public Sector'. Chartered Management Institute, May 2003.

Chemers, M.M, *An Integrative Theory of Leadership*. Mahwah, NJ: Lawrence Erlbaum Associates.

Chemers, M.M., Watson, C.B. and May, S.T. (2000). 'Dispositional Affect and Leadership Effectiveness: A Comparison of Self-esteem, Optimism, and Efficacy.' *Personality and Social Psychology Bulletin*, 26, pp.267–277.

Clark (1993). *Managing Personal Learning and Change*. McGraw Hill, p.47.

Clawson (1996). 'Mentoring in the Information Age.' *Leadership and Organization Development Journal*, 17(3), pp.6–15.

Conger (1992). *The Art of Transforming Managers into Leaders, Learning to Lead.* San Francisco, CA: Jossey-Bass.

Conger, J.A. and Benjamin, B. (1999). *Building Leaders: How Successful Companies Develop the Next Generation.* San Francisco, CA: Jossey-Bass.

Conger, J.A. and Kanungo, R.N. (1987). 'Toward a Behavioral Theory of Charismatic Leadership in Organizational Settings.' *Academy of Management Review*, 12, pp.637–647.

Cotton, Julie (1995). *The Theory of Learning.* Kogan Page, pp.9–39, pp.46–48, p.112 and p.121.

Coulson-Thomas (1992). *Transforming the Company.* Kogan Page.

CPI (2002). *Who Learns at Work.* CIPD.

CPI (2002). *The Cambridge Programme for Industry.*

Cribbin (1981). *Leadership Strategies for Organisational Affectiveness.* AMACOM NY, p.175.

Crosbie (2005). 'Learning the Soft Skills of Leadership.' *Industrial and Commercial Training*, 37(1), pp.45–51.

Cummins and Mullin (2002). *Sales Promotion.* Kogan Page, p.12. See also extracts in Published Texts.

Cunningham (1994). *The Wisdom of Strategic Learning.* McGraw Hill.

Dalton M. Swigert, S., VanVelsor, E., Bunker, K., Wachholz, J. (1999). *The Learning Tactics Inventory.* San Francisco, CA: Jossey-Bass/Pfeiffer.

Deetz (1992). *Democracy in An Age of Corporate Colonisation.* New York: State University of New York.

Delozier (1976). *The Marketing Communications Process.* New York: McGraw Hill, p.1.

Dixon, P. (1995a). 'Releasing middle management potential: Part 1', *Executive Development*, 8(5), pp.23–25.

Dixon, P. (1995b). 'Releasing Middle Management Potential: Part 2.' *Executive Development*, 8(7), pp.11–13.

Doyle (2000). *Value Based Marketing*. Chichester: Wiley.

Easterby-Smith (1994). *Evaluation of Management Development, Training and Education*. Aldershot: Gower.

Eluned Price (2006). 'The Future is Becoming Transparent.' *The Daily Telegraph*, 18 May 2006, p. A1.

Engel, Warshaw and Kinnear (1994). *Promotional Strategy*. Chicago: Irwin. See Blythe (2003), p.2.

Faison, (1961). *Advertising*. Wiley.

Felder–Silverman Learning Model, quoted by Sloman (2003) p.41 has five learning styles.

Festinger (1962). *A Theory of Cognitive Dissonance*. London: Tavistock.

Fill C. (2002). *Marketing Communications*. FT Prentice Hall, p.33 and pp.35–36.

Forsyth, Joliffe and Stevens (1999). *The Complete Guide to Teaching a Course – 'Planning a course'*, 2nd edition. Kogan Page, p.89 and pp.117–123.

Frances and Roland Bee (1994). *Training Needs Analysis*. Institute of Personnel Development.

Francis (1999). *Cognition Knowledge and Organisations*. JAI Press.

Gardner and Avolio (1998). Conger, J.A., Kanungo, R.N. (1987), *'Toward a Behavioral Theory of Charismatic Leadership in Organizational Settings.' Academy of Management Review* 12, pp.637–647.

Gibber, D., Carter, L. and Goldsmith, M. (Eds) (1999). *Best Practices in Leadership Development Handbook*. Lexington, MA: Linkage Press, Lexington, MA. p.2.

Gill, Roger (2002). 'The Impact of Leadership and Leadership Development.' The Research Centre for Leadership Studies Working paper no. LT-RG-02-16, August.

Goldman and Newman (1998). *Empowering Students to Transform Schools.* Corwin Press Inc.

Gower (1997). *Planning and Designing Training Programmes* Gower p.7 (extension of definition), p.14 (Figure 1.8), p.61, p.55 pp.70–71, p.87 are other refs of interest in series of Gower quotes.

Gredler (2001). *Learning and Instruction.* Prentice Hall.

Hardy (1988). *Understanding Voluntary Organisations.* Harmondsworth: Penguin, p.117.

Hart and Stapleton (1977). *Glossary of Marketing Terms.* London: Heinemann. Definition of Marketing p.117 given by CIM in 1975.

Harvey-Jones (1988). *Making it Happen.* Fontana, pp.398–399.

Hermann (1988). *The Creative Brain.* Lake Lure, NC: Brain Books.

Honey (1994). *101 Ways to Develop Your People Without Really Trying.* Maidenhead.

Honey and Mumford (1995). *Using Your Learning Styles.* Maidenhead.

Hovland, Janis and Kelley (1953). *Communication and Persuasion.* Yale University Press.

Hughes, Ginnett and Curphey (2002). *Leadership – Enhancing the Lessons of Experience.* McGraw Hill.

Hunt *Managing People at Work.* London: Pan.

Kardes (1988) 'Spontaneous Inference Processes in Advertising, the Effects of Conclusion Omission and Involvement on Persuasion.' *Journal of Consumer Research,* 15(September), pp.203–214.

Katz and Lazarsfield (1964). *Personal Influence.* New York: Free Press, pp.29–30, mentioned by Burns (1978), p.259 also by Blythe (2003) p.3.

Kegan R. (2000). *'What 'form' transforms?* A constructive-developmental approach to transformative learning.

Kelloway, K.E., Barling, J. and Helleur, J. (2000). 'Enhancing Transformational Leadership: The Role of Training and Feedback.' *Leadership and Organization Development Journal,* 21(3), p.145.

Kilcourse, T. (1995). 'The Business of Business Schools.' *The Learning Organization,* 2(2), pp.32–35.

Klas Mellander (1993). *The Power of Learning*. Irwin.

Klatt (1991). *The Ultimate Training Workshop Handbook.* McGraw Hill, p.16, p.57, pp.66–73 and p.87.

Kolb (1983). *Experiential Learning*. Englewood Cliffs, CA.

Kolb (1985). *Learning Style Inventory: Self Scoring Inventory and Interpretation Booklet*. Boston, MA: McBer and Company.

Kotter (1988). *The Leadership Factor*. New York, NY: Free Press.

Kouzes and Posner (2002). *The Leadership Challenge,* 3rd edition. Jossey-Bass and by John Wiley and Son.

Limerick, D., Passfield, R. and Cunnington, B. (1994). *'Transformational Change: Towards an Action Learning Organization.' The Learning Organization,* 1(2), pp.29–40.

Lorange, P. (1996). 'A business school as a Learning Organization.' *The Learning Organization,* 3(5), pp.5–13.

Maccoby (1981). *The Leader*. Simon and Shuster.

Management Charter Initiative (MCI), Lane and Robinson (1995). 'The Development of Standards of Competence for Senior Management.' *Executive Development,* 8(6), pp.4–8.

Mantovani (1996). *New Communications Environments*. London: Taylor and Francis London.

Margolis and Bell (1986). *Instructing for Results*. Lakewood Pubs.

Marquadt (2000). 'Action Learning and Leadership.' *The Learning Organisation*, 7(5), pp.233–241.

McCall, Lombardo and Robinson (1988). *The Lessons of Experience: How Successful Executives Develop on the Job*. Lexington, MA: Lexington Books.

McCauley, C.D. and Van Velsor, E. (Eds) (2004). *The Center for Creative Leadership Handbook of Leadership Development*, 2nd edition. San Francisco, CA: Jossey-Bass.

McKenna, S.D. (1994). 'Leveraging Complexity: The Middle Manager's Dilemma.' *The Learning Organization*, 1(2), pp.6–14.

McNulty, N.G. and Canty, G.R. (1995). 'Proof of the Pudding.' *Journal of Management Development*, 14(1), pp.53–66.

Merriam and Caffarella (1994). *Learning in Adulthood*. Jossey Bass.

Mezirow (1994). *Transformational Dimensions of Adult Learning*. San Francisco, CA: Jossey Bass, p.222.

Mole (2000). *Managing Management Training*. Oxford: Oxford Uuniversity Press, p.19.

Mullin (2001). *Value For Money Marketing*. London: Kogan Page.

Mullins, Laurie J. (2005). *Management and Organisational Behaviour*, 7th edition. Pearson Education Limited by Financial Times Pitman Publishing, p.245.

Mumford, A. (1994). 'Four Approaches to Learning from Experience.' *The Learning Organization*, 1(1), pp.4–10.

Mumford (1995). 1996, 'Effective Learners in Action Learning Sets,' *The Journal of Workplace Learning*, 8(6), pp.3–10.

O'Neill (1996). 'A Study of the Role of Learning Advisers in Action Learning.' *The Journal of Workplace Learning*, 8(6), pp.39–44.

Onkvisit and Shaw (1994). *Consumer Behaviour, Strategy Analysis*. Oxford: Maxwell Macmillan International, quoted by Blythe (2003), p.12.

Osborne, R.L. and Cowen, S.S. (1995). 'Business Schools Must Become Learning Organizations – Or Else.' *The Learning Organization*, 2(2), pp.28–31.

Oshagbemi, T. (1995). 'Management Development and Managers' Use of Their Time.' *Journal of Management Development*, 14(8) pp.19–34, p.32.

Parker and Stone (2003). *Developing Management Skills for Leadership*. Prentice Hall.

Peters and Smith (1996). *'Developing High Potential Staff: An Action Learning Approach.' The Journal of Workplace Learning*, 8(3), pp.6–11, esp. p.8.

Peterson (1992). *Training Needs Analysis in the Workplace*. Kogan Page.

Pfeffer (1992). *Managing with Power: Politics and Influence in Organizations*. Boston, MA: Harvard Business School Press, p.397.

Phillips, R. (1996). 'Coaching for Higher Performance.' *The Journal of Workplace Learning*, 8(4), pp.29–32.

Popper (2005). 'Main Principles and Practices in Leader Development.' *Leadership and Organisational Development Journal*, 26(1), pp.62–75.

Popper, Amit, Gal, Sinai, Lissak (2004). 'The Capacity to Lead.' *Military Psychology*, 16(4), pp.245–263.

Pringle, Hamish (2004). Interview, 4 February 2005.

Raz, G. (2001). *'Socialization for Leadership.'* Doctoral dissertation, Department of Psychology, University of Haifa, Haifa (in preparation).

Reynolds, Caley and Mason (2002). *How Do People Learn?* CPI for CIPD.

Reynolds, Caley and Mason (2002). *The Cambridge Programme for Industry*. CPI.

Ricketts, Cliff (2003). *Leadership: Persona! Development and Career Success*, 2nd edition. Delmar, a division of Thomson Learning, p.31, pp.56–68 and pp.76–78.

Sadler-Smith, E. (1998). *'Cognitive Style and the Self-Management of Learning.'* Conference Proceedings, Lancaster–Leeds Collaborative Conference, Leeds.

Schon, D. (1987). *Educating the Reflective Practitioner: Toward a New Design for Teaching and Learning in the Professions*. San Francisco, CA: Jossey Bass.

Schramm (1948). *Mass Communications*. Urbana, IL: University of Illinois Press.

Schramm (1955). *How Communications Works*. Urbana, IL: University of Illinois Press, pp.3–26.

Shannon and Weaver (1962). *The Mathematical Theory of Communication*. University of Illinois Press, quoted by Fill, C. (2002) *Marketing Communications* FT Prentice Hall, p.32.

Shaw, G.B. (1903). *Man and Superman*. Constable and Co.

Shaw and Merrick (2005). *Marketing Payback*. Harlow: Pearson Education Limited.

Shenhar and Renier (1996). 'How to Define Management: A Modular Approach.' *Management Development Review*, 9(1), pp.25–31.

Sloman (2003). *Training Needs Analysis*. Institute of Personnel Development, p.v, p.xiii, p.xiv and p.16.

Smith, Berry and Pulford (1999). *Strategic Marketing Communications*, 2nd edition. Kogan Page, pp.29–31.

Smith, P.R. and Taylor, J. (2004). *Marketing Communications: An Integrated Approach*. Kogan Page, p.42.

Stapleton (1975). *Teach Yourself Marketing*. London: Teach Yourself Books, quoted in Hart and Stapleton (1977), p.118.

Steinberg, B.S. (2001). 'The Making of Female Presidents and Prime Ministers: The Impact of Birth Order, Sex of Siblings and Father-Daughter Dynamics.' *Political Psychology*, 22, pp.89–114.

Stevenson, Lord (2004). *Market Research*. Lecture to WCM: Gibson Hall, 25 November.

Tannenbaum, S.I. (1997). 'Enhancing Continuous Learning: Diagnostic Findings from Multiple Companies.' *Human Resource Management*, 36(4), pp.437–452.

Taylor (2000) 'Building upon the Theoretical Debate: A Critical Review of the Empirical Studies of Mezirow's 1997.'

Teare (1997). 'Supporting Managerial Learning in the Workplace.' *International Journal of Contemporary Hospitality Management*, 9(7), pp.304–319.

Vaill, P. (1999). *Spirited Leading and Learning: Process Wisdom for a New Age.* San Francisco, CA: Jossey-Bass.

Valarino et al. (2005). 'Value Based Marketing – the Future.' MBA Dissertation, University of Southampton.

Van der Sluis (2002). *Management Learning: Interaction between Learning Behaviour and Learning Opportunities.* Rotterdam: Tinbergen Institute, also reports research by Spreitzer et al. (1997), Megginson (1996), Thijssen (1996), Hoeksema (1995) and Vermunt (1992).

Varey (2000). *Internal Marketing.* New York, NY: Routledge.

WCM Pamphlet (2004). *A Guide to Understanding One Key Source of Shareholder Value,* June, pp.2–3, extract in Published Texts.

Williams and Green (1994). *Dealing with Difference; How Trainers Can Take Account of Cultural* Diversity. Aldershot: Gower.

Williamson, M. (1993). *Training Needs Analysis.* Library Associations Publications, p.12.

Yeshin, Tony (1998). *Marketing Communications Strategy.* Oxford: Butterworth Heinemann.

Zakay and Scheinfeld (1993). 'Outstanding Battalion Commanders.' Research report, School of Leadership Development, Israel Defense Forces Military Educational Publishing Corps, Tel Aviv (in Hebrew).

Zaleznik A., and Kets de Vries, M. (1975). *Power and the Corporate Mind.* Boston, MA: Houghton Mifflin, pp.31–38 express basic leadership strategies but no definition, p.264 reflects on the present selecting and training of leaders through socialisation perpetuates the isolated self.

Zemke, R. and Zemke, S. (1995). 'Adult Learning: What Do We Know for Sure?' *Training,* pp.27–33.

Zuber-Skerritt, O. (1995). 'Developing a Learning Organization through Management Education by Action Learning.' *The Learning Organization,* 2(2), pp.36–46.

Index

Page numbers in **bold** refer to key or significant entries.

For Product Safety Concerns and Information please contact our EU representative GPSR@taylorandfrancis.com Taylor & Francis Verlag GmbH, Kaufingerstraße 24, 80331 München, Germany

Printed and bound by CPI Group (UK) Ltd, Croydon, CR0 4YY

01/05/2025

01858368-0006